Advanced Criminal Litigation in Practice

Authors

Joseph Barry, Barrister, Lecturer, The City Law School

Colin Bobb-Semple, Solicitor, Senior Lecturer, The City Law School

Peter Fortune, Barrister, Gray's Inn

James Griffiths, Barrister, Senior Lecturer, The City Law School

Peter Hungerford-Welch, Barrister, Associate Dean, The City Law School

Shamini Jayanathan, Barrister, former Lecturer, ICSL

Barbara Mensah, Barrister, former Senior Lecturer, The City Law School

James Robinson, Barrister, former Lecturer, ICSL

John Sprack, Employment Tribunal Chairman, former Reader, ICSL

Nikki Walsh, Solicitor, Lecturer, The City Law School

Editor

James Griffiths, Barrister, Senior Lecturer, The City Law School

Series Editor

Julie Browne, Barrister, Senior Lecturer, The City Law School

Advanced Criminal Litigation in Practice

The City Law School, City University, London

OXFORD
UNIVERSITY PRESS

OXFORD

UNIVERSITY PRESS

Great Clarendon Street, Oxford OX2 6DP

Oxford University Press is a department of the University of Oxford.
It furthers the University's objective of excellence in research, scholarship,
and education by publishing worldwide in

Oxford New York
Auckland Cape Town Dar es Salaam Hong Kong Karachi
Kuala Lumpur Madrid Melbourne Mexico City Nairobi
New Delhi Shanghai Taipei Toronto

With offices in

Argentina Austria Brazil Chile Czech Republic France Greece
Guatemala Hungary Italy Japan Poland Portugal Singapore
South Korea Switzerland Thailand Turkey Ukraine Vietnam

Oxford is a registered trade mark of Oxford University Press
in the UK and in certain other countries

Published in the United States
by Oxford University Press Inc., New York

British Library Cataloguing in Publication Data

Data available

Library of Congress Cataloging in Publication Data

Data available

Typeset by Laserwords Private Limited, Chennai, India
Printed in Great Britain on acid-free paper by
Ashford Colour Press, Gosport, Hampshire

ISBN 978-0-19-957917-4

10 9 8 7 6 5 4 3 2 1

FOREWORD

I am delighted to write this foreword to the manuals which are written by practitioners and staff of the Inns of Court School of Law (ICSL [now The City Law School]).

The manuals are designed primarily to support the training on the Bar Vocational Course (BVC). They now cover a wide range, embracing both the compulsory and the optional subjects of the BVC. They provide an outstanding resource for all those concerned to teach and acquire legal skills wherever the BVC is taught.

The manuals for the compulsory subjects are updated and revised annually. The manuals for the optional subjects are revised every two years. To complement the Series, the publishers will maintain a website for the manuals which will be used to keep them up-to-date throughout the academic year.

The manuals, continually updated, exemplify the practical and professional approach that is central to the BVC. I congratulate staff of The City Law School who have produced them to an excellent standard, and Oxford University Press for its commitment in securing their publication. As my predecessor the Hon. Mr Justice Gross so aptly said in a previous foreword, the manuals are an important ingredient in the constant drive to raise standards in the public interest.

Lord Justice Etherton
Chairman of the Advisory Board of the Institute of Law
City University, London

OUTLINE CONTENTS

DETAILED CONTENTS

TABLE OF CASES

TABLE OF LEGISLATION

Introduction

This Manual provides an introduction to areas of criminal law, practice and procedure with which the pupil or junior barrister must be familiar but which fall outside the syllabus of criminal law as a core subject and the Criminal Litigation and Sentencing module of the Bar Vocational Course. While it is intended primarily for students taking the Advanced Criminal Litigation Option on the Vocational Course, it also provides a general introduction to these topics which may be of use to students and junior practitioners.

Part I of this Manual deals with certain areas of procedure which are of crucial practical importance to the criminal practitioner. **Chapter 3** deals with the issues relating to search and seizure. It looks at the question of powers to search for and seize evidence, and the consequences at trial if those powers are exceeded. **Chapter 4** covers the doctrine of abuse of process. It examines the circumstances in which the court may exercise its discretion to stay a prosecution which it considers to be an abuse of its own process.

Part II covers chosen areas of substantive law. **Chapter 5** is devoted to the offences connected with dangerous drugs, **Chapter 6** deals with a variety of offences against public order and **Chapter 7** covers offensive weapons. Road traffic is an area which is particularly required for the barrister in the first few years of practice, and it is covered in **Chapters 8, 9** and **10** which deal with some of the most common offences and the penalty system for driving offences.

Part III provides an opportunity to practise some of the skills utilised by the criminal practitioner on a realistic set of papers for a trial in prospect. You are instructed for the defence in a Crown Court trial, the indictment containing counts of grievous bodily harm with intent, violent disorder, attempted robbery and driving while unfit through drink or drugs. The papers contain many of the documents with which the criminal practitioner is constantly dealing, eg the custody record and the plea and case management questionnaire. **Chapter 11** describes the way in which the papers might be used. To start with, they form the instructions to write an Advice on Evidence and draft a Defence Statement. Thereafter, they can form the basis for preparing a conference with the client. Finally, they can be used in order to plan the advocacy tasks necessary for a trial. The papers themselves appear in **Chapter 12**. In **Chapter 13**, there is a sample Advice on Evidence and a sample Defence Statement prepared in response to the instructions in the brief.

The law is stated as at 13 August 2009.

2

Sources for further study and preparation of cases

2.1 This Manual

This Manual is designed to introduce you to some of the main topics that the practitioner will meet from the early years of practice onwards. Subjects that are already covered in the main *Criminal Litigation* and *Evidence Manuals* are not covered here and a knowledge of those areas is assumed. This Manual does not provide you with all the materials you will need to undertake the case you will meet on the Advanced Criminal Litigation Option. You will find it necessary, in addition, to undertake further legal research which will require the use of practitioner texts and primary sources.

2.2 Primary sources

2.2.1 Statutory materials

You should be familiar with accessing statutory material through electronic and hard-copy sources so that you are prepared for all circumstances.

2.2.1.1 Electronic sources

The commercial providers (Lawtel, LexisNexis, Butterworths and Westlaw) all provide statutes and statutory instruments online. Useful information is also available through government websites such as the Office of Public Sector Information (formerly HMSO) (http://www.opsi.gov.uk), where both existing and draft legislation is available, the Home Office (http://www.homeoffice.gov.uk), where consultation on legislative proposals is available and the Ministry of Justice (http://www.justice.gov.uk), where the Criminal Procedure Rules, legislative consulation and draft legislation is available. The UK Statute Law Database (http://www.statutelaw.gov.uk) contains all the official revised editions of the primary legislation of the United Kingdom. However, caution should be exercised when using the Database as the official revised versions may not contain the more recent amendments to the legislation. Other commercial providers such as Crime line (http://www.crimeline.info) provide a certain amount of free relevant news and updating. For further guidance on electronic sources, see the *Case Preparation Manual*.

2.2.1.2 Paper sources

For proceedings in the Crown Court, the two main practitioners' texts, *Archbold: Criminal Pleading, Evidence and Practice* and *Blackstone's Criminal Practice*, should include most of the provisions you will need. For proceedings in the magistrates' court, you could additionally refer either to *Stone's Justices' Manual* or *Archbold Magistrates' Courts Criminal Practice*. For road traffic offences, you should refer to *Wilkinson's Road Traffic Offences*.

Richardson, J., and Thomas QC, D. (ed.), *Archbold: Criminal Pleading, Evidence and Practice* (London: Sweet & Maxwell, annual).

Murphy, P., and Stockdale, E. (ed.), *Blackstone's Criminal Practice* (Oxford: Oxford University Press, annual).

Carr, P., and Turner, A. (ed.), *Stone's Justices' Manual* (London: LexisNexis UK, annual). Padfield, N. (ed.), *Archbold Magistrates' Courts Criminal Practice* (Oxford: Oxford University Press, annual).

Swift, K., and McCormac, K. (ed.), *Wilkinson's Road Traffic Offences* (London: Sweet & Maxwell, updated).

2.2.2 Law reports

Many criminal cases are reported in the ordinary reports with which you are acquainted (eg AC, QB, WLR, All ER). However, you must develop familiarity with the specialist series which frequently report cases that are not reported elsewhere:

Criminal Appeal Reports (Cr App R)

Criminal Appeal Reports (Sentencing) (Cr App R (S))

Criminal Law Review (Crim LR)

Road Traffic Reports (RTR)

The *Criminal Appeal Reports* are published ten times per year, the *Criminal Appeal Reports (Sentencing)* six times per year, the *Criminal Law Review* is published monthly. They are usually quicker to report cases than the general series of law reports. The *Criminal Law Review* is often the quickest of the three, and case reports are frequently followed by a commentary providing useful analysis. Cases reported in any of the main or specialist series may easily be accessed through the main electronic services: Lawtel, LexisNexis, Casetrack and Westlaw.

2.3 Practitioner works

You will need to make regular use of practitioner texts. The two main texts are:

Richardson, J., and Thomas QC, D. (ed.), *Archbold: Criminal Pleading, Evidence and Practice* (London: Sweet & Maxwell, annual).

Hooper, L. J., and Ormerod, D., and Murphy, P. (ed.), *Blackstone's Criminal Practice* (Oxford: Oxford University Press, annual).

Archbold is regarded by most criminal practitioners as the standard text for practice in the Crown Court. However, *Blackstone's* is often preferred by the junior practitioner and those practising in the magistrates' courts, not least because it provides more extensive coverage of issues particular to those courts.

Oxford University Press provide a monthly updating service for readers of *Blackstone's* via the *Blackstone's Criminal Practice Companion Website*. The *Blackstone's Criminal Practice Bulletin* is published quaterly and is available as a printed version or online.

For road traffic offences you should refer to:

Swift, K., and McCormac, K. (ed.), *Wilkinson's Road Traffic Offences* (London: Sweet & Maxwell, updated).

You may also find the Legal Guidance section of the CPS website a useful resource (http://www.cps.gov.uk/legal/index.html). The website provides a summary of most of the important areas of criminal law and is used by some practitioners. However, it should not be regarded as a substitute for a practitioner text.

2.4 Periodicals

You may also find reference to the specialist journals and periodicals useful for keeping up to date with current developments and as a source of insightful commentary. Also, articles on criminal law and evidence appear regularly in all the main general legal periodicals.

2.4.1 Specialist journals

The leading specialist journal is the *Criminal Law Review*, containing articles, comment, case notes, reports and reviews.

Other journals of particular interest include the *Journal of Criminal Law*, the *Modern Law Review* and the *Law Quarterly Review*.

2.4.2 Updating periodicals

Archbold News, published ten times per year, provides access to updated developments, including cases, legislation and commentary in the field of criminal law. Significantly, it includes reports of cases that are not reported elsewhere.

Criminal Law Week, published weekly, is a comprehensive digest of developments in the criminal law. It is available as a printed version and online at http://www.criminal-law.co.uk.

The monthly and weekly publications, *Legal Action* and *New Law Journal*, are also useful for up-to-date information on recent cases, often before they have been reported, and articles surveying a particular topic, often from a highly practical perspective.

2.5 Online sources

CrimeLine is the largest circulation criminal law update. Each issue digests the latest cases, legislation and news. Students can subscribe at the CrimeLine website (www.crimeline.info) where previous editions of the update, together with other useful resources, are available.

Part I

Evidence and procedure

3

Entry, search and seizure

3.1 Introduction

This chapter is concerned with the legal powers:

- to enter premises for the purpose of searching for persons or things (search); and
- to seize such persons or things if found (seizure).

The powers range from the general to the very specific and emphasis will here be placed upon the main powers. By far the most important statutory provisions are to be found in the Police and Criminal Evidence Act (PACE) 1984 backed up by PACE Code of Practice B.

This chapter is not concerned with situations where one person enters and remains on another's premises with that other's consent (but see PACE Code of Practice B, para 5), nor with the powers of the police to stop and search an individual or vehicle without entering premises (for important examples of such powers see PACE 1984, ss 1–3 and s 32(1) and (2)(a), Misuse of Drugs Act 1971, s 23(2)—see generally PACE Code of Practice A).

Perhaps the main distinction to be drawn when considering the powers to enter premises is between:

- powers which can be exercised without a warrant; and
- those which can only be exercised with a warrant.

In this context, the warrant referred to is an express authorisation given by 'the court' to enter premises. Such warrants are often called search warrants and are to be distinguished from arrest warrants. Further details about search warrants are given below at **3.4**.

For the evidential consequences of a failure to comply with the rules on search and seizure described in this chapter, see **3.6** below.

3.2 Powers of search exercisable without a warrant

3.2.1 Police and Criminal Evidence Act 1984, s 17

A constable may enter and search premises without a warrant for the purpose of, *inter alia*:

(a) executing a warrant of arrest issued in connection with or arising out of criminal proceedings;

(b) arresting a person for an indictable offence;

(c) arresting a person for an offence under the Public Order Act 1936, s 1, the Public Order Act 1986, s 4, the Criminal Law Act 1977, ss 6, 7, 8 or 10, the Road Traffic Act 1988, ss 4 or 163 or the Animal Welfare Act 2006, ss 4–8;

(d) arresting, in pursuance of the Children and Young Persons Act 1968, s 32(1A), any child or young person who has been remanded or committed to local authority accommodation under s 23(1) of that Act;

(e) recapturing a person unlawfully at large while liable to be detained in a prison, remand centre, young offenders institution, or secure training centre, or in pursuance of the Powers of Criminal Courts (Sentencing) Act 2000, s 92 in any other place;

(f) recapturing a person who is unlawfully at large and whom he is pursuing;

(g) saving life or limb or preventing serious damage to property.

Except for the purpose specified in (g), these powers are exercisable only if the constable has reasonable grounds for believing that the person whom he is seeking is on the premises. Also, the power of entry to arrest for the offences under the Criminal Law Act 1977 mentioned in (c) above, is exercisable only by a constable in uniform. While there is a general duty to inform an occupier for the reasons for entry, where a constable is exercising his power under s 17 that is not always mandatory, for example where it is impossible, impracticable or undesirable to do so (*Baker v Crown Prosecution Service* (2009) 173 JP 215).

Section 17(5) provides that, subject to s 17(6), all the common law rules under which a constable has power to enter premises without a warrant are abolished. Section 17(6) preserves the common law power of entry to deal with or prevent a breach of the peace. The scope of this common law power was considered in *Thomas v Sawkins* [1935] 2 KB 249. Although it seems to be a wide power, the police do not in practice appear to rely on it heavily. This may be due partly to the narrowness of the definition of 'breach of the peace' used by the Court of Appeal in *Howell* [1982] QB 416, *viz.* 'an act done or threatened to be done which either actually harms a person or, in his presence, his property, or is likely to cause such harm, or which puts someone in fear of such harm'.

3.2.2 Police and Criminal Evidence Act 1984, s 18

A constable may (subject to s 18(3)–(8)) enter and search any premises occupied or controlled by a person who is under arrest for an indictable offence, if he has reasonable grounds for suspecting that there is on the premises evidence other than items subject to legal privilege relating to that offence or to some other indictable offence which is connected with, or similar to, that offence. The constable may seize and retain anything for which he may search (s 18(2)).

Section 18(3)–(7) provide that:

(a) the extent of the search is limited to that which is reasonably required for the purpose of discovering the type of evidence specified (s18(3));

(b) the power is exercisable only if an officer of the rank of inspector or above has authorised it in writing (see *Badham* [1987] Crim LR 202), *unless* it is exercised before the arrested person is taken to a police station or released on 'street bail' under s 30A of the Act and that person's presence at a place other than a police station is necessary for the effective investigation of the offence (in such an exceptional case the constable in question must inform an officer of the rank of inspector or above that he has made the search as soon as practicable after he has made it) (s18(5),(5A) and (6)). Note here the effect of s 107(2), permitting a sergeant to assume the powers of an inspector if he has been authorised by an officer of at least the rank of superintendent;

(c) the officer who authorises (or is informed of) the search must keep a written record of the grounds for the search and the nature of the evidence sought (s18(7)).

In *Khan v Commissioner of Police of the Metropolis* The Times, 16 June 2008, the Court of Appeal rejected an argument that a search should be lawful where a police officer had a reasonable belief that the premises are owned or occupied by the arrested person. There could be no justification for reading s 18 other than in accordance with its plain words: the power may be exercised only at premises 'occupied or controlled' by the person under arrest.

3.2.3   Police and Criminal Evidence Act 1984, s 32

By s 32(2)(b) (subject to s 32(3)–(7)), in any case where a person has been arrested for an indictable offence at a place other than a police station, a constable shall have the power to enter and search any premises in which the arrested person was when arrested or immediately before he was arrested (whether or not he was the occupier or controller of such premises, *cf* s 18 above) for evidence relating to the offence for which he was arrested.

Section 32(3)–(7) provide that:

(a) the extent of the search is limited to that which is reasonably required for the purpose of discovering the type of evidence specified (s 32(3));

(b) a constable may not undertake a s 32(2)(b) search unless he has reasonable grounds for believing that there is evidence on those premises for which such search is permitted (s 32(6));

(c) insofar as the s 32(2)(b) search relates to premises consisting of two or more separate dwellings, it is limited to a search of the dwelling in which the arrest took place or in which the person arrested was immediately before his arrest and any parts of the premises which the occupier of such dwelling uses in common with the occupiers of any other dwellings comprised in the premises (s 32(7)).

There is a common law power to similar effect (see *Ghani v Jones* [1970] 1 QB 693 and *R (Rottman) v Commissioner of Police of the Metropolis* [2002] 2 AC 692).

3.2.4   Misuse of Drugs Act 1971, s 23

By s 23(1), a constable (or other person authorised by a general or special order of the Secretary of State) shall, for the purposes of the execution of this Act, have power to enter the premises of a person carrying on business as a producer or supplier of any controlled drugs and to demand the production of, and to inspect, any books or documents relating to dealings in any such drugs and to inspect any stocks of any such drugs. Section 23(2) further provides that a constable who has reasonable grounds to suspect that a person is in possession of a controlled drug in contravention of the Act may search that person (or any vehicle or vessel in which it is suspected the drug may be found) and seize and detain anything which appears to him to be evidence of an offence under the Act. Section 23(4) creates a range of offences relating to the obstruction of a person exercising the powers contained in s 23(1).

3.2.5 Other statutory powers

The main powers of entry without a warrant have now been dealt with. However, there are several specific statutory powers which, in very limited circumstances, permit a search of premises to be authorised by a senior police officer (usually a superintendent). See, for example, the Terrorism Act 2000, the Explosives Act 1875, the Official Secrets Act 1911, Proceeds of Crime Act 2002, s 289.

3.3 Powers of search with a warrant

3.3.1 Police and Criminal Evidence Act 1984, s 8

By s 8(1), on an application made by a constable, a justice of the peace may issue either:

(a) A *Specific Premises Warrant*. This is a warrant which authorises a constable to enter and search one or more sets of premises specified in the application; or

(b) An *All Premises Warrant*. This is a warrant which authorises a constable to enter and search any premises occupied or controlled by a person specified in the application.

In *Redknapp v Commissioner of Police of the Metropolis* [2008] 1 All ER 229 it was stated obiter that whilst the Act distinguishes descriptively between 'a specific premises warrant' and an 'all premises warrant', there is no indication in PACE itself that one warrant cannot include both types.

A justice of the peace may only issue a *Specific Premises Warrant* if satisfied that there are reasonable grounds for believing:

(a) that an indictable offence has been committed; *and*

(b) that there is material on such premises which is likely to be of substantial value (whether by itself or together with other material) to the investigation of the offence; *and*

(c) that the material is likely to be relevant and admissible in evidence at a trial; *and*

(d) that it does not consist of or include items subject to legal privilege, excluded material or special procedure material; *and*

(e) that in relation to each set of premises specified in the application it is not practicable to communicate with any person entitled to grant entry to the premises, or although it is practicable to communicate with such person it is not practicable to communicate with any person entitled to grant access to the evidence, or that entry to the premises will not be granted unless a warrant is produced, or that the purpose of a search may be frustrated or seriously prejudiced unless a constable arriving at the premises can secure immediate entry to them. A failure to specify on the application form which of the four conditions applies will render the issue of a warrant unlawful (*Redknapp v Commissioner of Police of the Metropolis* [2008] 1 All ER 229, DC).

(For the definition of 'excluded material' and 'special procedure material' and the special procedures relating to such material, see **3.4.2** below.)

A justice of the peace may only issue an *All Premises Warrant* if additionally satisfied:

(a) that because of the particulars of the offence, there are reasonable grounds for believing that it is necessary to search premises occupied or controlled by the person in question which are not specified in the application in order to find the material sought; and

(b) that it is not reasonably practicable to specify in the application all the premises which he occupies or controls and which might need to be searched.

When applying for an *All Premises Warrant*, s 15(2A)(b) requires the constable to specify as many sets of premises which it is desired to enter and search as it is reasonably practicable to specify, why it is necessary to search more premises than those specified and why it is not reasonably practicable to specify all the premises which it is desired to enter and search (see **3.4.1**). Where an *All Premises Warrant* is issued, premises other than those specified in the warrant may only be searched if a police officer of at least the rank of inspector has given written authorisation (s 16(3A); see **3.4.1**).

In either case, it is unnecessary to have already tried other methods of entry and failed, nor is it necessary to demonstrate that other methods would be bound to fail, when applying for a warrant.

By s 8(2), a constable may seize and retain anything for which a search has been authorised under s 8(1).

Either type of warrant may authorise entry to and search of premises on more than one occasion if the justice of the peace is satisfied that it is necessary to authorise multiple entries in order to achieve the purpose for which the warrant is issued. If it authorises multiple entries, the number of entries authorised may be unlimited, or limited to a maximum. However, no premises may be searched for the second or subsequent time under a warrant authorising multiple entries unless an officer of at least the rank of inspector has given written authorisation (s 16(3B); see **3.4.1**).

Once the police have a search warrant, the date and time of its execution are a matter for them to decide. However, the warrant will cease to be valid three months after the date of its issue; also, execution should occur at a reasonable hour (unless this would frustrate the purpose of the search).

Section 8 warrants may be issued in respect of any indictable offence. However, there are further specific statutory powers to issue warrants in relation to particular offences. These powers are considered below. It should be noted that the power to issue such warrants differs from the power under s 8 in two significant respects. First, the criteria that must be satisfied before a warrant can be issued are different from those under s 8 and, second, in some cases, the powers extend to summary offences.

3.3.2   Misuse of Drugs Act 1971, s 23(3)

If a justice of the peace is satisfied by information on oath that there is reasonable ground for suspecting:

• that any controlled drugs are, in contravention of this Act, in the possession of a person on any premises; or

• that a document relating to a transaction or dealing which was (or would if carried out be) an offence under this Act is in the possession of a person on any premises, he may grant a warrant authorising any constable acting for the police area in which the premises are situated to enter, if need be by force, the premises named in the warrant and to search the premises and any persons found therein, and if there is reasonable ground for suspecting that an offence under this Act has been committed in relation to any drugs or document found, to seize and detain those drugs or that document. See also the Drug Trafficking Act 1994, ss 55 and 56.

3.3.3   Theft Act 1968, s 26

If it is made to appear by information or order before a justice of the peace that there is reasonable cause to believe that any person has in his custody or possession or on his premises any stolen goods, the justice may grant a warrant to search for and seize the same. The warrant must be addressed to a constable (unless a particular enactment expressly provides otherwise).

3.3.4   Criminal Damage Act 1971, s 6

If it is made to appear by information on oath before a justice of the peace that there is reasonable cause to believe that a person has in his custody, his control or on his premises something which there is reasonable cause to believe has been used or is intended for use without lawful excuse, to destroy or damage either property belonging to another or his own property (if damage to it would endanger the life of another), the justice may grant a warrant to search for and seize the same.

3.3.5   Other statutory powers

The powers of entry with a warrant which are of most general application have now been dealt with. However, there are numerous specific statutory powers of entry with a warrant. For important examples, see the Offences Against the Person Act 1861, s 65, the Obscene Publications Act 1959, s 3, the Forgery and Counterfeiting Act 1981, ss 7 and 24, the Criminal Justice Act 1987, s 2, the Copyright, Designs and Patents Act 1988, s 109, the Public Order Act 1986, s 24 and the Serious Organised Crime and Police Act 2005, s 66.

3.4   Search warrants—general rules and restrictions

3.4.1   Procedure

Although PACE 1984 left intact many specific statutory powers to search *with a warrant*, the Act, in ss 15 and 16, laid down rules and restrictions of general application to search warrants issued to a constable under *any enactment* (the rules and restrictions also apply to Customs and Excise Officers and Environmental Protection Officers).

Since these sections contain relatively straightforward procedural rules, they are set out in full below. The procedure is augmented by Code of Practice B, paras 3–6.

> *15.—(1) This section and section 16 below have effect in relation to the issue to constables under any enactment, including an enactment contained in an Act passed after this Act, of warrants*

to enter and search premises; and an entry on or search of premises under a warrant is unlawful unless it complies with this section and section 16 below.

(2) Where a constable applies for any such warrant, it shall be his duty—

    (a) to state—

        (i) the ground on which he makes the application; and

        (ii) the enactment under which the warrant would be issued; and

        (iii) if the application is for a warrant authorising entry and search on more than one occasion, the ground on which he applies for such a warrant, and whether he seeks a warrant authorising an unlimited number of entries, or (if not) the maximum number of entries desired;

    (b) to specify the matters set out in subsection (2A) below; and

    (c) to identify, so far as is practicable, the articles or persons to be sought.

(2A) The matters which must be specified pursuant to subsection (2)(b) above are—

    (a) if the application is for a specific premises warrant made by virtue of section 8(1A)(a) above or paragraph 12 of Schedule 1 below, each set of premises which it is desired to enter and search;

    (b) if the application is for an all premises warrant made by virtue of section 8(1A)(b) above or paragraph 12 of Schedule 1 below—

        (i) as many sets of premises which it is desired to enter and search as it is reasonably practicable to specify;

        (ii) the person who is in occupation or control of those premises and any others which it is desired to enter and search;

        (iii) why it is necessary to search more premises than those specified under sub-paragraph (i); and

        (iv) why it is not reasonably practicable to specify all the premises which it is desired to enter and search.

(3) An application for such a warrant shall be made ex parte and supported by an information in writing.

(4) The constable shall answer on oath any question that the justice of the peace or judge hearing the application asks him.

(5) A warrant shall authorise an entry on one occasion only unless it specifies that it authorises multiple entries.

(5A) If it specifies that it authorises multiple entries, it must also specify whether the number of entries authorised is unlimited, or limited to a specified maximum.

(6) A warrant—

    (a) shall specify—

        (i) the name of the person who applies for it;

        (ii) the date on which it is issued;

        (iii) the enactment under which it is issued; and

        (iv) each set of premises to be searched, or (in the case of an all premises warrant) the person who is in occupation or control of premises to be searched, together with any premises under his occupation or control which can be specified and which are to be searched; and

    (b) shall identify, so far as is practicable, the articles or persons to be sought.

(7) Two copies shall be made of a warrant which specifies only one set of premises and does not authorise multiple entries; and as many copies as are reasonably required may be made of any other kind of warrant.

(8) The copies shall be clearly certified as copies.

16.—(1) A warrant to enter and search premises may be executed by any constable.

(2) Such a warrant may authorise persons to accompany any constable who is executing it.

(2A) A person so authorised has the same powers as the constable whom he accompanies in respect of—

(a)   the execution of the warrant, and

(b)   the seizure of anything to which the warrant relates.

(2B) But he may exercise those powers only in the company, and under the supervision, of a constable.

(3) Entry and search under a warrant must be within three months from the date of its issue.

(3A) If the warrant is an all premises warrant, no premises which are not specified in it may be entered or searched unless a police officer of at least the rank of inspector has in writing authorised them to be entered.

(3B) No premises may be entered or searched for the second or any subsequent time under a warrant which authorises multiple entries unless a police officer of at least the rank of inspector has in writing authorised that entry to those premises.

(4) Entry and search under a warrant must be at a reasonable hour unless it appears to the constable executing it that the purpose of a search may be frustrated on an entry at a reasonable hour.

(5) Where the occupier of premises which are to be entered and searched is present at the time when a constable seeks to execute a warrant to enter and search them, the constable—

(a)   shall identify himself to the occupier and, if not in uniform, shall produce to him documentary evidence that he is a constable;

(b)   shall produce the warrant to him; and

(c)   shall supply him with a copy of it.

(6) Where—

(a)   the occupier of such premises is not present at the time when a constable seeks to execute such a warrant; but

(b)   some other person who appears to the constable to be in charge of the premises is present,

subsection (5) above shall have effect as if any reference to the occupier were a reference to that other person.

(7) If there is no person present who appears to the constable to be in charge of the premises, he shall leave a copy of the warrant in a prominent place on the premises.

(8) A search under a warrant may only be a search to the extent required for the purpose for which the warrant was issued.

(9) A constable executing a warrant shall make an endorsement on it stating—

(a)   whether the articles or persons sought were found; and

(b)   whether any articles were seized, other than articles which were sought and,

unless the warrant is a warrant specifying one set of premises only, he shall do so separately in respect of each set of premises entered and searched, which he shall in each case state in the endorsement.

(10) A warrant shall be returned to the appropriate person mentioned in subsection (10A) below—

(a)   when it has been executed; or

(b)   in the case of a specific premises warrant which has not been executed, or an all premises warrant, or any warrant authorising multiple entries, upon the expiry of the period of three months referred to in subsection (3) above or sooner.

(10A) The appropriate person is—

(a)   if the warrant was issued by a justice of the peace, the designated officer for the local justice area in which the justice was acting when he issued the warrant;

(b)   if it was issued by a judge, the appropriate officer of the court from which he issued it.

(11) A warrant which is returned under subsection (10) above shall be retained for 12 months from its return—

    (a) by the designated officer for the local justice area, if it was returned under paragraph (i) of that subsection; and

    (b) by the appropriate officer, if it was returned under paragraph (ii).

(12) If during the period for which a warrant is to be retained the occupier of premises to which it relates asks to inspect it, he shall be allowed to do so.

3.4.2 Protected material: special procedures

Although PACE 1984 creates a general power to issue search warrants in cases where there are reasonable grounds for believing that an indictable offence has been committed (see **3.3.1**), three categories of material are to a greater or lesser extent protected from being the object of search. These categories are:

- legally privileged material;
- excluded material; and
- special procedure material.

3.4.2.1 Legally privileged material

This category should require no introduction—see *Evidence Manual* at **19.2.2**. Since:

- PACE 1984 provides no power to search for legally privileged material; and
- the Act states, in s 9(2), that any Act preceding PACE 1984 shall cease to have effect insofar as it authorises a search for *any* of the three protected categories; and
- no subsequent Act provides a power to grant a warrant to search for legally privileged items,

legally privileged material may be treated as being fully protected (at least until a subsequent Act alters the position).

However, while there may be no power to issue a warrant to *search* for legally privileged material, a constable may nevertheless *seize* such material in certain circumstances (see the Criminal Justice and Police Act 2001, ss 50 and 51, and **3.5.2** below).

3.4.2.2 Excluded material

Excluded material is defined by PACE 1984, s 11 as follows:

- personal records acquired, or created, in the course of any trade, business, profession or other occupation or for the purposes of any paid or unpaid office, and which are held in confidence;
- human tissue or tissue fluid taken for the purposes of diagnosis or medical treatment and held in confidence;
- journalistic material held in confidence.

Personal records include medical records and spiritual and welfare counselling records about an individual (whether living or dead) who can be identified from them (s 12). A special warrant to search for such material may be obtained by leave of a circuit judge (for the procedure, see **3.4.2.4**).

3.4.2.3 Special procedure material

Special procedure material consists of any material (falling outside the first two categories) which a person acquired, or created, in the course of any trade, business, profession or other occupation or for the purpose of any paid or unpaid office, and which he holds subject to an express or implied undertaking to keep it confidential, and journalistic material (even if not held in confidence) (s 14). A special warrant to search for such material may be obtained by leave of a circuit judge (for the procedure, see **3.4.2.4**).

3.4.2.4 Special warrants

As noted above (at **3.3.1**) an ordinary search warrant (under s 8 of PACE 1984) cannot be issued in relation to items subject to legal privilege, excluded material or special procedure material. However, as regards excluded or special procedure material, if the procedure laid down in Sch 1 to PACE 1984 is followed (see below), a circuit judge may order that such material should be produced or that access to it should be given. If the person to whom the order is addressed fails to comply with the order, the judge may then issue a special warrant (pursuant to Sch 1, para 12).

Schedule 1 to PACE 1984 states:

1. *If on an application made by a constable a judge is satisfied that one or other of the sets of access conditions is fulfilled, he may make an order under paragraph 4 below.*

2. *The first set of access conditions is fulfilled if—*
   (a) *there are reasonable grounds for believing—*
       (i) *that an indictable offence has been committed;*
       (ii) *that there is material which consists of special procedure material or also includes special procedure material and does not also include excluded material on premises specified in the application, or on premises occupied or controlled by a person specified in the application (including all such premises on which there are reasonable grounds for believing that there is such material as it is reasonably practicable so to specify);*
       (iii) *that the material is likely to be of substantial value (whether by itself or together with other material) to the investigation in connection with which the application is made; and*
       (iv) *that the material is likely to be relevant evidence;*
   (b) *other methods of obtaining the material—*
       (i) *have been tried without success; or*
       (ii) *have not been tried because it appeared that they were bound to fail; and*
   (c) *it is in the public interest, having regard—*
       (i) *to the benefit likely to accrue to the investigation if the material is obtained; and*
       (ii) *to the circumstances under which the person in possession of the material holds it, that the material should be produced or that access to it should be given.*

3. *The second set of access conditions is fulfilled if—*
   (a) *there are reasonable grounds for believing that there is material which consists of or includes excluded material or special procedure material on premises specified in the application, or on premises occupied or controlled by a person specified in the application (including all such premises on which there are reasonable grounds for believing that there is such material as it is reasonably practicable so to specify);*
   (b) *but for section 9(2) above a search of such premises for that material could have been authorised by the issue of a warrant to a constable under an enactment other than this Schedule; and*
   (c) *the issue of such a warrant would have been appropriate.*

4. *An order under this paragraph is an order that the person who appears to the judge to be in possession of the material to which the application relates shall—*

(a) *produce it to a constable for him to take away; or*

(b) *give a constable access to it, not later than the end of the period of seven days from the date of the order or the end of such longer period as the order may specify.*

. . .

12. *If on an application made by a constable a judge—*

(a) *is satisfied—*

    (i) *that either set of access conditions is fulfilled; and*

    (ii) *that any of the further conditions set out in paragraph 14 below is also fulfilled in relation to each set of premises specified in the application; or*

(b) *is satisfied—*

    (i) *that the second set of access conditions is fulfilled; and*

    (ii) *that an order under paragraph 4 above relating to the material has not been complied with,*

he may issue a warrant authorising a constable to enter and search the premises or (as the case may be) all premises occupied or controlled by the person referred to in paragraph 2(a)(ii) or 3(a), including such sets of premises as are specified in the application (an 'all premises warrant').

12A. *The judge may not issue an all premises warrant unless he is satisfied—*

(a) *that there are reasonable grounds for believing that it is necessary to search premises occupied or controlled by the person in question which are not specified in the application, as well as those which are, in order to find the material in question; and*

(b) *that it is not reasonably practicable to specify all the premises which he occupies or controls which might need to be searched.*

13. *A constable may seize and retain anything for which a search has been authorised under paragraph 12 above.*

14. *The further conditions mentioned in paragraph 12(a)(ii) above are—*

(a) *that it is not practicable to communicate with any person entitled to grant entry to the premises;*

(b) *that it is practicable to communicate with a person entitled to grant entry to the premises but it is not practicable to communicate with any person entitled to grant access to the material;*

(c) *that the material contains information which—*

    (i) *is subject to a restriction or obligation such as is mentioned in section 11(2)(b) above; and*

    (ii) *is likely to be disclosed in breach of it if a warrant is not issued;*

(d) *that service of notice of an application for an order under paragraph 4 above may seriously prejudice the investigation.*

It is permissible for the police to seek voluntary disclosure even if there would be no chance of an application under Sch 1 succeeding (see *Singleton* [1995] 1 Cr App R 431).

Note: There is a distinction between (i) cases where protected material is sought in an investigation into whether a criminal offence has been committed; and (ii) cases where such material is sought for the purposes of an investigation (as part of confiscation proceedings) into whether any person has benefited from any criminal conduct. In the latter situation, an order may be granted under the Proceeds of Crime Act 2002, s 352 (these are not dealt with here as confiscation is a specialist area). Section 354 expressly provides that a warrant issued for this purpose does not confer a right to seize privileged or excluded material. However, as the section is silent on special procedure material, it is submitted that such material may be seized under this type of warrant. The fact that an incidental effect of confiscation proceedings (and orders under s 352) might be to reveal the commission of an offence will not be a bar to the making of such an order (see *Crown Court at Southwark, ex p Bowles* [1998] AC 641).

3.5 Seizure

3.5.1 PACE 1984

Section 19 of PACE 1984 contains general provisions regarding the seizure of things in circumstances where a constable is lawfully on any premises. The powers of seizure are supplemented by Code of Practice B, paras 7(a), (c) and (d). Under s 19, a constable may seize anything which is on the premises if he has reasonable grounds for believing:

(a) that it has been obtained in consequence of the commission of an offence; and that it is necessary to seize it in order to prevent it being concealed, lost, damaged, altered or destroyed; or

(b) that it is evidence in relation to an offence which he is investigating or any other offence; and that it is necessary to seize it in order to prevent the evidence being concealed, lost, altered or destroyed.

The constable may require any information which is stored in any electronic form and is accessible from the premises to be produced in a form in which it can be taken away and in which it is visible and legible or from which it can readily be produced in a visible and legible form if he has grounds for believing:

(a) that
    (i) it is evidence in relation to an offence which he is investigating or any other offence; or
    (ii) it has been obtained in consequence of the commission of an offence; and

(b) that it is necessary to do so in order to prevent it being concealed, lost, tampered with or destroyed.

It will be noted that these are very wide powers. They are restricted by the operation of s 19(6) which provides that no power of seizure conferred on a constable under *any* enactment (including an Act passed after the 1984 Act) is to be taken to authorise the seizure of an item which the constable exercising the power has reasonable grounds for believing to be subject to legal privilege. This provision does not apply to the powers of seizure exercisable under ss 50 and 51 of the Criminal Justice and Police Act 2001 which permit the seizure of legally privileged material in certain circumstances (see 3.5.2 below).

Under s 21, the officer in charge of an investigation is required to allow access to or provide copies or photographs of things seized unless allowing such access would prejudice the investigation in which the thing was seized (or related investigations) (s 21(4)–(8)). However, things seized may be retained by the police for as long as is necessary in all the circumstances (s 22(1)). Retention will, for example, be necessary if a photograph or copy is insufficient for police purposes, or because the thing is stolen or might be used to cause damage or injury.

3.5.2   Criminal Justice and Police Act 2001

The statutory powers of seizure under PACE 1984 have been considerably widened by the new 'seize and sift' provisions in the Criminal Justice and Police Act (CJPA) 2001. The powers are augmented by Code of Practice B, para 7(b). It should be noted that the new 'search and sift' provisions apply not only to powers of seizure under PACE but also to a wide range of other statutory powers of seizure (see further CJPA 2001, Sch 1, Part 1).

CJPA 2001, s 50 is designed to address two problematic areas, namely:

(a) where it cannot be determined during the course of the search whether an item, or its contents, are subject to a power of seizure; and

(b) where material is discovered during a search which *is* subject to a power of seizure but it is inextricably linked to other material, including legally privileged, excluded or special procedure material, for which there is no power of seizure.

Under s 50(1) of the Act, where a person who is lawfully on any premises finds something that he has reasonable grounds for believing may be, or may contain, something for which he is authorised to search and which he is entitled to seize but, in the circumstances, it is not reasonably practicable to determine whether he is in fact entitled to seize it, then he may seize so much of what he has found as is necessary to enable that to be determined. When considering whether or not it would be reasonably practicable to make such a determination, regard must be had to the list of criteria in s 50(3) which includes the length of time that it would take, the number of persons that would be involved, the nature of any equipment required and whether the process would be likely to involve damage to property.

Under s 50(2), where a person is lawfully on any premises and finds something which he would be entitled to seize but for its being comprised in other material that he has no power to seize and, in all the circumstances, it is not reasonably practicable for the seizable property to be separated on the premises, then that person may seize both the seizable and the other property. This power is particularly relevant to information held on computer media. Significantly, PACE 1984, s 19(6) does not apply to this provision (s 50(4)) and so a person conducting a search would be entitled to seize legally privileged material. When considering whether it would be reasonably practicable for seizable material to be separated from the other material in which it is comprised, regard must be had to the criteria in s 50(3).

Section 53 provides that an initial examination of property seized must be carried out as soon as is reasonably practicable after its seizure for the purpose of assessing which property must be returned and which may be retained. Section 53(3) provides that property must be returned unless:

(a) it is property for which the person seizing it had power to search and which does not have to be returned under s 54 on the ground that it is legally privileged material;

(b) it is property the retention of which is authorised by s 56; or

(c) it is material which, in all the circumstances, it will not be reasonably practicable, following the examination, to separate from property falling within category (a) or (b) above without prejudicing the use of the rest of that property.

By s 54, there is an obligation to return any legally privileged material (or material in which a legally privileged item is comprised) as soon as is reasonably practicable after its seizure. However, where the legally privileged item is comprised in other material then there is no duty to return it if:

(a) the property in which it is comprised is:
  (i) property for which the person seizing it had power to search when he made the seizure but does not fall to be returned under s 54 (on the grounds that it is legally privileged) or under s 55 (by virtue of its being excluded or special procedure material); or
  (ii) property the retention of which is authorised under s 56; and
(b) in all the circumstances, it is not reasonably practicable for the legally privileged item to be separated from the rest of the property without prejudicing the use of the rest of that property.

By s 56, property seized on any premises by a constable (or a person accompanying a constable) who was lawfully on the premises may be retained if there are reasonable grounds for believing that:

  (i) it is property obtained in consequence of the commission of an offence and it is necessary for it to be retained in order to prevent its being concealed, lost, damaged, altered or destroyed; or
  (ii) there are reasonable grounds for believing that it is evidence in relation to any offence and that it is necessary for it to be retained in order to prevent its being concealed, lost, damaged, altered or destroyed.

Where legally privileged, excluded or special procedure material has been seized because it is inextricably linked to material for which the police were entitled to search, it may only be examined, copied or put to any other use where to do so is necessary to facilitate the use of the material in which it is comprised in any investigation or proceedings (s 62).

The retention of any property that has been seized under s 50 is additionally subject to PACE 1984 s 22 (see **3.5.1**).

The Act makes provision for anyone with an interest in the seized property to apply to a judge of the Crown Court for its return on the grounds that its seizure or retention is unlawful (s 59).

3.6 Evidential consequences of breach of rules on search and seizure

At common law, evidence obtained by illegal search or seizure is admissible (*Jeffrey v Black* [1978] QB 490). However, a court may exclude such evidence by virtue of the discretion under PACE 1984, s 78. In order to do so, it must be satisfied that the admission of the evidence would adversely effect the fairness of the proceedings. In *Rotherham Magistrates' Court, ex p Todd*, unreported, 16 February 2000, DC, Lord Justice Simon Brown said:

Absent bad faith or a flagrant and deliberate breach of one of the codes of practice issued pursuant to the 1984 Act, or some other matter affecting the quality of the evidence, the mere fact that evidence is discovered in the course of an unlawful search is unlikely to render the admission of the evidence unfair.

Thus, an accused will ordinarily have to point to some prejudice over and above the unlawfulness of the search before a court will exclude evidence obtained during an illegal search. See also *Khan, Sakkaravej and Pamarapa* [1997] Crim LR 508.

3.7 Further reading

Stone, R., *The Law of Entry, Search, and Seizure*, 4th edn (Oxford: Oxford University Press, 2005).

Zander, M., *The Police and Criminal Evidence Act 1984*, 5th edn (London: Sweet & Maxwell, 2005).

4

Abuse of process

4.1 Introduction

The criminal courts have discretion to prevent a prosecution proceeding against a defendant by staying (ie suspending) the proceedings. Traditionally, it was thought that the court could only properly stay proceedings:

(a) where the indictment was found to be defective, eg because it is duplicitous;

(b) where a plea in bar was tried and resolved in favour of the defendant, eg *autrefois acquit* (where the defendant claims he faces double jeopardy because he has already been acquitted of the alleged offence);

(c) where a *nolle prosequi* is entered by the Attorney-General (where the Attorney-General steps in to stop proceedings, eg where a person is considered permanently unfit to stand trial);

(d) where the indictment discloses no offence that the court has jurisdiction to try, eg an indictment alleging adultery or wearing an offensive shirt.

A fifth category was added to the list in the case of *Connelly v DPP* [1964] AC 1254, HL:

(e) where the criminal proceedings are considered by the court to be an abuse of its own process.

This chapter deals with this particular area of judicial discretion.

4.2 Abuse of process

In *DPP v Humphrys* [1977] AC 1, HL, Lord Salmon stated at 46:

It is only if the prosecution amounts to an abuse of the process of the court and is oppressive and vexatious that the judge has the power to intervene. Fortunately, such prosecutions are hardly ever brought but the power of the court to prevent them is, in my view, of great constitutional importance and should be jealously preserved. For a man to be harassed and be put to the expense of perhaps a long trial and then given an absolute discharge is hardly from any point of view an effective substitute for the exercise by the court of the power to which I have referred.

In *Beckford* [1996] 1 Cr App R 94, CA, the Court of Appeal reviewed the case law and identified two principles on which proceedings could be stayed for abuse of process:

(a) where the defendant could not receive a fair trial; and

(b) where it would be unfair to try the defendant.

Applications to stay proceedings on the grounds of abuse of process have been granted in a wide variety of situations. The circumstances most commonly or resulting in stays for abuse of process applications are:

(a) where there has been substantial delay in commencing a prosecution;

(b) where the prosecution have failed to honour an undertaking given to the defendant;

(c) where the police, or another investigative agency, have entrapped the defendant into committing an offence;

(d) where the prosecution have failed to secure or even destroyed potentially exculpatory evidence; and

(e) where the prosecution have manipulated particular procedures so as to deprive a defendant of some right.

We will consider each of these categories in more detail. It is important to realise that this list is not exhaustive and is merely illustrative of some of the most commonly occurring situations in which the courts have stayed proceedings as an abuse of process.

4.2.1 Delay

Delay in bringing a prosecution may amount to an abuse of process. In the *Attorney-General's Reference (No 1 of 1990)* [1992] QB 630, the Court of Appeal held that a stay should only be imposed on the grounds of delay in exceptional circumstances. In principle, even where the delay can be said to be unjustifiable, the imposition of a stay should be the exception rather than the rule. Still more rare should be cases where a stay can properly be imposed in the absence of any fault on the part of the complainant or prosecution. Delay due merely to the complexity of the case or contributed to by the actions of the defendant himself should never be the foundation for a stay. In order for a stay to be granted, the defendant must show on the balance of probabilities that owing to the delay he will suffer serious prejudice to the extent that no fair trial can be held. In assessing whether there is likely to be prejudice, and, if so, whether it can properly be described as serious, the following matters should be borne in mind: first, the power of the judge at common law and under the Police and Criminal Evidence Act 1984 to regulate the admissibility of evidence; second, the trial process itself, which should ensure that all relevant factual issues arising from delay will be placed before the jury as part of the evidence for their consideration, together with the powers of the judge to give appropriate directions to the jury before they consider their verdict.

The relevant JSB Specimen Direction (see http://www.jsboard.co.uk/criminal_law/cbb/index.htm) is as follows:

> 37. Delay
>
> We are now concerned with events which are said to have taken place a long time ago. You must appreciate that because of this there may be a danger of real prejudice to a defendant. This possibility must be in your mind when you decide whether the prosecution has made you sure of the defendant's guilt.
>
> 1. (Where appropriate:) You are entitled to consider why these matters did not come to light sooner. Is that a reflection on the reliability of the complaint? Or does it arise from the conduct of the defendant? You have been given an explanation for this, which is [...]
>
> 2. You should make allowances for the fact that with the passage of time memories fade. Witnesses, whoever they may be, cannot be expected to remember with crystal clarity events

which occurred [many years ago]. Sometimes the passage of time may even play tricks on memories.

3. You should also make allowances for the fact that from the defendant's point of view, the longer the time since an alleged incident, the more difficult it may be for him to answer it. [For example, has the passage of time deprived him of the opportunity to put forward an alibi and evidence in support of it?] You only have to imagine what it would be like to have to answer questions about events which are said to have taken place [...] years ago to appreciate the problems which may be caused by delay. Even if you believe that the delay in this case is understandable, if you decide that because of this the defendant has been placed at a real disadvantage in putting forward his case, take that into account in his favour when deciding if the prosecution has made you sure of his guilt.

4. (Where appropriate in the case of a defendant of good character i.e. either here, or when giving the second limb of the good character direction on page 23.2, add:) Having regard to what you know about this defendant and in particular the [...] years since the date of the alleged offence [and (if it be the case) that no similar allegation has been made against him] you may think he is entitled to ask you to give considerable/more than usual weight to his good character when deciding whether the prosecution has satisfied you of his guilt.

In *S* [2006] 2 Cr App R 23, the Court of Appeal held that the correct approach for a judge to whom an application for a stay for abuse of process on the ground of delay is made, could be summarised as follows:

(i) even where delay is unjustifiable, a permanent stay should be the exception rather than the rule;

(ii) where there is no fault on the part of the complainant or the prosecution, it will be very rare for a stay to be granted;

(iii) no stay should be granted in the absence of serious prejudice to the defence so that no fair trial can be held;

(iv) when assessing possible serious prejudice, the judge should bear in mind his or her power to regulate the admissibility of evidence and that the trial process itself should ensure that all relevant factual issues arising from delay will be placed before the jury for their consideration in accordance with appropriate direction from the judge;

(v) if, having considered all these factors, a judge's assessment is that a fair trial will be possible, a stay should not be granted.

In determining whether a defendant has been so prejudiced by the delay that a fair trial would be impossible, the court ought to look at the nature of the defence proposed; whether any admissions were made; whether independent witnesses present at the time may be traced or, if they were traced, their ability to recall events; contamination of evidence between prosecution witnesses, inconsistencies in prosecution evidence and the ability of the defence, given the delay, to adequately test those inconsistencies, for example, by calling other witnesses; the reason for the delay (eg, the extent to which defendant was responsible for the delay) and any other factors that are relevant to the particular issues in the case. Each case will turn on its facts, however, and the above list is not exhaustive.

Where the delay is deliberate or attributable to bad faith on the part of the prosecutor then proceedings are likely to be stayed an abuse of process. See, for example, *Brentford Justices, ex p Wong* [1981] QB 445.

Under Article 6 of the European Convention on Human Rights, a defendant has a right to the determination of a criminal charge within a reasonable time. With the coming into force of the Human Rights Act 1998, the question arose as to whether the reasonable time requirement of Article 6 gave an absolute entitlement to a trial within a reasonable time so that where proceedings are not brought within such time, the defendant is automatically entitled to a stay of proceedings without the obligation to prove that the delay had resulted in prejudice.

The position was clarified by the *Attorney-General's Reference (No 2 of 2001)* [2004] 2 AC 72. The House of Lords held that where the defendant's rights are breached because a criminal charge is not determined within a reasonable time, the defendant is entitled to such remedy as is just and proportionate. However, proceedings should not be stayed on the grounds that there has been a breach of the reasonable time requirement under Article 6 without the defendant demonstrating that he was so prejudiced by the delay that there was no possibility of a fair trial or that it would otherwise be unfair for him to be tried. A stay of proceedings would therefore not be appropriate if a lesser remedy would adequately vindicate the defendant's Convention right. The Privy Council reviewed the Strasbourg case law in *Spiers v Ruddy* [2008] 1 AC 873 and concluded that where there has (or may have) been such delay in the conduct of proceedings as to breach a party's right to trial within a reasonable time but the fairness of the trial has not been or will not be compromised, such delay does not give rise to a continuing breach which cannot be cured save by a discontinuation of proceedings. It gives rise to a breach which can be cured, even where it cannot be prevented, by expedition, reduction of sentence or compensation, provided always that the breach, where it occurs, is publicly acknowledged and addressed. The European court does not prescribe what remedy will be effective in any given case, which is a matter for the national court.

4.2.2 Going back on a promise

In certain circumstances, the police may promise a suspect that they will not institute proceedings against him. For example, where the suspect provides assistance to the police in conducting other investigations. Similarly, a prosecuting authority may promise a defendant that it will not continue with an existing prosecution. For example, where a defendant faces two or more charges, the prosecution may take the view that guilty pleas to some but not all of the charges adequately reflect the gravity of the defendant's conduct and that it would not be in the public interest to proceed to trial in relation to the remainder. Prosecution counsel will then indicate his intentions to the defendant and subsequently either offer no evidence on the counts to which guilty pleas were not entered or request that they are left to 'lie on the file' marked not to be proceeded with without leave of the court or the Court of Appeal. A similar situation arises where prosecution counsel decides not to proceed with an indictment or a count in an indictment because he believes that it would be unjust to do so, notwithstanding that the prosecution can be justified in law. Again, in such circumstances, prosecution counsel may indicate his intentions to the defendant. What approach should the courts adopt if the prosecution go back on such promises?

In *Bloomfleld* [1997] 1 Cr App R 135, prosecution counsel took the view that it would be wrong to proceed against the defendant because he agreed with the defence contention that the police had 'set up' the offence. At the plea and directions hearing (now the plea and case management hearing), prosecution counsel informally advised defence counsel of his intention and told the judge the same in chambers. Prosecution counsel successfully applied for the matter to be adjourned to another day so that no evidence could be offered. The Crown Prosecution Service did not agree with the course taken by counsel and sought to proceed with the case. It was held that to allow the prosecution to do so would be an abuse of process as it would bring the administration of justice into disrepute. It was irrelevant whether prosecution counsel had the authority to discontinue the case; the defence were entitled to assume that counsel had such authority and to rely upon the promise.

In *Horseferry Road Magistrates' Court, ex p DPP* [1999] COD 441, a stipendiary magistrate (now district judge) stayed a prosecution where an earlier assurance that no action would be taken had been given to the defendant's solicitor. The Divisional Court quashed the stay, stating that breach of an earlier promise would not, on its own, justify staying the proceedings; there would have to be some particular prejudice or special circumstances. For example, in *Bloomfleld*, above, no evidence would have been offered but for the prosecution's request for an adjournment which they made for their convenience.

In *D* [2000] 1 Archbold News 1, it was held to be an abuse of process to reinstate proceedings in relation to an allegation of indecent assault against a 10-year-old boy some years after the defendant had received a letter informing him that a final decision had been taken not to prosecute him. In the interim period, the law had changed so that the boy's allegation no longer required corroboration. The prejudice pointed to was that exculpatory evidence was no longer available.

An analogous situation arose in *Jones v Whalley* [2007] 1 AC 63. Following an investigation into an assault committed by Jones, the police decided that he should be formally cautioned and not prosecuted for the offence. Jones was notified that the effect of the caution was that he would not have to go before a criminal court in connection with the matter. Subsequently, Whalley brought a private prosecution against Jones. It was held that the officer's assurance had led Jones to believe that if he agreed to be cautioned he would not be prosecuted for that offence. Although Whalley could have challenged the lawfulness of the caution, and, if successful, would have been free to bring his prosecution, as long as the formal caution stood, it was an abuse of the court's process for the trial to proceed.

In *R v Abu Hamza* [2007] QB 659, the Court of Appeal reviewed the authorities and concluded that it is not likely to constitute an abuse of process to proceed with a prosecution unless (i) there has been an unequivocal representation by those with the conduct of the investigation or prosecution of a case that the defendant will not be prosecuted; and (ii) that the defendant has acted on that representation to his detriment. Even then, if facts come to light which were not known when the representation was made, these may justify proceeding with the prosecution despite the representation.

See also *DPP v B* [2008] Crim LR 707.

4.2.3 Entrapment

Entrapment refers to a situation where agents of the state lure its citizens into committing acts forbidden by the law and then seek to prosecute them for doing so. The House of Lords in *Looseley; Attorney-General's Reference (No 3 of 2000)* [2002] 1 Cr App R 29 made clear that the appropriate course of action, where it is alleged that there has been entrapment, is to apply for a stay on the grounds of abuse of process.

In such cases, the defendant need not necessarily show that he has been prejudiced or that he would not have a fair trial. Rather, the stay is granted on the basis that it would be unfair for the defendant to be tried (ie, the second limb of *Beckford*). The overriding principle in such applications is that the rule of law must be maintained and that the integrity of the executive agents of the state, responsible for law enforcement, is maintained. Ultimately, the overall consideration is always whether the conduct of the police or other law enforcement agency was so seriously improper as to bring the administration of justice into disrepute.

In *Looseley*, it was held that in determining whether actions of the prosecuting authority fall into this category, the court must have regard to all the circumstances of the case, including:

(a) the nature of the offence. The use of pro-active techniques is more needed and, hence, more appropriate, in some circumstances than others. The secrecy and difficulty of detection, and the manner in which the particular criminal activity is carried on, are relevant considerations;

(b) the reason for the particular police operation. It goes without saying that the police must act in good faith and not, for example, as part of a malicious vendetta against an individual or group of individuals. Having reasonable grounds for suspicion is one way good faith may be established, but having grounds for suspicion of a particular individual is not always essential. For example, suspicion may be centred on a particular place, such as a particular public house;

(c) the nature and extent of police participation in the crime. The greater the inducement held out by the police, and the more forceful or persistent the police overtures, the more readily may a court conclude that the police overstepped the boundary; and

(d) the defendant's criminal record. The defendant's criminal record is unlikely to be relevant unless it can be linked to other factors grounding reasonable suspicion that the defendant is currently engaged in criminal activity.

4.2.4 Failing to obtain, losing and destroying evidence

The police and other investigative agencies may fail to obtain evidence that was available to them during the course of an investigation. Even where evidence has successfully been gathered, it may subsequently be lost or destroyed. Difficulties arise where such evidence potentially exonerated the defendant. How should the court approach these problems?

The leading case in this area is *R (Ebrahim) v Feltham Magistrates' Court* [2001] 2 Cr App R 23 which concerned CCTV video tapes but, it is submitted, is equally relevant to other types of evidence that the investigator has either failed to obtain or retain. *Ebrahim* reviewed the earlier authorities. The first question to be asked was the extent to which the investigator was under a duty to obtain and/or retain the material in question. In answering this question, consideration should be given to the code of practice issued under the Criminal Procedure and Investigations Act 1996 and the *Attorney-General's Guidelines: Disclosure of Information in Criminal Proceedings*. If there was no duty to obtain and/or retain the material before the defence first sought it, then there could be no grounds to stay the proceedings. If there was a breach of the duty to obtain and/or retain the material, then the defence must establish on the balance of possibilities that as a result of the breach the defendant is seriously prejudiced. By 'seriously prejudiced' the Court in *Ebrahim* meant 'could not have a fair trial'. It was stressed that the normal forum for challenges to the prosecution case was the trial process itself which was well equipped to deal with most complaints about how the investigators or the prosecution have behaved. It follows, therefore, that the presumption seems to be in favour of refusing to stay. The Divisional Court went on to say that a stay should also be granted if the behaviour complained of was so bad that it was in a general sense unfair to subject the defendant to trial.

4.2.5 Manipulation of procedure

An application to stay the proceedings may be an appropriate remedy where the defence contend that the prosecution has wrongfully manipulated a particular procedure. Is the prosecution, for example, entitled to proceed on summary-only offences, so as to deprive the defendant of a right to jury trial, where triable either way offences would ordinarily be appropriate?

In *Canterbury and St Augustine Justices, ex p Klisiak* [1982] QB 398, it was held that the court should only interfere with the prosecution's decision as to what offences to proceed upon 'in the most obvious circumstances which disclose blatant injustice'. In *Sheffleld Justices, ex p DPP* [1993] Crim LR 136, it was said that it would only be appropriate for the court to interfere where it concluded that the prosecution was acting in bad faith, ie deliberately manipulating the system to deprive a defendant of his rights. In *Rotherham JJ, ex p Brough* [1991] Crim LR 522, the prosecution deliberately delayed proceedings so that the defendant could not be tried in the youth court and had to be tried in the Crown Court. This was held not to be an abuse of process as the court perceived the behaviour of the prosecution as amounting to an error of judgement rather than bad faith. The court was also of the view that the defendant faced no prejudice as the sentencing judge in the Crown Court would, in giving the defendant credit for his youth, focus on the age he was when he committed the offence and not his age at the sentencing hearing. In *Gleaves v Insall* [1999] 2 Cr App R 466, DC, the prosecution was refused a summons in one magistrates' court and so it renewed its application in another. Unsurprisingly, perhaps, this was held to be an abuse of process.

4.3 Procedural issues

4.3.1 The magistrates' court

The magistrates' court has the power to stay criminal proceedings for abuse of process. However, in *Horseferry Road Magistrates' Court, ex p Bennett* [1994] 1 AC 42, it was held that the power of the magistrates to stay proceedings as an abuse of process should be strictly confined to matters directly affecting the fairness of the trial of the particular accused with whom it is dealing, such as delay or unfair manipulation of court procedures. It did not extend to the wider supervisory jurisdiction to uphold the rule of law, the responsibility for which belongs to the High Court. Should an issue falling in this category arise, a magistrate should allow an adjournment so that an application can be made to the Divisional Court.

4.3.2 The burden and standard of proof

In *Attorney-General's Reference (No 1 of 1990)* [1992] QB 630, it was stated per Lord Lane that in order for a stay to be granted, the defendant must show on the balance of probabilities that he will suffer serious prejudice to the extent that no fair trial can be held. However, in *S* [2006] 2 Cr App R 23, it was held that the discretionary decision whether or not to grant a stay as an abuse of process, is an exercise in judicial assessment dependent on judgment rather than on any conclusion as to fact based on evidence. It is, therefore, potentially misleading to apply to the exercise of that discretion the language of burden and standard of proof, which is more apt to an evidence-based fact-finding process. Accordingly, the Court of Appeal doubted whether, today, in the light of intervening authorities in relation to the exercise of judicial discretion, Lord Lane would have expressed himself as he did. It should be noted that while *Attorney-General's Reference (No 1 of 1990)* [1992] QB 630 and *S* [2006] 2 Cr App R 23 concerned abuse of process on the grounds of delay, it is submitted that the decisions are of general application.

4.3.3   The time of an application for a stay

Typically, the time to apply to stay proceedings will be before plea although there is no reason why the application cannot be made at a later stage (*Aldershot Youth Court, ex p A* [1997] 3 Archbold News 2, DC (CO/1911/96)).

4.3.4   The Consolidated Criminal Practice Direction

The Consolidated Criminal Practice Direction, Part IV.36 lays down the procedure to be followed where an abuse of process application is made in the Crown Court:

IV.36.1 In all cases where a defendant in the Crown Court proposes to make an application to stay an indictment on the grounds of abuse of process, written notice of such application must be given to the prosecuting authority and to any co-defendant not later than 14 days before the date fixed or warned for trial ('the relevant date'). Such notice must:

(a) *give the name of the case and the indictment number;*

(b) *state the fixed date or the warned date as appropriate;*

(c) *specify the nature of the application;*

(d) *set out in numbered sub-paragraphs the grounds upon which the application is to be made;*

(e) *be copied to the chief listing officer at the court centre where the case is due to be heard.*

IV.36.2 Any co-defendant who wishes to make a like application must give a like notice not later than seven days before the relevant date, setting out any additional grounds relied upon.
IV.36.3 In relation to such applications, the following automatic directions shall apply:

(a) *the advocate for the applicant(s) must lodge with the court and serve on all other parties a skeleton argument in support of the application at least five clear working days before the relevant date. If reference is to be made to any document not in the existing trial documents, a paginated and indexed bundle of such documents is to be provided with the skeleton argument;*

(b) *the advocate for the prosecution must lodge with the court and serve on all other parties a responsive skeleton argument at least two clear working days before the relevant date, together with a supplementary bundle if appropriate.*

IV.36.4 All skeleton arguments must specify any propositions of law to be advanced (together with the authorities relied upon in support, with page references to passages relied upon) and, where appropriate, include a chronology of events and a list of dramatis personae. In all instances where reference is made to a document, the reference in the trial documents or supplementary bundle is to be given.
IV.36.5 The above time limits are minimum time limits. In appropriate cases the court will order longer lead times. To this end in all cases where defence advocates are, at the time of the plea and directions hearing, considering the possibility of an abuse of process application, this must be raised with the judge dealing with the matter, who will order a different timetable if appropriate, and may wish, in any event, to give additional directions about the conduct of the application.

This practice direction only applies to proceedings before the Crown Court. In magistrates' court proceedings there is no set procedure. However, the common practice is for the defence to flag up any potential abuse of process argument at the pre-trial review stage and to lodge and serve a skeleton argument in support of their application in advance of the abuse of process hearing. The prosecution will be required to lodge and serve a skeleton argument in reply.

4.4 Further reading

Choo, A. L.-T., *Abuse of Process and Judicial Stays of Criminal Proceedings* (Oxford: Oxford University Press, 2008).

Corker, D., *Abuse of Process and Fairness in Criminal Proceedings*, 3rd edn (London: Butterworths, 2009).

Jackson, J., and Johnstone, J., 'The Reasonable Time Requirement: An Independent and Meaningful Right' [2005] Crim LR 3–23.

Webster, A., 'Delay and Article 6(1): An End to the Requirement of Prejudice?' [2001] Crim LR 786–94.

Wells, C., *Abuse of Process: A Practical Approach* (London: Legal Action Group, 2006).

Part II

Substantive law

Dangerous drugs

5.1 'Controlled drugs'

The Misuse of Drugs Act 1971 applies to 'controlled drugs'. Section 2 of the Act defines this term as the substances listed in Sch 2 to the Act. Schedule 2 divides controlled drugs into three classes: A (eg, cocaine, lysergide (LSD), methylamphetamine (crystal meth), morphine and diamorphine (heroin)), B (eg, cannabis, amphetamine and codeine) and C (eg, diazepam and temazepam). The relevance of this distinction is that offences involving class A drugs attract a more severe sentence than offences involving class B drugs, and class B drug offences are more serious than class C drug offences. This distinction is based on the degree of harm a particular drug can do.

To be controlled, the substance must be listed in Sch 2. So the coco-leaf (from which cocaine may be extracted) is specifically listed. Prior to the implementation of the Drugs Act 2005, s 21, the magic mushroom, from which psilocin (a controlled drug) may be extracted, was not listed *per se* and so in its natural state the magic mushroom was not a controlled drug but only became a controlled drug once it had been made into a 'preparation' or 'product' containing psilocin (*Hodder v DPP* [1989] Crim LR 261). However, the Drugs Act 2005, s 21 amended Sch 2 so as to make any fungus which contains psilocin or an ester of psilocin a class A drug. As a result 'magic mushrooms', even in their natural state, are now a controlled drug.

Whether or not the particular substance in question is a controlled drug has to be proved by chemical analysis (*Hunt* [1987] AC 352; *Hill* (1993) 96 Cr App R 456). However, it was said in *Chatwood* [1980] 1 WLR 874, that an admission by the defendant that the substance is a controlled drug is prima facie evidence as to the nature of the substance, and so such an admission can found a case to answer.

Note that cannabis and cannabis resin are listed separately, and so the prosecution must specify which is alleged (*Best* (1979) 70 Cr App R 21).

For full details on offences relating to drugs, see *Blackstone's Criminal Practice*, B20.

5.2 The offences

5.2.1 Import/export

Section 3 of the Misuse of Drugs Act 1971 prohibits the export and import of controlled drugs. However, the section by itself does not create an offence. The offence is committed under s 50(3) of the Customs and Excise Management Act 1979, which creates the offence of importing or being concerned with the importing of any goods contrary to any prohibition with intent to evade that prohibition or s 170(2) of the same

Act which creates the offence of being knowingly concerned in the fraudulent evasion (or attempted evasion) of any prohibition. The latter offence covers both import and (unlike s 50) export of prohibited goods.

5.2.2 Production

Section 4 of the Misuse of Drugs Act 1971 creates these offences:

(a) producing a controlled drug (s 4(2)(a)). Section 37(1) defines 'producing' as including manufacture or cultivation. Growing cannabis can be charged under this section or under s 6 which deals specifically with cannabis;

(b) being concerned in the production of a controlled drug by another person (s 4(2)(b)) (this is a sort of statutory conspiracy).

Converting one controlled drug into another controlled drug amounts to production (eg, converting cocaine hydrochloride into freebase cocaine, ie 'crack') (*Russell* (1991) 94 Cr App R 351).

5.2.3 Supply/offer to supply

Under s 4(3)(a) of the Misuse of Drugs Act 1971, it is an offence to supply or offer to supply a controlled drug to another person (ie, drug dealing).

5.2.3.1 Supply

The meaning of 'supply' was considered by the House of Lords in *Maginnis* [1987] AC 303. The defendant in that case was found to be in possession of some cannabis. He said that he was looking after it for a friend who was going to retrieve it later. It was held that a person who was in unlawful possession of a controlled drug which had been deposited with him by another person for safekeeping had the necessary intent to supply it to another if it was the defendant's intention to return it to the person who had given it to him for that other person's purposes. The handing over must be for the recipient to use the thing handed over for his or her own purposes, but it was not necessary that the supply be made out of the defendant's own personal resources. It follows that a person who hands another a drug for temporary safekeeping and intending to reclaim it does not commit an offence, since the person looking after it cannot use it for his own purposes. In *Dempsey* (1985) 82 Cr App R 291, a registered drug addict who was in lawful possession of a controlled drug, asked someone to hold some of the drug for him while he went into the toilet to inject himself with the rest of it. The police then arrested both of them. The Court of Appeal held that, on the facts of the particular case, there was no act of supply. The addict had not transferred the drugs to his friend so that she could use them herself or pass them on to someone else (and her return of the drugs to him was not an unlawful supply, since he was lawfully entitled to possession of the drugs).

In *Panton* [2001] EWCA Crim 611 The Times, 27 March 2001, the defendant was charged with possession of controlled drugs with intent to supply. He relied on the defence of duress, claiming that he had been an involuntary custodian of the drugs for unnamed depositors, following threats made to himself and his family after he had failed to settle drug-related debts. The jury rejected the defence of duress. It was held, following *Maginnis*, that the ordinary and natural meaning of the word 'supply' is to furnish or provide a person with something which that person wants or requires for that person's purposes. It follows that a return of goods to a depositor by a custodian, who had held those goods for safekeeping, constitutes a supply. For the purposes of ss 4(1) and 5(3) of the Misuse of Drugs Act 1971, it is irrelevant whether the custodian was a voluntary or involuntary custodian of the drugs.

5.2.3.2 Offering to supply

If the defendant offers to supply one controlled drug, thinking mistakenly that it is another controlled drug, the offence is still made out. If the defendant offers to supply what he or she believes to be a controlled drug but which in fact is not a controlled drug, the offence is nonetheless committed (*Haggard v Mason* [1976] 1 WLR 187). Further, an offence is committed even if the defendant did not in fact intend to supply the drug he was offering to supply (*Gill* (1993) 97 Cr App R 215).

In *Dhillon* [2000] Crim LR 760, the defendant was charged with offering to supply a controlled drug (s 4(1)(b)). He argued that by the date specified in the charge, the offer had been accepted and so it could no longer be treated as an offer. The Court of Appeal rejected this argument, holding that it would be wrong to introduce the principles of the law of contract into the trial of a person charged with this offence.

5.2.3.3 Being concerned in supply

Under s 4(3)(b), it is an offence to be concerned in the supplying of a controlled drug to another person. Under s 4(3)(c), it is an offence to be concerned in the making of an offer to supply a controlled drug to another person.

The last two offences require the prosecution to prove:

- supply/offer to supply (by someone other than the defendant);
- that the defendant is a participant in the supply/offer;
- that the defendant knows the nature of the enterprise.

See *Hughes* (1985) 81 Cr App R 344.

'Another person' in this context cannot be someone who is charged in the same count, though it may be someone who is charged under a different count in the same indictment (*Connelly* [1992] Crim LR 296, CA).

A person may be concerned by being involved at a distance in the making of an offer to supply a controlled drug (*Blake* (1978) 68 Cr App R 1) (one person introducing another to someone who could supply a controlled drug).

5.2.4 Possession/possession with intent to supply

Section 5(2) of the Misuse of Drugs Act 1971 creates the offence of being in possession of a controlled drug. Section 5(3) creates the offence of being in possession of a controlled drug with intent to supply it to another person.

5.2.4.1 Possession

The only definition of 'possession' given by the 1971 Act is that contained in s 37(3). This says that a person is in possession of something even if it is in the custody of someone else, provided that it is subject to the control of the possessor. However, this section is dealing with the fairly unusual situation where custody and control are separated.

In *Lambert* [2002] 2 AC 545, it was held by the House of Lords that there are two elements to possession: the physical element and the mental element. The House confirmed the approach taken by the House in the earlier cases of *Warner v Metropolitan*

Police Commissioner [1968] 2 All ER 356 and *Boyesen* [1982] 2 All ER 161, and by the Court of Appeal in *McNamara* (1988) 87 Cr App R 246.

So far as the physical element is concerned, this requires proof that the thing is in the custody of the defendant or subject to his or her control. So far as the mental element is concerned, the essential point is that a person must know that he or she is in possession of something which is, in fact, a controlled drug. To satisfy this element, the defendant need not know the true nature of the thing: so long as the defendant knows that the thing, whatever it is, is under his or her control, then it is in his or her possession. It follows, therefore, that a person does not possess something of which he or she is completely unaware, and so if drugs are put into someone's pocket without their knowledge, that person is not in possession of those drugs.

It also follows that ignorance of (or mistake as to) the nature of the substance in question does not prevent the accused being in possession of it, provided that the substance turns out to be a controlled drug. Thus, if the substance turns out to be heroin, it is irrelevant (so far as the meaning of possession is concerned) that the accused believed the substance to be aspirin.

Where a controlled drug is in a container, it was held in *Lambert* that, if the defendant is in possession of the container and knows that there is something in it, he or she will be taken to be in possession of the contents of the container. It follows that where the drugs are in a container, it is sufficient for the prosecution to prove that the defendant had control of the container, that he or she knew of its existence and knew that there was something in it, and that the something was in fact the controlled drug which the prosecution alleges it to be. The prosecution does not have to prove that the accused knew that the thing was a controlled drug.

The exception to this is where the accused had no right to open the container and ascertain its contents. In such a case, it is probable that the accused is not in possession of the contents (according to dicta in *Warner* and *McNamara*).

Even if the accused is, as a matter of law, in possession of drugs according to the case law set out above, he or she may nonetheless have a statutory defence (see **5.3** below).

Where more than one person has the right to draw on drugs which form a common pool, all those having such control may be charged with possession (*Searle* [1971] Crim LR 592). Everyone who has the right to say what is done with the drugs possesses them (*Strong* The Times, 26 January 1990).

The issue in *Boyesen* (mentioned above) was whether one can be said to be in possession of a quantity of a controlled drug which is so minute that it is not 'usable'. The answer given by the House of Lords was yes, provided that the prosecution are able to prove possession and provided that the drug is 'visible, tangible, measureable and capable of manipulation' (per Lord Scarman at 166).

5.2.4.2 Proving intent to supply

The greater the quantity of drugs, the less likely it is that they were for the accused's personal use, making a charge of possession with intent to supply more likely.

If the accused is seen to be supplying a substance to other people, and that substance turns out to be an illegal drug, it can be inferred that any of the drug still in his or her possession was held with the intent to supply it to other people.

The Drugs Act 2005 adds subsections 5(4A) and (4B) to the 1971 Act. These provide that if it is proved that the defendant had an amount of a controlled drug in his possession which is not less than the 'prescribed amount' (ie, an amount prescribed in regulations under the Act), the court must assume that the defendant intended to supply those drugs unless evidence is adduced which is sufficient to raise an issue that he or she may not have had the drug in his possession with that intent. It should be noted that the burden on the defendant is an evidential, not legal, burden. These provisions are not yet in force.

Experienced police officers are entitled to give expert evidence on some matters. For example, in *Hodges* [2003] 2 Cr App R 15, the prosecution case, that the defendants were commercial drug dealers, relied on the evidence of a police officer who stated that the drugs found were in too great a quantity for personal use. The officer had 16 or 17 years' experience; he obtained his information through training, observation and speaking to other officers, people arrested and informers. The Court of Appeal upheld the trial judge's decision to allow this evidence to be adduced. The defence argued that the officer's evidence should not be admitted if the people who supplied the information on which he based his opinion were not also called as witnesses. The court rejected this argument, holding that it is not necessary for the various people to whom the witness had spoken to be called before the witness could give expert evidence based upon what they had said. The court added that it is relevant that the defence can challenge the officer's evidence through cross-examination.

Intent to supply can also be inferred from the 'paraphernalia' of drug dealing—for example, scales and packaging materials.

In *Morris* [1995] 2 Cr App R 69, it was held that evidence of large amounts of money in the possession of a defendant, or of an extravagant life style, prima facie explicable only if derived from drug dealing, can be admissible as part of the proof of intent to supply. An explanation by the defendant for the possession of the money does not render the evidence inadmissible, since the Crown may have evidence to rebut that explanation. If the judge decides that such evidence is admissible as a matter of law, he or she must then decide, as a matter of discretion, whether or not to admit it (having regard to both its probative value and its prejudicial effect). If the evidence is admitted, the judge must direct the jury as to the possible probative significance of the evidence, making it clear that the jury must decide whether or not it in fact has that probative significance. The judge must also warn the jury that, if they conclude that the defendant is a drug dealer, this is not of itself either evidence of possession of drugs on a particular occasion or a basis for disbelieving the defendant.

In *Gordon* [1995] 2 Cr App R 61, the Court of Appeal noted that where a defendant is charged with possession with intent to supply, the intention to supply has to relate to the drugs found in the possession of the defendant. In order to be admissible, evidence of cash or other property found in the possession of the defendant, or of financial dealings by the defendant, must therefore be relevant to the intention to supply the particular drugs in order to be admissible.

Grant [1996] 1 Cr App R 73 confirms that the finding of money either in the home or the possession of the accused (in conjunction with a substantial quantity of drugs) is capable of being relevant to the issue of whether there was an intent to supply. It is a matter for the jury to decide whether the presence of money is in fact indicative of an ongoing trade in the drugs, so that the presence of the drugs at the time of the arrest is capable of being construed as possession with intent to supply. However, where such evidence is admitted, the jury should be directed that any innocent explanation put forward by the accused must first be rejected before they can regard the finding of the money as relevant to the offence. If they conclude that the presence of the money indicates not merely past dealing but an ongoing dealing in drugs, then finding the money (together with the drugs in question) is a matter that they can take into account in considering whether the necessary intent has been proved.

> The relevant JSB Specimen Direction is as follows:
>
> 36. Drugs—Allegation of Supply—Money Found in Possession of Defendant/Evidence of Extravagant Lifestyle etc.
>
> The prosecution has called evidence that D [eg, was found to be in possession of £ . . .] (and/or to the effect that he) [was living to a standard which they suggest was much higher than that which might be expected of a man of his means].
>
> That evidence, if you accept it, does not by itself prove anything against D. However, if you are sure that:
>
> (a) D's explanation for the [money][standard of living] is untrue; (adding, in a supply or intent to supply case)
>
> (b) the [money][standard of living] can only be explained by continuing dealing in drugs as opposed to drug dealing in the past,
>
> you may, if you think fit, take that evidence into account when deciding whether D [was in possession of drugs][intended to supply drugs to another person][supplied drugs to another person] as alleged in the indictment.

In certain circumstances, drugs paraphernalia and quantities of money may fall within the definition of 'bad character' under the Criminal Justice Act 2003, s 98. Where this is the case, the evidence will only be admissible under CJA 2003, s 101. See further *Evidence Manual*, **Chapter 9**.

5.2.5 Expert evidence

As well as expert evidence proving that the substance in question is indeed a controlled drug (see **5.1**), a police officer in the drugs squad is entitled to give expert evidence on the street value of drugs and on the use of paraphernalia by drug dealers (eg, giving evidence that certain equipment is commonly used by drug dealers to produce crack cocaine). However, in *Jeffries* [1997] Crim LR 819, it was held that a police officer was not entitled to say that, in her opinion, a list containing dates, names and figures related to the sale of drugs: to do so would amount to her giving as her opinion that the defendant is guilty as charged. See also *Hodges* [2003] 2 Cr App R 247.

5.3 Statutory defences

The dicta on the meaning of possession set out in **5.2.4.1** must be related to the defences contained in the Misuse of Drugs Act 1971, s 28. Section 28(2), which applies, *inter alia* to s 4(2) and (3) and s 5(2) and (3), creates the defence that the defendant 'neither knew of nor suspected nor had any reason to suspect the existence of some fact alleged by the prosecution which it is necessary for the prosecution to prove if he is to be convicted of the offence charged'.

Section 28(3) further provides that where the prosecution have to prove that a particular substance was a controlled drug, it is *not* a defence for the defendant to show that he did not realise that it was the particular controlled drug alleged by the prosecution; however, it *is* a defence that the defendant did not realise (and could not reasonably have realised) that the substance was a controlled drug at all. So, it is a statutory defence to a charge of possession of cocaine to say 'I reasonably believed the substance to be aspirin' but it is not a defence to say 'I thought it was cannabis.'

In *Leeson* [2000] 1 Cr App R 233, the defendant was charged with unlawful possession of a controlled drug, namely cocaine, with intent to supply (contrary to s 5(3) of the 1971 Act). The defendant said that he believed that the drug was 'speed' (amphetamine). It was held that, under s 5(3), all that the prosecution has to establish is that the defendant had in his possession 'a' controlled drug with intent to supply the substance which was in his possession to another. It was not necessary to prove an intention to supply the specified drug. Therefore, the possibility of mistake by the defendant as to the nature of the drug in his possession does not afford him any defence under s 28 of the Act.

It had been thought that the burden of proof under s 28 rested on the defendant (to prove the defence on the balance of probabilities). However, in *Lambert* [2002] 2 AC 545 the House of Lords said that such a burden would amount to a violation of the presumption of innocence enshrined in Article 6 of the European Convention on Human Rights. However, by invoking s 3 of the Human Rights Act 1998, s 28 could be read in a way that is compatible with the Convention. This requires s 28 to be construed as imposing no more than an evidential burden on the accused (ie, a burden to raise the issue). If sufficient evidence is adduced by the defence to raise the issue, it will then be for the prosecution to show, beyond reasonable doubt, that the s 28 defence is not made out. It is for the judge to determine whether the evidential burden is discharged by the defendant and, if it is, it is for the jury to determine whether the legal burden is discharged by the prosecution. The evidential burden is discharged by the defendant whenever there is sufficient evidence adduced on the defence to satisfy the judge that it could result in a finding in the defendant's favour.

The s 28 defence is only available in respect of offences under the 1971 Act. It is not therefore available in a case where common law conspiracy is charged instead (*McGowan* [1990] Crim LR 399).

As well as the general defence in s 28, s 5(4) makes it a defence to a charge of being in possession of a controlled drug that the defendant was in possession of the drug in order to deliver it to someone who could lawfully take custody of it. The defendant bears the burden of proving this defence (on the balance of probabilities). The defence will only succeed if it is shown that the defendant's purpose was to act in accordance with s 5(4) (*Dempsey* (1985) 82 Cr App R 291 (CA)).

5.4 Occupiers of premises

Section 8 of the Misuse of Drugs Act 1971 applies to a person who is the occupier of premises or concerned in the management of the premises. The occupier is the person who has a legal right to exercise sufficient control over the premises as to be able to prevent the forbidden activities from taking place.

Such a person commits an offence if he or she knowingly permits or allows specified activities to take place on the premises including:

- producing a controlled drug;
- supplying/offering to supply a controlled drug;
- smoking cannabis, cannabis resin or opium.

In *Bett* [1999] 1 All ER 600, the defendant was charged with permitting premises to be used for supplying a controlled drug (contrary to s 8(b) of the Misuse of

Drugs Act 1971). The trial judge directed the jury that it had to be proved that the defendant knowingly permitted the premises to be used for supplying *a* controlled drug but that it was not necessary to prove that he knew the particular identity or class of the drug that was in fact being supplied. The Court of Appeal upheld this direction.

5.5 Permitted uses of controlled drugs

Many of the controlled drugs have legitimate medical uses (eg, morphine, a class A drug, is a painkiller and drugs such as lorazepam, diazepam and temazepam, all class C drugs, are very commonly prescribed sleeping tablets). So, s 7 of the 1971 Act requires the making of regulations to permit doctors, dentists, pharmacists and veterinary surgeons to produce and supply controlled drugs. The regulations in question are the Misuse of Drugs Regulations 2001 (SI 2001/3998) and the Misuse of Drugs (Designation) Regulations 2001 (SI 2001/3997). Effectively, these regulations permit the appropriate use of drugs for medicinal purposes or which are contained in a medicinal product.

Accordingly, one must first check Sch 2 to the Misuse of Drugs Act 1971 to see if the drug in question is a controlled drug and then check the 2001 Regulations to see if the particular use of the particular drug in question is authorised.

5.6 Enforcement

5.6.1 Search and seizure

The Misuse of Drugs Act 1971, s 23(2) says that a constable who has reasonable grounds to suspect that a person is in possession of a controlled drug may detain and search that person, stop and search a vehicle in which the constable suspects that drugs may be found, and seize and detain anything found in the course of the search which appears to be evidence of an offence under the Act. See also **Chapter 3**.

Section 23(3) empowers a justice of the peace to grant a search warrant if satisfied by information given on oath that there are reasonable grounds for suspecting that controlled drugs are on any premises, or that there is on the premises a document relating to unlawful dealing in controlled drugs.

Section 55 of PACE 1984 provides that where a suspect is under arrest and an officer of at least the rank of inspector has reasonable grounds for believing that that person may have a class A drug concealed on him which he was in possession of before his arrest, he may authorise an intimate search of that person. Where consent is refused without good cause an adverse inference can be drawn against the suspect by the court when determining if there is a case to answer and by the court or jury when determining whether he is guilty of the offence.

By virtue of PACE 1984, s 55A, if an officer of at least the rank of inspector has reasonable grounds for believing that a person who has been arrested for an offence and is in police detention may have swallowed a class A drug which he was in possession of before his arrest, then he may authorise that an X-ray is taken of the person or an ultrasound scan is carried out on the person (or both). Refusal to consent without good cause will again permit such inferences as appear proper to be drawn by the court when determining if there is a case to answer and by the court or jury when determining whether that person is guilty of the offence.

5.6.2 Penalties: sentencing guidelines

The maximum sentences are set out in the Misuse of Drugs Act 1971, Sch 4.

Cases involving class A drugs attract more severe sentences than those involving class B drugs, which in turn attract more severe sentences than cases involving class C drugs. Importation and production are generally regarded as the most serious offences, followed by supply and possession with intent to supply, followed by possession for personal use. A custodial sentence is usually appropriate for all drugs offences, except those involving possession for personal use. All acts of supply are seen as serious. For example, in *Luke* [1999] 1 Cr App R (S) 389, the defendant was a university student. He supplied cannabis to some friends. He made no profit from the transaction and the cannabis was intended for personal use by the recipients. The Court of Appeal held that a sentence of immediate custody was appropriate.

Factors relevant to determining the sentence include the following:

(a) First and foremost, the type and quantity of the drug. The severest sentences are reserved for cases involving class A drugs (see *Richardson* The Times, 18 March 1994, where the Lord Chief Justice speaks of the harm done by hard drugs). Guidelines in cases of importing drugs were laid down by the Court of Appeal in *Aramah* (1982) 76 Cr App R 190 and *Bilinski* (1987) 86 Cr App R 146. Those guidelines are based on the street value of the drug in question. However, in *Aranguren and others* (1994) 99 Cr App R 347, the Court of Appeal issued fresh guidelines for class A drugs, such as heroin and cocaine, to the effect that the sentence should be based on the weight of the drugs seized (at 100% purity) rather than their street value. The purity of the drug is to be taken into account in determining its weight. Guidelines for sentencing in cases involving Ecstasy were given in *Warren & Beeley* [1996] 1 Cr App R 100, for cases involving LSD in *Hurley* [1998] 1 Cr App R (S) 299, for cases involving importation of cannabis in *Ronchetti* [1998] Crim LR 227, and for cases involving importation of amphetamine in *Wijs* [1998] 2 Cr App R (S) 436. In *Chamberlain*, The Independent, 19 May 1997, the Court of Appeal said that being concerned in the management of premises used for the production of a controlled drug should, for sentencing purposes, be considered analogous to importing controlled drugs, thus attracting sentences at the higher end of the scale.

(b) If the defendant has provided information to the authorities, this will result in a lower sentence (partly because it shows remorse). However, regard will be had to the actual value of the assistance and to the risk of possible reprisals faced by the offender or his family (*Richardson, supra*); the information must actually be useful to the authorities, assisting in the speedy arrest of other offenders and the prevention of further distribution of drugs (*M* The Times, 1 March 1994).

(c) The court must consider not only what the defendant in fact did, but also what he thought he was doing. If the defendant thinks he is importing cannabis when in fact it is heroin, the sentence should be reduced (*Bilinski, supra*). Similarly, if the defendant thinks he is importing high-quality heroin when in fact its purity is only 1%, the sentence will take account of the low purity of the heroin (*Afzal and Arshad* The Times, 25 June 1991). In *Purcell* [1996] 1 Cr App R (S) 190, the appellant believed that he was carrying 'speed' (amphetamine sulphate, a class B drug). Later analysis showed that the substance was not, in fact, a controlled drug. He was convicted of attempting to import a controlled drug. In light of this (and the fact that he confessed at the earliest opportunity, and that, as a courier, he would have received very little profit), the Court of Appeal reduced his sentence from three years to two years.

(d) The degree of organisation and planning, and any steps taken to avoid detection will be relevant to the sentence (*Kouadio* The Times, 21 February 1991).

(e) How 'high up in the drug operation' the defendant is, is also relevant to the sentence (*Hussain* The Times, 27 June 1990).

(f) As to those who are simply drug couriers, see *Attuh-Benson* [2005] 2 Cr App R (S) 392.

In *Morris* [2001] 1 Cr App R 4, the Court of Appeal gave further detailed guidance. It was said that, in considering the need to test for the purity of drugs for the purposes of sentencing defendants convicted of drugs offences, courts should take account of the following matters: the amount of class A or B drugs with which a defendant is involved is a very important, but not solely determinative, factor. Evidence as to the scale of dealing can come from many sources other than the amount of drugs with which a defendant is directly connected. Amount should generally be based on the weight of drug involved at 100% purity, not on its street value. Reference to the street value of the same weight of different drugs may, however, be pertinent by way of cross-check. Purity of drugs such as cocaine or heroin, not in tablet or dosage form and often contaminated by other substances, and amphetamine powder, can appropriately be determined only by analysis. The weight of drugs such as Ecstasy, in tablet form, or LSD, in dosage form, can generally be assessed by reference to the number of tablets or doses and an assumed average purity of 100 mg of Ecstasy and 50 microgrammes (μg) of LSD, unless prosecution or defence expert evidence shows to the contrary. Purity analysis is essential for sentencing purposes for cases of importation or in other circumstances where 500g or more of cocaine, heroin or amphetamine are seized, and may be desirable in respect of smaller quantities. However, bearing in mind the cost of purity analysis and that analysis may cause delay, analysis will not generally be necessary or desirable on behalf of prosecution or defence where a defendant is in possession of only a small quantity of cocaine, heroin or amphetamine consistent with personal use or only limited supply to others. In such a case, the court can be expected to sentence on the basis of low-level retail dealing only, but taking into account all the other circumstances of the case. However, as purity can indicate proximity to the primary source of supply, if there is a reason for the prosecution to believe that a defendant in possession of a small quantity of drugs is close to the source of supply, and is wholesaling rather than retailing, it will be necessary for purity analysis to be undertaken before a court can be invited to proceed on this more serious basis. In the absence of purity analysis or expert evidence, it is not open to a court to find or assume levels of purity, except in the case of ecstasy and LSD in the circumstances referred to above.

In due course, these guidelines will be superseded by guidance issued by the Sentencing Guidelines Council.

The Drugs Act 2005 inserts a s 4A into the Misuse of Drugs Act, making it an aggravating factor if the drug dealing happens in or near school premises *and* a courier under the age of 18 is used to deliver drugs or drug money.

5.6.3   Forfeiture

Section 27(1) of the 1971 Act allows the court to order forfeiture (and destruction, if appropriate) of 'anything shown to the satisfaction of the court to relate to the offence'. In *Cuthbertson* [1980] 2 All ER 401, Lord Diplock said (at 406) that forfeiture orders apply to 'tangible' items such as 'the drugs involved, apparatus for making them, vehicles used for transporting them [as in *Bowers* (1994) 15 Cr App R (S) 315], or cash ready to be, or having just been handed over for them'.

The point was made in *Cuthbertson* that the aim of forfeiture orders was not to strip drug traffickers of the profits of their crime. That objective is achieved instead through the Proceeds of Crime Act 2002.

5.7   Confiscation orders under the Proceeds of Crime Act 2002

The Proceeds of Crime Act (PCA) 2002 replaces the pre-existing dual scheme for the confiscation of the proceeds of crime, previously contained in the Drug Trafficking Act 1994 and the Criminal Justice Act 1988. The new scheme applies to criminal offences generally but it is of particular application to drugs offences.

The PCA 2002 uses concepts that were developed under the previous legislation and it is submitted that much of the case law decided under that legislation applies equally to confiscation orders made under the PCA 2002.

5.7.1   Making of confiscation order

The basic procedure for making a confiscation order under the PCA 2002 is set out in s 6.

The power to make a confiscation order arises if the defendant is:

(a) convicted of one or more offences in the Crown Court; or

(b) committed to the Crown Court for sentence in respect of one or more offences under ss 3, 4 or 6 of the Powers of Criminal Courts (Sentencing) Act 2000; or

(c) committed to the Crown Court in respect of one or more offences under s 70 of the PCA 2002, which empowers the magistrates' court to commit a defendant to the Crown Court with a view to a confiscation order being considered.

The PCA 2002 abolishes the power of magistrates to make confiscation orders. However, the Serious Organised Crime and Police Act 2005, s 97, empowers the Secretary of State to make such provision as he considers appropriate for or in connection with enabling confiscation orders of up to £10,000 to be made by magistrates' courts. To date, no such provision has been made.

A confiscation order can only be made if either:

- the prosecutor asks the court to proceed under s 6; or

- the court believes it is appropriate for it to proceed under s 6.

Where the prosecutor makes such a request or the court forms that view, then the court must proceed to consider making a confiscation order (*Hockney* [2008] 1 Cr App R (S) 279; *Brack* [2007] EWCA 1205). In *Morgan* [2008] 4 All ER 890, it was held that where on the facts of the case it would be oppressive to make an order, it could amount to an abuse of process and so entitle the judge to stay the proceedings.

However, in *N* [2009] Crim LR 811, the Court of Appeal criticised this approach, holding that an abuse of process argument could not be founded on the basis that the consequences of the proper application of the legislative structure might produce an 'oppressive' result with which the judge might be unhappy.

Where s 6 is invoked, the court has to proceed as follows:

(a) the court must first decide whether the defendant has 'a criminal lifestyle';

(b) if it decides that the defendant has a criminal lifestyle, it must then decide whether he or she has benefited from 'general criminal conduct';

(c) if the court decides that the defendant does not have a criminal lifestyle and has not benefited from 'general criminal conduct', it must then decide whether the defendant has benefited from 'particular criminal conduct' (ie, the offence(s) of which he or she has been convicted in the present proceedings);

(d) if the court decides that the defendant has benefited from general criminal conduct or particular criminal conduct, the court must go on to:

(i)   decide the recoverable amount; and

(ii) make a confiscation order requiring the defendant to pay that amount.

If the court believes that any victim of the defendant's criminal conduct has started, or intends to start, proceedings against the defendant in respect of loss, injury or damage sustained in connection with the conduct, then the court is no longer obliged to decide the recoverable amount and to make a confiscation order; nonetheless, the court retains the power to do so in such a case.

In deciding whether the defendant has a criminal lifestyle, whether he has benefited from particular or general criminal conduct, and in determining the recoverable amount, the court must decide any question which arises on a balance of probabilities (s 6(7)).

The phrase 'criminal lifestyle' is comprehensively defined in s 75. Under s 75(2), a defendant has a criminal lifestyle if (and only if) the offence, or any of the offences:

(a) is specified in Sch 2 to the Act (s 75(2)(a));

(b) constitutes conduct forming part of a course of criminal activity and the offender has obtained benefit from this conduct of at least £5,000 (s 75(2)(b)); or

(c) is an offence committed over a period of at least six months, and the defendant has obtained benefit of at least £5,000 from the conduct which constitutes the offence (s 75(2)(c)).

The offences specified in Sch 2 include:

(a) drug trafficking: offences under the Misuse of Drugs Act 1971, s 4(2) or (3), 5(3), 8 and 20; offences under the Customs and Excise Management Act 1979, s 50(2) or (3), 68(2) or 170 (if committed in connection with a prohibition or restriction on importation or exportation which has effect by virtue of the Misuse of Drugs Act 1971); offences under the Criminal Justice (International Co-operation) Act 1990, s 10 or 19;

(b) money laundering: offences under the PCA 2002, s 327 or 328;

(c) directing terrorism (the Terrorism Act 2000, s 56);

(d) people trafficking (the Immigration Act 1971, s 25(1));

(e) arms trafficking: offences under the Customs and Excise Management Act 1979, s 68(2) or 170 (if committed in connection with a firearm or ammunition) or under the Firearms Act 1968, s 3(1);

(f) counterfeiting (the Forgery and Counterfeiting Act 1981, ss 14, 15, 16 or 17);

(g) intellectual property: offences under the Copyright, Designs and Patents Act 1988, s 107(1) or (2), 198(1) or 297A or under the Trade Marks Act 1994, s 92(1), (2) or (3);

(h) pimps and brothels: offences under the Sexual Offences Act 1956, ss 33 or 34 or under the Sexual Offences Act 2003, ss 14, 48, 49, 50, 52 and 53;

(i) blackmail (the Theft Act 1968, s 21);

(j) doing an act capable of encouraging or assisting the commission of an offence specified in the PCA 2002, Sch 2; and

(k) inchoate offences of attempt, conspiracy or incitement of an offence specified above or aiding, abetting, counselling or procuring the commission of such an offence.

Under s 75(3), conduct forms part of a course of criminal activity for the purposes of s 75(2)(b) where the offender has benefited from the conduct, and:

(a) in the proceedings in which he was convicted, he was convicted of three or more other offences, each of three or more of them constituting conduct from which he has benefited (s 75(3)(a)); or

(b) in the period of six years ending with the day when those proceedings were started (or, if there is more than one such day, the earliest day), he was convicted on at least two separate occasions of an offence constituting conduct from which he has benefited (s 75(3)(b)).

Under s 75(5), relevant 'benefit', for the purposes of s 75(2)(b), is benefit from conduct which constitutes the offence, or benefit from any other conduct which forms part of the course of criminal activity and which constitutes an offence of which the offender has been convicted, or benefit from conduct which constitutes an offence which has been or will be taken into consideration in sentencing, and relevant 'benefit' for the purposes of s 75(2)(c) is benefit from conduct which constitutes the offence, or benefit from conduct which constitutes an offence which has been or will be taken into consideration in sentencing.

The terms 'criminal conduct', 'general criminal conduct' and 'particular criminal conduct' are defined in s 76:

(a) 'Criminal conduct' is conduct which constitutes an offence in England and Wales.

(b) 'General criminal conduct' is all the offender's criminal conduct, it being irrelevant whether the conduct occurred before or after the passing of the PCA 2002, or whether property constituting a benefit from conduct was obtained before or after the passing of the Act.

(c) 'Particular criminal conduct' is all the offender's criminal conduct which is:
   (i) conduct which constitutes the offence or offences concerned,
   (ii) conduct which constitutes offences of which he was convicted in the same proceedings, or

(iii) conduct which constitutes offences which the court will be taking into consideration in sentencing.

There is no infringement of the presumption of innocence in Article 6(2) where the court makes a confiscation order for the value of the benefit that the defendant has obtained as a result of an offence about which the court has heard evidence at trial but with which he was not charged and which he denied (*Briggs-Price* [2009] 2 WLR 1101; but cf *Geerings v The Netherlands* (2007) 46 EHRR 1212).

5.7.2 Recoverable amount

Section 7(1) of the PCA 2002 defines the 'recoverable amount' for the purposes of s 6 as being 'an amount equal to the defendant's benefit from the conduct concerned'. However, under s 7(2), if the defendant shows that the available amount is less than that benefit, the recoverable amount is 'the available amount' or, if the available amount is nil, a nominal amount. This reverse burden of proof has been held not to offend against Article 6(1) of the ECHR (*Grayson v UK* (2009) 48 EHRR 30). Section 7(5) states that the court must include in the confiscation order a statement of its findings as to the matters relevant for deciding the available amount.

Section 8 of the PCA 2002 provides that, in deciding whether the defendant has benefited from conduct, and in deciding his benefit from the conduct, the court must take account of conduct occurring up to the time it makes its decision and must take account of property obtained up to that time.

Section 9 provides that, for the purposes of deciding the recoverable amount, the 'available amount' is the aggregate of:

(a) the total of the values (at the time the confiscation order is made) of all the free property (ie, property that is not subject to a forfeiture order: see s 82) then held by the defendant minus the total amount payable in pursuance of obligations which then have priority (ie, a fine in respect of an earlier conviction or a preferential debt as defined by s 386 of the Insolvency Act 1986); and

(b) the total of the values (at that time) of all tainted gifts (if the court has decided that the defendant has a criminal lifestyle, a gift is to be regarded as tainted if either:

(i) it was made by the defendant at any time during the period of six years before the start of the proceedings for the present offence; or

(ii) it was made by the defendant at any time and was of property obtained by the defendant as a result of, or in connection with, general criminal conduct,

if the court has decided that the offender does not have a criminal lifestyle, a gift is to be regarded as tainted if it was made by the defendant at any time after the date on which the present offence was committed: see s 77).

Under s 9(2), an obligation has priority if it is an obligation of the defendant:

(a) to pay an amount due in respect of a fine or other order of a court which was imposed or made on conviction of an offence and at any time before the time the confiscation order is made; or

(b) to pay a sum which would be included among the preferential debts if the defendant's bankruptcy had commenced on the date of the confiscation order or his or her winding up had been ordered on that date.

Under s 76(4) and (7), a person 'benefits' from conduct if he or she obtains property as a result of, or in connection with, the conduct. The 'benefit' is the value of the property so obtained. If a person obtains a pecuniary advantage as a result of, or in connection with the conduct, he or she is to be regarded as having obtained a sum of money equal to the value of the pecuniary advantage (s 76(5)). In *May* [2008] 1 AC 1028, the House of Lords stated that in determining whether the defendant has obtained property or a pecuniary advantage and, if so, the value of any property or advantage so obtained, the court should apply ordinary common law principles, according to which mere couriers or custodians or other very minor contributors to an offence, rewarded by a specific fee and having no interest in the property or the proceeds of sale, are unlikely to be found to have obtained that property. In *Jennings* [2008] 2 AC 1046, the House of Lords added that a defendant cannot be deprived of what he has never gained and so it is not sufficient that a person is instrumental in property being obtained as a person may contribute to property being obtained without actually obtaining it. It is important to note that the benefit is not net profit derived after the deduction of any expenses but the whole value of the property obtained (*Smith* (1989) 11 Cr App R 290; *Simpson* [1998] 2 Cr App R (S) 111). However, in *Versluis* [2005] 2 Cr App R (S) 144, it was held that there might nevertheless be cases in which it would be appropriate to take account of expenses incurred in the purchase of drugs. For examples of cases where such an approach has been taken, see *Comiskey* (1991) 93 Cr App R (S) 227 and *Cukovic* [1996] 1 Cr App R (S) 131.

Valuation of property obtained by a defendant from his or her criminal conduct is dealt with by s 80 of the PCA 2002. Under s 80(2), the value of the property at the material time (the court makes its decision) is the greater of the following:

- the value of the property (at the time the person obtained it) adjusted to take account of later changes in the value of money; and
- the value (at the material time) of the property found under s 80(3).

The property found under s 80(3) is as follows:

- if the person holds the property obtained, the property found under this subsection is that property;
- if he or she holds no part of the property obtained, the property found under this subsection is any property which directly or indirectly represents it in their hands;
- if he or she holds part of the property obtained, the property found under this subsection is that part and any property which directly or indirectly represents the other part in their hands.

In *Islam* [2009] 3 WLR 1, the House of Lords held that the court may take account of the black market value of drugs when valuing the benefit obtained by the defendant, although such drugs have a nil market value after seizure for the purposes of assessing the amount available for confiscation.

In *Ahmed* [2005] 1 WLR 102, the Court of Appeal said that, when assessing realisable assets for the purpose of making a confiscation order (under the Criminal Justice Act 1988), the court is bound to include the convicted person's share in the value of the matrimonial home, irrespective of whether that might prejudice the interests of the spouse or family. If the court is later asked to make an order for the sale of the matrimonial home, Article 8 of the ECHR is engaged, and the court will have to consider whether or not it would be proportionate to make the order in the circumstances of the particular case.

5.7.3   Criminal lifestyle: assumptions

Section 10 of the PCA 2002 states that if the court decides that the defendant has a criminal lifestyle it must make four assumptions for the purpose of deciding whether the defendant has benefited from general criminal conduct, and deciding the value of the benefit from that conduct. Those assumptions are as follows:

(a) that any property transferred to the defendant at any time after the relevant day was obtained as a result of the general criminal conduct, and at the earliest time the defendant appears to have held it;

(b) that any property held by the defendant at any time after the date of conviction was obtained as a result of the general criminal conduct, and at the earliest time the defendant appears to have held it;

(c) that any expenditure incurred by the defendant at any time after the relevant day was met from property obtained by the defendant as a result of his or her general criminal conduct; and

(d) that, for the purpose of valuing any property obtained (or assumed to have been obtained) by the defendant, he or she obtained it free of any other interests in it.

Under s 10(8), the 'relevant day' is the first day of the period of six years ending with the day when proceedings for the present offence were started against the defendant or, if there are two or more offences and proceedings for them were started on different days, the earliest of those days.

With regard to the second assumption, it is to be noted that there is no stipulation that the property must have been acquired at a specific time. The assumption applies to all property held by the defendant after the date of his conviction, regardless of when it was acquired.

In drugs cases, the courts may infer, in the absence of an alternative credible explanation, the expenditure that would be required to purchase the drugs because those who traffic in drugs do not normally extend credit or trust to others (*Dellaway* [2001] 1 Cr App R (S) 77; see also *Green* [2007] 3 All ER 751). The third assumption therefore allows the court to presume that a drugs purchase was met from property obtained by the defendant as a result of his general criminal conduct. However, where the sentencing judge is of the view that it was a first time drug trafficking offence and that the drugs had been purchased on a single occasion, the assumption should not be made (*Butler* (1993) 14 Cr App R (S) 537).

By virtue of s 10(6), the court must not make a required assumption in relation to particular property or expenditure if either:

• the assumption is shown to be incorrect; or
• there would be a serious risk of injustice if the assumption were made.

Section 10(6) requires that the defendant prove on the balance of probabilities that the assumption is incorrect but the defendant is not required to prove a serious risk of injustice. Rather, the onus is on the judge to avoid any risk of injustice (*Benjafield* [2003] 1 AC 1099). The injustice must be an injustice in the operation of the assumptions in assessing the defendant's benefit from his general criminal conduct and not an injustice that may be caused as a consequence of making a confiscation order (*Jones* [2007] 1 WLR 7; see also *Dore* [1997] 2 Cr App R (S) 152; *Ahmed* [2005] 1 WLR 122 at **5.7.2**; and *Neuberg* [2008] 1 Cr App R (S) 481).

If the court does not make one or more of the required assumptions, it must state its reasons (s 10(7)).

In *Rezvi* [2002] UKHL 1; [2003] 1 AC 1099, the House of Lords held that similar assumptions to be made in confiscation proceedings under the CJA 1988 were not incompatible with the rights of a defendant under the ECHR. In *Benjafield* [2003] 1 AC 1099, the House of Lords reached the same conclusion as regards the assumptions in confiscation proceedings under the Drug Trafficking Act 1994. In *Phillips v UK* (2001) 11 BHRC 280, the European Court of Human Rights held that the statutory assumptions contained in the Drug Trafficking Act 1994 did not contravene Article 6 of the Convention.

5.7.4 Statements of information

Under s 16 of the PCA 2002, where the prosecutor has asked the court to proceed under s 6, the prosecutor must give the court a statement of information within the period specified by the court. A copy must also be served, as soon as practicable, on the defendant (Crim PR 58.1(1))

If the court is proceeding under s 6 of its own motion, it may order the prosecutor to give it a statement of information within a specified period.

If the prosecutor believes that the defendant has a criminal lifestyle, the statement of information must take the form of a statement of matters that the prosecutor believes are relevant in connection with deciding whether the defendant has a criminal lifestyle, whether he or she has benefited from his or her general criminal conduct and the amount of his or her benefit from the conduct. It must also include information the prosecutor believes to be relevant in connection with the making by the court of a required assumption under s 10 and for the purpose of enabling the court to decide if the circumstances are such that it must not make such an assumption (s 16(3), (4)). Further requirements as to the content of the statement of information may be found in Crim PR 58.1 (2).

If the prosecutor does not believe the defendant has a criminal lifestyle, the statement of information should take the form of a statement of matters which the prosecutor believes to be relevant in connection with deciding whether the defendant has benefited from particular criminal conduct and the benefit from that conduct (s 16(5)).

Under s 17(1), if the prosecutor gives the court a statement of information and a copy is served on the defendant, the court may order the defendant to indicate (within the period it orders) the extent to which he or she accepts each allegation in the statement and, insofar as he or she does not accept such an allegation, to give particulars of any matters he or she proposes to rely on. This must be done in writing to the prosecutor and a copy must be served on the court (Crim PR 58.1(3)).

If the defendant accepts to any extent an allegation in a statement of information, the court may treat this acceptance as conclusive of the matters to which it relates for the purpose of deciding the issues referred to in s 16(3) or (5): s 17(2).

If the defendant fails in any respect to comply with an order under s 17(1), he or she may be treated as accepting every allegation in the statement of information apart from any allegation in respect of which he or she has complied with the requirement and any allegation that he or she has benefited from general or particular criminal conduct.

Section 18 empowers the court, for the purpose of obtaining information to help it in carrying out its functions, to order the defendant to give it information specified in the order. Such information must be in writing and be served on the prosecutor if the court proceeded under PCA 2002, s 6 at their request.

If the defendant fails without reasonable excuse to comply with an order under s 18, the court may draw such inference as it believes is appropriate (s 18(4)). It should also be borne in mind that the failure to comply with the order could also amount to contempt of court.

If the prosecutor accepts to any extent an allegation made by the defendant in giving information required by an order under s 18, or in any other statement given to the court in relation to any matter relevant to deciding the available amount under s 9, the court may treat that acceptance as conclusive of the matters to which it relates.

5.7.5   Time for payment

Section 11 of the PCA 2002 provides that the amount ordered to be paid under a confiscation order must normally be paid when the order is made. However, where the offender is unable to pay immediately, the court may make an order allowing payment to be made within a specified period; this time must not exceed six months from the date on which the confiscation order is made. The offender may, in exceptional circumstances, apply to the court for an extension of that period (up to a total of 10 months from the date of the confiscation order).

5.7.6   Effect of the confiscation order on the sentencing powers of the court

Under s 13 of the PCA 2002, the court must take account of the confiscation order before imposing a fine on the defendant, or a forfeiture or deprivation order such as a forfeiture order under s 27 of the Misuse of Drugs Act 1971. Apart from that, the court must leave the confiscation order out of account in deciding the appropriate sentence for the defendant (s 13(4)).

If the court makes both a confiscation order and a compensation order under s 130 of the Powers of Criminal Courts (Sentencing) Act 2000 against the same person in the same proceedings, and the court believes that the offender does not have sufficient means to satisfy both the orders in full, the court must direct that so much of the compensation as it specifies is to be paid out of any sums recovered under the confiscation order. The amount it specifies must be the amount it believes will not be recoverable because of the insufficiency of the offender's means.

5.7.7   Enforcement

Detailed provisions on the enforcement of confiscation orders are contained in the PCA 2002, ss 34 to 69. Sections 38 and 39 provide for the setting of a term of imprisonment in default of payment of the amount ordered to be paid under a confiscation order. The maximum terms to be served in default are the same as in relation to fines (see *Blackstone's Criminal Practice*, E15.3).

Where the defendant is ordered to serve a term of imprisonment in default of payment of a confiscation order, this term does not start to run until the defendant has served any prison sentence imposed for the offence(s) which led to the confiscation order being made. If the defendant does serve a sentence in default of payment, that does not prevent the order from continuing to apply for the purposes of enforcement by other means (see s 38(5)).

Sections 40 to 69 deal with restraint orders and receivership. In *J v CPS* [2006] 1 WLR 182, the Court of Appeal gave guidance on restraint orders in connection with confiscation proceedings. Whilst in a case where dishonesty is charged, the risk of dissipation will generally speak for itself, prosecutors should nevertheless be alive to the possibility that there might be no risk in fact. If no asset dissipation has occurred over a long period, particularly after a defendant has been charged, the prosecutor should explain why asset dissipation is feared at the date of the application for a restraint order, when it had not been feared before. If the court considers that a prosecutor has failed to consider whether there is a risk of dissipation when he should have done, or has failed to put relevant documentary material before the court, but that the public interest still requires the making of a restraint order, the judge can deprive the prosecution of its costs, but still make the order. The duty to make full and frank disclosure applies as much to applicants for restraint orders as to applicants for freezing orders. The fact that the Crown acts in the public interest generally militates against the sanction of discharging the order because of a failure to disclose if the court thinks that an order is appropriate.

The Serious Organised Crime and Police Act 2005 inserts ss 245A–245D into the 2002 Act, providing for applications (made in the High Court) for 'property freezing orders'.

In *Crowther v UK* (App No 53741/00), The Times, 11 February 2005, the ECtHR held that Article 6(1) of the ECHR applies throughout the entirety of the proceedings for 'the determination of . . . any criminal charge', including proceedings whereby a sentence is fixed. Confiscation proceedings are analogous to the determination by a court of the amount of a fine or the length of a period of imprisonment to be imposed on a properly convicted offender. It follows that the authorities have to ensure that the proceedings are completed within a reasonable time.

5.7.8 Postponement

The court should normally proceed under s 6 of the PCA 2002 before it sentences the offender for the offence(s) of which the defendant has been convicted. However, s 14 enables the court to postpone proceedings under s 6 for a specified period. Such a period of postponement may be extended, but it should not (unless there are exceptional circumstances) extend for more than two years from the date of conviction (s 14(3)).

If the offender appeals against sentence, proceedings under s 6 may be postponed for a period of up to three months after the appeal is determined or disposed of (s 14(6)). A postponement or extension may be made on application by the offender, the prosecutor or may be made by the court of its own motion.

Section 15 provides that if proceedings under s 6 are postponed, the court may proceed to sentence the offender for the offence(s), but must not impose a fine or make a compensation order. When the postponement period comes to an end, the court may vary the sentence by imposing one or more of the financial orders, but it must do so within 28 days of the end of the postponement period (s 15(4)).

5.7.9 Reconsideration

Sections 19 to 22 of the PCA 2002 enable questions relating to confiscation orders to be reopened. Section 19 provides that where the court did not proceed against the offender under s 6, and there is now evidence available to the prosecutor which was not then available, the prosecutor may apply to the Crown Court for consideration of the evidence at any time prior to the end of the period of six years from the date of conviction.

Section 20 provides that where the court proceeded against the offender under s 6 but found that he or she had not benefited from general criminal conduct, or particular criminal conduct, and there is now evidence available to the prosecutor which was not then available, the prosecutor may apply to the Crown Court for consideration of the evidence at any time prior to the end of the period of six years from the date of conviction.

Section 21 provides that where the court has made a confiscation order, and there is now evidence available to the prosecutor which was not then available, the prosecutor may apply to the Crown Court to make a new calculation of the offender's benefit from the conduct concerned.

Sections 22 to 25 allow for applications to be made to the court for reconsideration of the available amount, and for variation or discharge of the confiscation order in light of the inadequacy of the available amount.

Where there is a right to reopen the issue of confiscation (reopening the issues of the amount of benefit or the amount that might be realised), then the reasonable time requirement extends throughout the period in question. Reconsideration therefore has to take place within a reasonable time (see *Re Saggar* [2005] 1 WLR 2693).

5.7.10   Appeals by the prosecution

Section 31 of the PCA 2002 enables the prosecutor to appeal to the Court of Appeal against a decision of the court not to make a confiscation order, or in respect of the amount of a confiscation order which has been made.

5.7.11   Useful websites containing information on the PCA 2002

The following sites contain useful information about the operation of the PCA 2002:
Serious Organised Crime Agency: http://www.soca.gov.uk
Joint Money Laundering Steering Group: http://www.jmlsg.org.uk

5.8   Further reading

Bucknell, P., *Misuse of Drugs*, 3rd edn (London: Sweet & Maxwell, 1996).

Forston, R., *Misuse of Drugs: Offences, Confiscation and Money Laundering*, 5th edn (London: Sweet & Maxwell, 2005).

Gumpert, B., *Proceeds of Crime Act 2002: A Practical Guide* (Bristol: Jordans, 2003).

Millington, T., and Sutherland Williams, M., *The Proceeds of Crime: Law and Practice of Restraint, Confiscation, Condemnation, and Forfeiture* (Oxford: Oxford University Press, 2007).

Mitchell, A., *Mitchell, Taylor and Talbot on Confiscation and the Proceeds of Crime*, 3rd edn (London: Sweet & Maxwell, 2002).

Public order offences

6.1 Introduction

Offences relating to public order have been created by a number of statutes. The main statutes dealt with in this chapter are the Criminal Law Act 1977, the Sporting Events (Control of Alcohols etc) Act 1985, the Public Order Act 1986, the Football Spectators Act 1989, the Football (Offences) Act 1991, the Criminal Justice and Public Order Act 1994, the Protection from Harassment Act 1997, the Crime and Disorder Act 1998, the Criminal Justice and Police Act 2001, the Football (Disorder) Act 2000 and the Serious Organised Crime and Police Act 2005.

Details of the relevant provisions are to be found in *Blackstone's Criminal Practice*, B11 and B13.

6.2 Riot

Riot is the most serious offence against public order and is triable only on indictment. It is defined by the Public Order Act 1986, s 1, as follows:

> *(1) Where 12 or more persons who are present together use or threaten unlawful violence for a common purpose and the conduct of them (taken together) is such as would cause a person of reasonable firmness present at the scene to fear for his personal safety, each of the persons using unlawful violence for the common purpose is guilty of riot.*
>
> *(2) It is immaterial whether or not the 12 or more use or threaten unlawful violence simultaneously.*
>
> *(3) The common purpose may be inferred from conduct.*
>
> *(4) No person of reasonable firmness need actually be, or be likely to be, present at the scene.*
>
> *(5) Riot may be committed in private as well as in public places.*

Section 1(6) of the Act provides for a maximum penalty of a term of ten years, or a fine or both.

Section 6(1) of the Act provides that a person is guilty of riot only if he intends to use violence or is aware that his conduct may be violent. Section 6(7) provides that s 6(1) does not affect the determination for the purposes of riot of the number of persons who use or threaten violence, thus one of 12 or more persons may be guilty of riot even though the *mens rea* of riot cannot be proved against the remaining persons.

As for aiding and abetting, see *Jefferson, Skerritt, Keogh and Readman* [1994] 1 All ER 270.

'Violence' is defined in s 8 of the Act as follows:

> *In this Part—*
>
>   . . .

'violence' means any violent conduct, so that—

(a) *except in the context of affray, it includes violent conduct towards property as well as violent conduct towards persons, and*

(b) *it is not restricted to conduct causing or intended to cause injury or damage but includes any other violent conduct (for example, throwing at or towards a person a missile of a kind capable of causing injury which does not hit or falls short).*

The Act makes special provision for the intoxicated defendant in s 6(5) and (6) as follows:

(5) *For the purposes of this section a person whose awareness is impaired by intoxication shall be taken to be aware of that of which he would be aware if not intoxicated, unless he shows either that his intoxication was not self-induced or that it was caused solely by the taking or administration of a substance in the course of medical treatment.*

(6) *In subsection (5) 'intoxication' means any intoxication, whether caused by drink, drugs or other means, or by a combination of means.*

6.3   Violent disorder

Violent disorder is an offence which is triable either way. Section 2(5) of the Public Order Act 1986 provides that it is punishable on indictment with a term of five years, or a fine or both, or on summary conviction, with six months' imprisonment, or a fine not exceeding the statutory maximum or both.

The offence is defined in s 2 of the Act as follows:

(1) *Where three or more persons who are present together use or threaten unlawful violence and the conduct of them (taken together) is such as would cause a person of reasonable firmness present at the scene to fear for his personal safety, each of the persons using or threatening unlawful violence is guilty of violent disorder.*

(2) *It is immaterial whether or not the three or more use or threaten unlawful violence simultaneously.*

(3) *No person of reasonable firmness need actually be, or be likely to be, present at the scene.*

(4) *Violent disorder may be committed in private as well as in public places.*

There is no need for a common purpose. Each of at least three persons must be using or threatening unlawful violence. See *Mahroof* (1989) 88 Cr App R 317; *Fleming* (1989) 153 JP 517; *Worton* (1990) 154 JP 201; *McGuigan* [1991] Crim LR 719; *Rothwell and Barton* [1993] Crim LR 626.

6.4   Affray

Affray is an offence which is triable either way. Section 3(7) of the Public Order Act 1986 provides that it is punishable on indictment with a term of three years, or a fine or both, or on summary conviction, with six months' imprisonment, or a fine not exceeding the statutory maximum or both.

The offence is defined in s 3 of the Act as follows:

(1) *A person is guilty of affray if he uses or threatens unlawful violence towards another and his conduct is such as would cause a person of reasonable firmness present at the scene to fear for his personal safety.*

(2) Where two or more persons use or threaten the unlawful violence, it is the conduct of them taken together that must be considered for the purposes of subsection (1).

(3) For the purposes of this section a threat cannot be made by the use of words alone.

(4) No person of reasonable firmness need actually be, or be likely to be, present at the scene.

(5) Affray may be committed in private as well as in public places.

In the context of this offence, 'violence' relates to persons and does not include violent conduct towards property. See s 8 and *Davison* [1992] Crim LR 31; *Charles* (1989) 11 Cr App R (S) 125; *Walsh* (1990) 12 Cr App R (S) 243; *DPP v Cotcher* [1993] COD 181; *Dixon* [1993] Crim LR 579; *Robinson* [1993] Crim LR 581; and *Stanley and Knight* [1993] Crim LR 618. Note further that it is the 'hypothetical, reasonable bystander who must be put in fear for his personal safety, not the victim himself', per Simon Brown LJ in *Sanchez* (1996) 160 JP 321 at 323.

See further, *Thind* [1999] Crim LR 842, where the Court of Appeal held that the conviction was not unsafe even though the judge's summing up had not made it sufficiently clear that the person put in fear had to be the hypothetical bystander.

The threat of unlawful violence must, however, be directed towards a person or persons present at the scene (*I and others v DPP* [2001] 2 WLR 765). It was held in this case that where a group of young people had been arrested in possession of petrol bombs, the offence of affray had not been committed, as there was no use or threat of unlawful violence 'towards another'. The notional bystander had to be in the presence of both the offender and the victim and there was no evidence that there was a victim.

6.5   Fear or provocation of violence

The offence under s 4 of the Public Order Act 1986 is triable summarily only and is punishable with six months' imprisonment, or a fine not exceeding level 5 or both. The offence is defined as follows:

(1) A person is guilty of an offence if he—

    (a)   uses towards another person threatening, abusive or insulting words or behaviour, or

    (b)   distributes or displays to another person any writing, sign or other visible representation which is threatening, abusive or insulting,

with intent to cause that person to believe that immediate unlawful violence will be used against him or another by any person, or to provoke the immediate use of unlawful violence by that person or another, or whereby that person is likely to believe that such violence will be used or it is likely that such violence will be provoked.

(2) An offence under this section may be committed in a public or a private place, except that no offence is committed where the words or behaviour are used, or the writing, sign or other visible representation is distributed or displayed, by a person inside a dwelling and the other person is also inside that or another dwelling.

The four ways in which the offence may be committed were set out in *Winn v DPP* (1992) 156 JP 881. See also *Loade v DPP* [1990] 1 QB 1052; *Horseferry Road Metropolitan Stipendiary Magistrate, ex p Siadatan* [1991] 1 QB 260; *O'Brien* [1993] Crim LR 70; *Afzal* [1993] Crim LR 791; *Rukwira and others v DPP* [1993] Crim LR 882; and *Swanston v DPP* (1997) 161 JP 203.

It was held by the Divisional Court in *DPP v Ramos* [2000] Crim LR 768 that a letter threatening that a bomb would be detonated, but which did not state when the detonation would take place, was capable of being a threat, as it is the state of mind of the victim that was crucial rather than the statistical risk of violence occurring within a very short space of time.

'Dwelling' is defined in s 8 as follows:

In this Part—

'dwelling' means any structure or part of a structure occupied as a person's home or as other living accommodation (whether the occupation is separate or shared with others) but does not include any part not so occupied, and for this purpose 'structure' includes a tent, caravan, vehicle, vessel or other temporary or movable structure.

A police cell is not a dwelling for the purposes of the Act (*Francis* [2007] 1 WLR 1021).

6.5.1   Intentional harassment, alarm or distress

The offence under s 4A of the Public Order Act 1986 is triable summarily only and is punishable with six months' imprisonment, or a fine not exceeding level 5, or both. The offence is defined as follows:

4A.—(1)   A person is guilty of an offence if, with intent to cause a person harassment, alarm or distress, he—

(a)   uses threatening, abusive or insulting words or behaviour, or disorderly behaviour, or

(b)   displays any writing, sign or other visible representation which is threatening, abusive or insulting,

thereby causing that or another person harassment, alarm or distress.

(2)   An offence under this section may be committed in a public or a private place, except that no offence is committed where the words or behaviour are used, or the writing, sign or other visible representation is displayed, by a person inside a dwelling and the person who is harassed, alarmed or distressed is also inside that or another dwelling.

[(3)   provides a specific defence.]

. . .

(5)   A person guilty of an offence under this section is liable on summary conviction to imprisonment for a term not exceeding 6 months or a fine not exceeding level 5 on the standard scale or both.

The following statutory defence is provided in s 4A(3) as follows:

(3) It is a defence for the accused to prove—

(a)   that he was inside a dwelling and had no reason to believe that the words or behaviour used, or the writing, sign or other visible representation displayed, would be heard or seen by a person outside that or any other dwelling, or

(b)   that his conduct was reasonable.

The words 'harassment, alarm or distress' have been held to be relatively strong words befitting an offence which may result in a prison sentence. 'Distress' connotes real emotional disturbance or upset which, while it does not have to be grave, ought not to be trivialised (*R (R) v DPP* (2006) 170 JP 661). A police cell is not a dwelling (*Francis* [2007] 1 WLR 1021). Where a person sees for the first time a copy of threatening, abusive or insulting material months after it was originally published on the Internet, if it was published with the requisite intention for s 4A and if the viewer suffers harassment, alarm or distress, an offence is committed: *S v DPP* [2008] 1 WLR 2847.

6.6   Harassment, alarm or distress

The offence under s 5 of the Public Order Act 1986 is triable summarily only and is punishable with a fine not exceeding level 3. The offence is defined as follows:

(1) A person is guilty of an offence if he—

(a)   *uses threatening, abusive or insulting words or behaviour, or disorderly behaviour, or*

(b)   *displays any writing, sign or other visible representation which is threatening, abusive or insulting,*

within the hearing or sight of a person likely to be caused harassment, alarm or distress thereby.

[(2) and (3) concern the place of commission of the offence and a specific defence.]

The words harassment, alarm or distress have been held to be relatively strong words. 'Distress' connotes real emotional disturbance or upset which, while it does not have to be grave, ought not to be trivialised (*R (R) v DPP* (2006) 170 JP 661). See also *Lodge v DPP* The Times, 26 October 1988; *DPP v Orum* [1989] 1 WLR 88; *Ball* (1990) 90 Cr App R 378; *Chappell v DPP* (1989) 89 Cr App R 82; *Groom v DPP* [1991] Crim LR 713; *DPP v Clarke* (1992) 94 Cr App R 359; *Chambers and Edwards v DPP* [1995] Crim LR 896; *Vigon v DPP* (1998) 162 JP 115; *Holloway v DPP* (2005) 169 JP 14; and *Taylor v DPP* (2006) 170 JP 485.

A specific defence is set out in s 5(3) as follows:

(3) It is a defence for the accused to prove—

(a)   *that he had no reason to believe that there was any person within hearing or sight who was likely to be caused harassment, alarm or distress, or*

(b)   *that he was inside a dwelling and had no reason to believe that the words or behaviour used, or the writing, sign or other visible representation displayed, would be heard or seen by a person outside that or any other dwelling, or*

(c)   *that his conduct was reasonable.*

See *Kwasi Poku v DPP* [1993] Crim LR 705 and *Morrow and others v DPP and others* [1994] Crim LR 58.

In *Percy v DPP* [2002] Crim LR 835, the defendant had defaced an American flag at an American airbase and had put it on the ground and stood on it. The Divisional Court held that her conviction of an offence under s 5 should be quashed as it was incompatible with the right to freedom of expression contained in Article 10 of the ECHR. See also *Norwood v DPP* [2003] Crim LR 888; *DPP v Hammond* The Times, 28 January 2004; and *Detial v CPS* (2005) 169 JP 581.

6.7   Harassment

Governmental concerns over stalking led to the enactment of the Protection from Harassment Act 1997 which creates a number of offences designed to address that particular mischief. However, the offences created under the Act are broadly defined and encompass public order situations.

The offence of harassment is only triable summarily. Section 2(2) provides that it is punishable with a term of six months' imprisonment, or a fine not exceeding level 5 on the standard scale. The offence is defined in ss 1 and 2 as follows:

1.—(1) A person must not pursue a course of conduct—

(a)   *which amounts to harassment of another, and*

(b)   *which he knows or ought to know amounts to harassment of the other.*

(1A) A person must not pursue a course of conduct—

(a)   *which involves harassment of two or more persons, and*

> (b)   which he knows or ought to know involves harassment of those persons, and
>
> (c)   by which he intends to persuade any person (whether or not one of those mentioned above)—
>
> > (i)   not to do something that he is entitled or required to do, or
> >
> > (ii)   to do something that he is not under any obligation to do.
>
> (2)   For the purposes of this section, the person whose course of conduct is in question ought to know that it amounts to or involves harassment of another if a reasonable person in possession of the same information would think the course of conduct amounted to or involved harassment of the other.
>
> 2.—(1)   A person who pursues a course of conduct in breach of section 1(1) or (1A) is guilty of an offence.

A 'course of conduct' is defined in s 7 of the Act in the following terms:

> (3)   A 'course of conduct' must involve—
>
> (a)   in the case of conduct in relation to a single person (see section 1(1)), conduct on at least two occasions in relation to that person, or
>
> (b)   in the case of conduct in relation to two or more persons (see section 1(1A)), conduct on at least one occasion in relation to each of those persons.
>
> (3A)   A person's conduct on any occasion shall be taken, if aided, abetted, counselled or procured by another—
>
> (a)   to be conduct on that occasion of the other (as well as conduct of the person whose conduct it is); and
>
> (b)   to be conduct in relation to which the other's knowledge and purpose, and what he ought to have known, are the same as they were in relation to what was contemplated or reasonably foreseeable at the time of the aiding, abetting, counselling or procuring.
>
> (4)   'Conduct' includes speech.
>
> (5)   References to a person, in the context of the harassment of a person, are references to a person who is an individual.

The incidents, however many there may be, must properly be said to be so connected in type and in context as to justify the conclusion that they can amount to a course of conduct (*Patel* [2005] 1 Cr App R 440). In *Lau v DPP* [2000] Crim LR 580, it was held that the fewer the occasions and the wider they are spread, the less likely it would be that a finding of harassment can reasonably be made. However, the court stated that it could conceive of circumstances where incidents, as far apart as a year, could constitute a course of conduct and harassment. At the other end of the scale, a short series of telephone calls made with a five minute period has been held to amount to a course of conduct as each call was sufficiently distinct to be a separate event (*Kelly v DPP* (2001) 166 JP 621; see also *Buckley v DPP* [2008] EWHC 136 (Admin)).

The following statutory defences are provided in s 1(3):

> (3)   Subsection (1) or (1A) 1 does not apply to a course of conduct if the person who pursued it shows—
>
> (a)   that it was pursued for the purpose of preventing or detecting crime,
>
> (b)   that it was pursued under any enactment or rule of law or to comply with any condition or requirement imposed by any person under any enactment, or
>
> (c)   that in the particular circumstances the pursuit of the course of conduct was reasonable.

Under s 3(6) of the Protection from Harassment Act 1997, where an injunction has been granted by the High Court or a county court to prevent an actual or apprehended breach of s 1(1) of the Act, it is an offence for the defendant, without reasonable excuse, to do anything which he is prohibited from doing by the injunction. The offence is triable either way and punishable on conviction on indictment to a term not exceeding five years' imprisonment, or a fine, or both, and on summary conviction to six months' imprisonment, or a fine not exceeding the statutory maximum, or both.

6.8 Putting people in fear of violence

The offence under s 4 of the Protection from Harassment Act 1997 is triable either way. Section 4(4) of the 1997 Act provides that it is punishable on indictment with a term not exceeding five years' imprisonment, or a fine, or both, or on summary conviction, a term not exceeding six months' imprisonment, or a fine not exceeding the statutory maximum, or both.

The offence is defined in s 4 of the Act as follows:

(1) *A person whose course of conduct causes another to fear, on at least two occasions, that violence will be used against him is guilty of an offence if he knows or ought to know that his course of conduct will cause the other so to fear on each of those occasions.*

(2) *For the purposes of this section, the person whose course of conduct is in question ought to know that it will cause another to fear that violence will be used against him on any occasion if a reasonable person in possession of the same information would think the course of conduct would cause the other so to fear on that occasion.*

The definition of a course of conduct is the same as for the offence of harassment (see 6.7).

The conduct must put the complainant in fear of violence, fear alone will not suffice (*Henly* [2000] Crim LR 852; *Caurti* [2002] Crim LR 131).

The following statutory defences are provided in s 4(3):

(3) *It is a defence for a person charged with an offence under this section to show that—*
  (a) *his course of conduct was pursued for the purpose of preventing or detecting crime,*
  (b) *his course of conduct was pursued under any enactment or rule of law or to comply with any condition or requirement imposed by any person under any enactment, or*
  (c) *the pursuit of his course of conduct was reasonable for the protection of himself or another or for the protection of his or another's property.*

Where the judge rules that there is no case to answer under s 4, the s 2 offence may be left to the jury (*Livesey* [2007] 1 Cr App R 35).

6.9 Harassment of a person in a dwelling

Harassment of a person in a dwelling is triable summarily and is punishable with a term of imprisonment not exceeding three months, or a fine not exceeding level 4 on the standard scale, or both. When the Criminal Justice Act 2003, s 281(5) is brought into force, the maximum penalty will be increased to 51 weeks' imprisonment. The offence is defined in s 42A of the Criminal Justice and Police Act 2001 as follows:

(1) *A person commits an offence if—*
  (a) *that person is present outside or in the vicinity of any premises that are used by any individual ('the resident') as his dwelling;*

(b)   that person is present there for the purpose (by his presence or otherwise) of representing to the resident or another individual (whether or not one who uses the premises as his dwelling), or of persuading the resident or such another individual—

(i)   that he should not do something that he is entitled or required to do; or

(ii)   that he should do something that he is not under any obligation to do;

(c)   that person—

(i)   intends his presence to amount to the harassment of, or to cause alarm or distress to, the resident; or

(ii)   knows or ought to know that his presence is likely to result in the harassment of, or to cause alarm or distress to, the resident; and

(d)   the presence of that person—

(i)   amounts to the harassment of, or causes alarm or distress to, any person falling within subsection (2); or

(ii)   is likely to result in the harassment of, or to cause alarm or distress to, any such person.

(2)   A person falls within this subsection if he is—

(a)   the resident,

(b)   a person in the resident's dwelling, or

(c)   a person in another dwelling in the vicinity of the resident's dwelling.

(3)   The references in subsection (1)(c) and (d) to a person's presence are references to his presence either alone or together with that of any other persons who are also present.

(4)   For the purposes of this section a person (A) ought to know that his presence is likely to result in the harassment of, or to cause alarm or distress to, a resident if a reasonable person in possession of the same information would think that A's presence was likely to have that effect.

'Dwelling' has the same meaning as in Part 1 of the Public Order Act 1986 (s 42A(7)) (see **6.5**).

6.10 Racially or religiously aggravated public order offences

Sections 31 and 32 of the Crime and Disorder Act (CDA) 1998 create racially or religiously aggravated offences. The public order offences which may be racially or religiously aggravated are offences contrary to ss 4, 4A and 5 of the Public Order Act 1986 and harassment contrary to ss 2 and 4 of the Protection from Harassment Act 1997. The racially and religiously aggravated forms of these offences carry higher maximum penalties. In addition, the aggravated form of the offences under the Public Order Act 1986, ss 4 and 4A and the Protection from Harassment Act 1997, s 2 are triable either way. The CDA 1998, ss 31 and 32 provide as follows:

31.—(1)   A person is guilty of an offence under this section if he commits—

(a)   an offence under section 4 of the Public Order Act 1986 (fear or provocation of violence);

(b)   an offence under section 4A of that Act (intentional harassment, alarm or distress); or

(c)   an offence under section 5 of that Act (harassment, alarm or distress),

which is racially or religiously aggravated for the purposes of this section.

. . .

(4)   A person guilty of an offence falling within subsection (1)(a) or (b) above shall be liable—

(a)   on summary conviction, to imprisonment for a term not exceeding six months or to a fine not exceeding the statutory maximum, or to both;

(b)   on conviction on indictment, to imprisonment for a term not exceeding two years or to a fine, or to both.

(5) *A person guilty of an offence falling within subsection (1)(c) above shall be liable on summary conviction to a fine not exceeding level 4 on the standard scale.*

32.—(1) *A person is guilty of an offence under this section if he commits—*

(a) *an offence under section 2 of the Protection from Harassment Act 1997 (offence of harassment); or*

(b) *an offence under section 4 of that Act (putting people in fear of violence),*

which is racially or religiously aggravated for the purposes of this section

. . .

(3) *A person guilty of an offence falling within subsection (1)(a) above shall be liable—*

(a) *on summary conviction, to imprisonment for a term not exceeding six months or to a fine not exceeding the statutory maximum, or to both;*

(b) *on conviction on indictment, to imprisonment for a term not exceeding two years or to a fine, or to both.*

(4) *A person guilty of an offence falling within subsection (1)(b) above shall be liable—*

(a) *on summary conviction, to imprisonment for a term not exceeding six months or to a fine not exceeding the statutory maximum, or to both;*

(b) *on conviction on indictment, to imprisonment for a term not exceeding seven years or to a fine, or to both.*

The definition of 'racially or religiously aggravated' is provided in s 28 of the Crime and Disorder Act 1998:

(1) *An offence is racially or religiously aggravated for the purposes of sections 29 to 32 below if—*

(a) *at the time of committing the offence, or immediately before or after doing so, the offender demonstrates towards the victim of the offence hostility based on the victim's membership (or presumed membership) of a racial or religious group; or*

(b) *the offence is motivated (wholly or partly) by hostility towards members of a racial or religious group based on their membership of that group.*

(2) *In subsection (1)(a) above—*

'membership', in relation to a racial or religious group, includes association with members of that group;

'presumed' means presumed by the offender.

(3) *It is immaterial for the purposes of paragraph (a) or (b) of subsection (1) above whether or not the offender's hostility is also based, to any extent, on any other factor not mentioned in that paragraph.*

(4) *In this section 'racial group' means a group of persons defined by reference to race, colour, nationality (including citizenship) or ethnic or national origins.*

(5) *In this section 'religious group' means a group of persons defined by reference to religious belief or lack of religious belief.*

In *Rogers* [2007] 2 AC 62, the defendant was alleged to have called three Spanish women 'bloody foreigners' and told them to 'go back to your own country'. The Court of Appeal certified for consideration by the House of Lords the question of whether those who are not of British origin constitute a racial group within s 28(4) of the Crime and Disorder Act 1998. The House held that they did, observing that the definition of a racial group in s 28(4) clearly goes beyond groups defined by their colour, race or ethnic origin and encompasses both nationality (including citizenship) and national origins. Moreover, whether the group is defined exclusively by reference to what its members are not or inclusively by reference to what they are, the criterion by which the group is defined, whether nationality or colour, is the same.

Whether the words used demonstrate racial hostility was a question of fact for the tribunal of fact (*Johnson v DPP* The Times, 9 April 2008; *DPP v Howard* [2008] EWHC 608 (Admin)).

As to the distinction between s 28(1)(a) and s 28(1)(b), see *G v DPP* (2004) 168 JP 313. In *G v DPP*, the court noted that the prosecution may well be able and entitled in any particular case to rely on both limbs of s 28(1) of the 1998 Act.

There is no requirement that the victim belong to a different racial group to the defendant (*White* [2001] 1 WLR 1352).

In *Norwood v DPP* [2003] Crim LR 888, the appellant, a regional director of the British National Party, had displayed a poster which contained information said to be offensive to Muslims. He appealed by way of case stated against his conviction for an offence of causing alarm, or distress under s 5(1)(b) of the Public Order Act 1986 which was religiously aggravated in the manner provided by ss 28 and 31 of the Crime and Disorder Act 1998, as amended by s 39 of the Anti-Terrorism, Crime and Security Act 2001. The Administrative Court held that the judge was justified in finding on the evidence before the court, that the aggravated offence had been made out and that the appellant's right to freedom of expression under Article 10(1) of the ECHR had not been restricted.

The Court of Appeal indicated in *Saunders* [2000] 1 Cr App R 458 and in *Kelly* [2001] 2 Cr App R (S) 341, that when sentencing for racially aggravated public order offences, the sentencer should consider the appropriate sentence for the offence in the absence of racial aggravation and then add a further term to reflect the racial element.

6.11 Offences of stirring up racial hatred

Sections 18 to 23 of the Public Order Act 1986 create six distinct offences. They are triable either way and are punishable on indictment with a term of two years' imprisonment or a fine or both, or on summary conviction, with six months' imprisonment, or a fine not exceeding the statutory maximum or both. Proceedings require the consent of the Attorney-General (s 27(3)).

6.11.1 Use of words or behaviour or display of written material stirring up racial hatred

The Public Order Act 1986, s 18 offence is defined as follows:

> (1) *A person who uses threatening, abusive or insulting words or behaviour, or displays any written material which is threatening, abusive or insulting, is guilty of an offence if—*
>   (a) *he intends thereby to stir up racial hatred, or*
>   (b) *having regard to all the circumstances racial hatred is likely to be stirred up thereby.*

'Racial hatred' is defined by s 17 as follows:

> *In this part 'racial hatred' means hatred against a group of persons in Great Britain defined by reference to colour, race, nationality (including citizenship) or ethnic or national origins.*

The *mens rea* of the offence is referred to in s 18(5):

> *A person who is not shown to have intended to stir up racial hatred is not guilty of an offence under this section if he did not intend his words or behaviour, or the written material, to be, and was not aware that it might be, threatening, abusive or insulting.*

Section 18(2) stipulates where the offence may be committed and s 18(4) sets out a statutory defence:

(2) An offence under this section may be committed in a public or a private place, except that no offence is committed where the words or behaviour are used, or the written material is displayed, by a person inside a dwelling and are not heard or seen except by other persons in that or another dwelling.

(4) In proceedings for an offence under this section it is a defence for the accused to prove that he was inside a dwelling and had no reason to believe that the words or behaviour used, or the written material displayed, would be heard or seen by a person outside that or any other dwelling.

No offence is committed where words or behaviour are used, or written material displayed, solely for the purpose of being included in a programme service (s 18(6)).

6.11.2 Publishing or distributing written material stirring up racial hatred

The Public Order Act 1986, s 19 offence is defined as follows:

(1) A person who publishes or distributes written material which is threatening, abusive or insulting is guilty of an offence if—

(a)   he intends thereby to stir up racial hatred, or

(b)   having regard to all the circumstances racial hatred is likely to be stirred up thereby.

6.11.3 Public performance of a play stirring up racial hatred

The Public Order Act 1986, s 20 offence is defined as follows:

(1) If a public performance of a play is given which involves the use of threatening, abusive or insulting words or behaviour, any person who presents or directs the performance is guilty of an offence if—

(a)   he intends thereby to stir up racial hatred, or

(b)   having regard to all the circumstances (and, in particular, taking the performance as a whole) racial hatred is likely to be stirred up thereby.

The following statutory defences are provided in s 20:

(2) If a person presenting or directing the performance is not shown to have intended to stir up racial hatred, it is a defence for him to prove—

(a)   that he did not know and had no reason to suspect that the performance would involve the use of the offending words or behaviour, or

(b)   that he did not know and had no reason to suspect that the offending words or behaviour were threatening, abusive or insulting, or

(c)   that he did not know and had no reason to suspect that the circumstances in which the performance would be given would be such that racial hatred would be likely to be stirred up.

(3) This section does not apply to a performance given solely or primarily for one or more of the following purposes—

(a)   rehearsal,

(b)   making a recording of the performance, or

(c)   enabling the performance to be included in a programme service, but if it is proved that the performance was attended by persons other than those directly concerned with the giving of the performance or the doing in relation to it of the things mentioned in paragraph (b) or (c), the performance shall, unless the contrary is shown, be taken not to have been given solely for the purposes mentioned above.

(4) For the purposes of this section—

    (a)   a person shall not be treated as presenting a performance of a play by reason only of his taking part in it as a performer,

    (b)   a person taking part as a performer in a performance directed by another shall be treated as a person who directed the performance if without reasonable excuse he performs otherwise than in accordance with that person's direction, and

    (c)   a person shall be taken to have directed a performance of a play given under his direction notwithstanding that he was not present during the performance;

and a person shall not be treated as aiding or abetting the commission of an offence under this section by reason only of his taking part in a performance as a performer.

6.11.4   Distributing, showing or playing a recording stirring up racial hatred

The Public Order Act 1986, s 21 offence is defined as follows:

(1) A person who distributes, or shows or plays, a recording of visual images or sounds which are threatening, abusive or insulting is guilty of an offence if—

    (a)   he intends thereby to stir up racial hatred, or

    (b)   having regard to all the circumstances racial hatred is likely to be stirred up thereby.

The following statutory defence is provided in s 21:

(3) In proceedings for an offence under this section it is a defence for an accused who is not shown to have intended to stir up racial hatred to prove that he was not aware of the content of the recording and did not suspect, and had no reason to suspect, that it was threatening, abusive or insulting.

(4) This section does not apply to the showing or playing of a recording solely for the purpose of enabling the recording to be included in a programme service.

6.11.5   Broadcasting or including a programme in programme service stirring up racial hatred

The Public Order Act 1986, s 22 offence is defined as follows:

(1) If a programme involving threatening, abusive or insulting visual images or sound is included in a programme service, each of the persons mentioned in subsection (2) is guilty of an offence if—

    (a)   he intends to stir up racial hatred, or

    (b)   having regard to all the circumstances racial hatred is likely to be stirred up thereby.

(2) The persons are—

    (a)   the person providing the programme service,

    (b)   any person by whom the programme is produced or directed, and

    (c)   any person by whom offending words or behaviour are used.

The following statutory defences are provided in s 22:

(3) If the person providing the service, or a person by whom the programme was produced or directed, is not shown to have intended to stir up racial hatred, it is a defence for him to prove that—

    (a)   he did not know and had no reason to suspect that the programme would involve the offending material, and

    (b)   having regard to the circumstances in which the programme was included in a programme service, it was not reasonably practicable for him to secure the removal of the material.

(4) *It is a defence for a person by whom the programme was produced or directed who is not shown to have intended to stir up racial hatred to prove that he did not know and had no reason to suspect—*

    (a)   *that the programme would be included in a programme service, or*

    (b)   *that the circumstances in which the programme would be so included would be such that racial hatred would be likely to be stirred up.*

(5) *It is a defence for a person by whom offending words or behaviour were used and who is not shown to have intended to stir up racial hatred to prove that he did not know and had no reason to suspect—*

    (a)   *that a programme involving the use of the offending material would be included in a programme service, or*

    (b)   *that the circumstances in which a programme involving the use of the offending material would be so included, or in which a programme so included would involve the use of the offending material, would be such that racial hatred would be likely to be stirred up.*

(6) *A person who is not shown to have intended to stir up racial hatred is not guilty of an offence under this section if he did not know, and had no reason to suspect, that the offending material was threatening, abusive or insulting.*

6.11.6   Possession of inflammatory material stirring up racial hatred

The Public Order Act 1986, s 23 offence is defined as follows:

(1) *A person who has in his possession written material which is threatening, abusive or insulting, or a recording of visual images or sound which are threatening, abusive or insulting, with a view to—*

    (a)   *in the case of written material, its being displayed, published, distributed, or included in a programme service, whether by himself or another, or*

    (b)   *in the case of a recording, its being distributed, shown, played, or included in a programme service, whether by himself or another;*

        is guilty of an offence if he intends racial hatred to be stirred up thereby or, having regard to all the circumstances, racial hatred is likely to be stirred up thereby.

(2) *For this purpose regard is to be had to such display, publication, distribution, showing, playing, or inclusion in a programme service as he has, or it may reasonably be inferred that he has, in view.*

A statutory defence is provided in s 23(3):

(3) *In proceedings for an offence under this section it is a defence for an accused who is not shown to have intended to stir up racial hatred to prove that he was not aware of the content of the written material or recording and did not suspect, and had no reason to suspect, that it was threatening, abusive or insulting.*

6.12   Offences of stirring up hatred on religious grounds or on the grounds of sexual orientation

Part 3A of the Public Order Act 1986 creates six offences involving stirring up hatred against persons on religious grounds or on grounds of sexual orientation. The offences, which are similar to those involving stirring up racial hatred (see **6.11**), are triable either way and are punishable on indictment with a term of seven years' imprisonment or a fine or both, or on summary conviction with not more than 12 months' imprisonment or a fine not exceeding the statutory maximum or both. Proceedings require the consent of the Attorney-General (s 29L(1)).

6.12.1 Use of words or behaviour or display of written material stirring up hatred on religious grounds or on grounds of sexual orientation

The Public Order Act 1986, s 29B offence is defined as follows:

> *(1) A person who uses threatening words or behaviour, or displays any written material which is threatening, is guilty of an offence if he intends thereby to stir up religious hatred or hatred on the grounds of sexual orientation.*

'Religious hatred' for the purposes of Part 3A of the 1986 Act is defined by s 29A in the following terms:

> *In this Part 'religious hatred' means hatred against a group of persons defined by reference to religious belief or lack of religious belief.*

'Hatred on the grounds of sexual orientation' is defined by s 29AB as follows:

> *In this Part "hatred on the grounds of sexual orientation" means hatred against a group of persons defined by reference to sexual orientation (whether towards persons of the same sex, the opposite sex or both).*

Freedom of expression on religious matters, including the right to proselytise, is protected by s 29J which provides that:

> *Nothing in this Part shall be read or given effect in a way which prohibits or restricts discussion, criticism or expressions of antipathy, dislike, ridicule, insult or abuse of particular religions or the beliefs or practices of their adherents, or of any other belief system or the beliefs or practices of its adherents, or proselytising or urging adherents of a different religion or belief system to cease practising their religion or belief system.*

Section 29JA allows for criticism of sexual conduct and practices. It provides as follows:

> *In this Part, for the avoidance of doubt, the discussion or criticism of sexual conduct or practices or the urging of persons to refrain from or modify such conduct or practices shall not be taken of itself to be threatening or intended to stir up hatred.*

Section 29B(2) stipulates where the offence may be committed and s 29B(4) sets out a statutory defence:

> *(2) An offence under this section may be committed in a public or a private place, except that no offence is committed where the words or behaviour are used, or the written material is displayed, by a person inside a dwelling and are not heard or seen except by other persons in that or another dwelling.*
>
> *(4) In proceedings for an offence under this section it is a defence for the accused to prove that he was inside a dwelling and had no reason to believe that the words or behaviour used, or the written material displayed, would be heard or seen by a person outside that or any other dwelling.*

No offence is committed where words or behaviour are used, or written material displayed, solely for the purpose of being included in a programme service (s 29B(5)).

6.12.2 Publishing or distributing written material stirring up religious hatred

The Public Order Act 1986, s 29C offence is defined as follows:

> *(1) A person who publishes or distributes written material which is threatening is guilty of an offence if he intends thereby to stir up religious hatred or hatred on the grounds of sexual orientation.*

6.12.3 Public performance of a play stirring up religious hatred

The Public Order Act 1986, s 29D offence is defined as follows:

(1) *If a public performance of a play is given which involves the use of threatening words or behaviour, any person who presents or directs the performance is guilty of an offence if he intends thereby to stir up religious hatred or hatred on the grounds of sexual orientation.*

The following statutory defences are provided by s 29D:

(2) *This section does not apply to a performance given solely or primarily for one or more of the following purposes—*

    (a) *rehearsal;*

    (b) *making a recording of the performance; or*

    (c) *enabling the performance to be included in a programme service;*

but if it is proved that the performance was attended by persons other than those directly connected with the giving of the performance or the doing in relation to it of the things mentioned in paragraph (b) or (c), the performance shall, unless the contrary is shown, be taken not to have been given solely or primarily for the purpose mentioned above.

(3) *For the purposes of this section—*

    (a) *a person shall not be treated as presenting a performance of a play by reason only of his taking part in it as a performer;*

    (b) *a person taking part as a performer in a performance directed by another shall be treated as a person who directed the performance if without reasonable excuse he performs otherwise than in accordance with that person's direction; and*

    (c) *a person shall be taken to have directed a performance of a play given under his direction notwithstanding that he was not present during the performance;*

and a person shall not be treated as aiding or abetting the commission of an offence under this section by reason only of his taking part in a performance as a performer.

6.12.4 Distributing, showing or playing a recording stirring up religious hatred

The Public Order Act 1986, s 29E offence is defined as follows:

(1) *A person who distributes, or shows or plays, a recording of visual images or sounds which are threatening is guilty of an offence if he intends thereby to stir up religious hatred or hatred on the grounds of sexual orientation.*

No offence is committed where the recording is shown or played solely for the purpose of enabling the recording to be included in a programme service (s 29E(3)).

6.12.5 Broadcasting or including a programme in programme service stirring up religious hatred

The Public Order Act 1986, s 29F offence is defined as follows:

(1) *If a programme involving threatening visual images or sounds is included in a programme service, each of the persons mentioned in subsection (2) is guilty of an offence if he intends thereby to stir up religious hatred.*

(2) *The persons are—*

    (a) *the person providing the programme service;*

    (b) *any person by whom the programme is produced or directed; and*

    (c) *any person by whom offending words or behaviour are used.*

6.12.6   Possession of inflammatory material stirring up religious hatred

The Public Order Act 1986, s 29G offence is defined as follows:

(1) A person who has in his possession written material which is threatening, or a recording of visual images or sounds which are threatening, with a view to—

    (a)   in the case of written material, its being displayed, published, distributed, or included in a programme service whether by himself or another; or

    (b)   in the case of a recording, its being distributed, shown, played, or included in a programme service, whether by himself or another;

    is guilty of an offence if he intends thereby to stir up religious hatred or hatred on the grounds of sexual orientation.

(2) For this purpose regard shall be had to such display, publication, distribution, showing, playing, or inclusion in a programme service as he has, or it may be reasonably be inferred that he has, in view.

6.13   Football and sporting offences

6.13.1   Throwing of objects, chanting of indecent or racialist nature, going onto playing area

Sections 2, 3 and 4 of the Football (Offences) Act 1991 create offences which are triable summarily only. The maximum penalty is a fine not exceeding level 3 on the standard scale (s 5(2)). They provide as follows:

2— It is an offence for a person at a designated football match to throw anything at or towards—

    (a)   the playing area, or any area adjacent to the playing area to which spectators are not generally admitted, or

    (b)   any area in which spectators or other persons are or may be present, without lawful authority or lawful excuse (which shall be for him to prove).

3.—(1) It is an offence to take part at a designated football match in chanting of an indecent or racialist nature.

    (2) For this purpose—

    (a)   'chanting' means the repeated uttering of any words or sounds in concert with one or more others; and

    (b)   'of racialist nature' means consisting of or including matter which is threatening, abusive or insulting to a person by reason of his colour, race, nationality (including citizenship) or ethnic or national origins.

4— It is an offence for a person at a designated football match to go onto the playing area, or any area adjacent to the playing area to which spectators are not generally admitted, without lawful authority or lawful excuse (which shall be for him to prove).

The Divisional Court held in *DPP v Stoke-on-Trent Magistrates' Court* [2003] 3 All ER 1096 that the use of the phrase 'You're just a town full of Pakis' chanted at a football match was insulting and racially abusive within the meaning of s 3(2)(b).

6.13.2   Alcohol offences at sporting events

Section 1 of the Sporting Events (Control of Alcohol etc) Act 1985 creates offences which are triable summarily only and are punishable by a fine not exceeding level 4 on the standard scale in the case of an offence under s 1(2), level 3 in the case of an offence under s 1(3), and level 2 in the case of an offence under s 1(4). The offences are defined as follows:

> (2) *A person who knowingly causes or permits alcohol to be carried on a vehicle to which this section applies is guilty of an offence—*
>> (a) *if the vehicle is a public service vehicle and he is the operator of the vehicle or the servant or agent of the operator, or*
>> (b) *if the vehicle is a hired vehicle and he is the person to whom it is hired or the servant or agent of that person.*
>
> (3) *A person who has intoxicating liquor in his possession while on a vehicle to which this section applies is guilty of an offence.*
>
> (4) *A person who is drunk on a vehicle to which this section applies is guilty of an offence.*

Section 2 offences are also triable summarily only and are punishable by a fine not exceeding level 3 on the standard scale, or by imprisonment for a term not exceeding three months or both in the case of an offence under s 2(1), and a fine not exceeding level 2 in the case of an offence under s 2(2). The offences are defined as follows:

> (1) *A person who has alcohol or an article to which this section applies in his possession—*
>> (a) *at any time during the period of a designated sporting event when he is in any area of a designated sports ground from which the event may be directly viewed, or*
>> (b) *while entering or trying to enter a designated sports ground at any time during the period of a designated sporting event at that ground, is guilty of an offence.*
>
> (2) *A person who is drunk in a designated sports ground at any time during the period of a designated sporting event at that ground or is drunk while entering or trying to enter such a ground at any time during the period of a designated sporting event at that ground is guilty of an offence.*

6.13.3 Banning orders

The Football Spectators Act 1989 provides that a court by or before which a person has been convicted of certain offences may make a banning order against him. The relevant offences are set out in Sch 1. It was held by the Court of Appeal in *Gough and Smith v Chief Constable of Derbyshire* [2002] 2 All ER 985 that international banning orders under the Act contravened neither European law on freedom of movement of persons nor the ECHR.

6.14 Offences relating to public processions, assemblies and demonstrations

6.14.1 Failure to give notice to the police

A person organising a public procession is required by s 11 of the Public Order Act 1986 to satisfy requirements concerning the giving of notice of the procession to the police.

The offence under s 11(7) of the Public Order Act 1986 is triable summarily only and is punishable with a fine not exceeding level 3. The offence is defined as follows:

> (7) *Where a public procession is held each of the persons organising it is guilty of an offence if—*
>> (a) *the requirements of this section as to notice have not been satisfied, or*
>> (b) *the date when it is held, the time when it starts, or its route, differs from the date, time or route specified in the notice.*

The following statutory defences are provided in s 11(8) and (9):

> *(8) It is a defence for the accused to prove that he did not know of, and neither suspected nor had reason to suspect, the failure to satisfy the requirements or (as the case may be) the difference of date, time or route.*

> *(9) To the extent that an alleged offence turns on a difference of date, time or route, it is a defence for the accused to prove that the difference arose from circumstances beyond his control or from something done with the agreement of a police officer or by his direction.*

As to what amounts to a procession for the purposes of s 11, see *R (Kay) v Commissioner of Police of the Metropolis* [2008] 1 WLR 2723.

6.14.2   Failure to comply with conditions imposed on a public procession

Under s 12 of the Public Order Act 1986, the police have power to make directions regarding public processions.

> *12.—(1) If the senior police officer, having regard to the time or place at which and the circumstances in which any public procession is being held or is intended to be held and to its route or proposed route, reasonably believes that—*
>
> > *(a)   it may result in serious public disorder, serious damage to property or serious disruption to the life of the community, or*
> >
> > *(b)   the purpose of the persons organising it is the intimidation of others with a view to compelling them not to do an act they have a right to do, or to do an act they have a right not to do,*
>
> *he may give directions imposing on the persons organising or taking part in the procession such conditions as appear to him necessary to prevent such disorder, damage, disruption or intimidation, including conditions as to the route of the procession or prohibiting it from entering any public place specified in the directions.*

'Senior police officer' is defined by s 12(2) as follows:

> *(2) In subsection (1) 'the senior police officer' means—*
>
> > *(a)   in relation to a procession being held, or to a procession intended to be held in a case where persons are assembling with a view to taking part in it, the most senior in rank of the police officers present at the scene, and*
> >
> > *(b)   in relation to a procession intended to be held in a case where paragraph (a) does not apply, the chief officer of police.*

Section 12(4)–(6) creates the following offences:

> *(4) A person who organises a public procession and knowingly fails to comply with a condition imposed under this section is guilty of an offence, but it is a defence for him to prove that the failure arose from circumstances beyond his control.*

> *(5) A person who takes part in a public procession and knowingly fails to comply with a condition imposed under this section is guilty of an offence, but it is a defence for him to prove that the failure arose from circumstances beyond his control.*

> *(6) A person who incites another to commit an offence under subsection (5) is guilty of an offence.*

The offences are triable summarily and the penalty for s 12(4) offence is imprisonment for a term not exceeding three months, or a fine not exceeding level 4, or both.

The penalty for the s 12(5) offence is a fine not exceeding level 3 and for the s 12(6) offence, imprisonment for a term not exceeding three months, or a fine not exceeding level 4, or both.

When the Criminal Justice Act 2003, s 280(2) is brought into force, the maximum penalty for the offences under s 12(4) and (6) will be increased to 51 weeks' imprisonment.

6.14.3   Contravening prohibition of a public procession

Section 13 of the Public Order Act 1986 enables a local authority to make an order prohibiting the holding of all public processions within a specified district for a period of up to three months.

13.—(1) *If at any time the chief officer of police reasonably believes that, because of particular circumstances existing in any district or part of a district, the powers under section 12 will not be sufficient to prevent the holding of public processions in that district or part from resulting in serious public disorder, he shall apply to the council of the district for an order prohibiting for such period not exceeding 3 months as may be specified in the application the holding of all public processions (or of any class of public procession so specified) in the district or part concerned.*

(2) *On receiving such an application, a council may with the consent of the Secretary of State make an order either in the terms of the application or with such modifications as may be approved by the Secretary of State.*

In the City of London and the metropolitan police district, such order can only be made by the Commissioner of Police for the City of London or the Commissioner of Police of the Metropolis, respectively (s 13(4)). The consent of the Secretary of State is again required.

Section 13(7)–(9) of the 1986 Act creates three offences:

(7) *A person who organises a public procession the holding of which he knows is prohibited by virtue of an order under this section is guilty of an offence.*

(8) *A person who takes part in a public procession the holding of which he knows is prohibited by virtue of an order under this section is guilty of an offence.*

(9) *A person who incites another to commit an offence under subsection (8) is guilty of an offence.*

The offences are triable summarily. The penalty for each of the s 13(7) and (9) offences is imprisonment for a term not exceeding three months or a fine not exceeding level 4 or both, and for the s 13(8) offence is a fine not exceeding level 3. When the Criminal Justice Act 2003, s 280(2) is brought into force, the maximum penalty for the offences under s 13(7) and (9) will be increased to 51 weeks' imprisonment.

6.14.4   Failure to comply with conditions imposed on a public assembly

Under s 14, the police have power to impose conditions on public assemblies.

14.—(1) *If the senior police officer, having regard to the time or place at which and the circumstances in which any public assembly is being held or is intended to be held, reasonably believes that—*

(a) *it may result in serious public disorder, serious damage to property or serious disruption to the life of the community, or*

(b) *the purpose of the persons organising it is the intimidation of others with a view to compelling them not to do an act they have a right to do, or to do an act they have a right not to do,*

he may give directions imposing on the persons organising or taking part in the assembly such conditions as to the place at which the assembly may be (or continue to be) held, its maximum duration, or the maximum number of persons who may constitute it, as appear to him necessary to prevent such disorder, damage, disruption or intimidation.

'Senior police officer' is defined in s 14(2) as follows:

> *(2) In subsection (1) 'the senior police officer' means—*
>
> > *(a) in relation to an assembly being held, the most senior in rank of the police officers present at the scene, and*
> >
> > *(b) in relation to an assembly intended to be held, the chief officer of police.*

Section 14(4)– (6) creates three offences:

> *(4) A person who organises a public assembly and knowingly fails to comply with a condition imposed under this section is guilty of an offence, but it is a defence for him to prove that the failure arose from circumstances beyond his control.*
>
> *(5) A person who takes part in a public assembly and knowingly fails to comply with a condition imposed under this section is guilty of an offence, but it is a defence for him to prove that the failure arose from circumstances beyond his control.*
>
> *(6) A person who incites another to commit an offence under subsection (5) is guilty of an offence.*

The offences are triable summarily. The penalty for the s 14(4) and (6) offences is imprisonment for a term not exceeding three months, or a fine not exceeding level 4, or both, and for the s 14(5) offence, a fine not exceeding level 3. When the Criminal Justice Act 2003, s 280(2) is brought into force, the maximum penalty for the offences under s 14(4) and (6) will be increased to 51 weeks' imprisonment.

6.14.5   Demonstrating without authorisation in the vicinity of Parliament

Under s 138 of the Serious Organised Crime and Police Act 2005, the Secretary of State may by order specify an area as a 'designated area'. The designated area must be within one kilometre from Parliament Square (s 138(3)). On its proper construction, s 132(1) includes demonstrations starting before the commencement of the Act as well as those starting after (*R (Haw) v Secretary of State for the Home Department* [2006] QB 780).

Section 132 makes it an offence to demonstrate in a designated area. The offence is defined as follows:

> *132.—(1)   Any person who—*
>
> > *(a)   organises a demonstration in a public place in the designated area, or*
> >
> > *(b)   takes part in a demonstration in a public place in the designated area, or*
> >
> > *(c)   carries on a demonstration by himself in a public place in the designated area,*
>
> *is guilty of an offence if, when the demonstration starts, authorisation for the demonstration has not been given under section 134(2).*

The following statutory defence is provided in s 132(2):

> *(2) It is a defence for a person accused of an offence under subsection (1) to show that he reasonably believed that authorisation had been given.*

The offences under s 132(1) are triable summarily only. The penalty for an offence under s 132(1)(a) is a term not exceeding 51 weeks, or a fine not exceeding level 4 on the standard scale, or both. The penalty for the offences under s 132(1)(b) and (c) is a fine not exceeding level 3 on the standard scale. The penalty for inciting another to either:

(a) do anything which would constitute an offence under s 132(1); or

(b) fail to do anything where the failure would constitute such an offence, is imprisonment for a term not exceeding 51 weeks, or a fine not exceeding level 4 on the standard scale, or both.

Section 132(1) does not apply in relation to demonstrations which are public processions or assemblies to which ss 11–13 of the Public Order Act 1986 apply (s 132(2)). Section 14 of the Public Order Act 1986 does not apply in relation to a public assembly which is also a demonstration in a public place in the designated area (s 132(6)).

Section 132 has been held not to infringe the right to freedom of peaceful assembly under Article 11 of the ECHR (*Blum v DPP* [2007] UKHRR 233).

6.14.6   Contravening conditions imposed on authorised demonstrations in the vicinity of Parliament

Authorisation for a demonstration may be sought in accordance with the terms of ss 133 and 134 of the Serious Organised Crime and Police Act 2005.

Section 134(7) of the 2005 Act creates the following offence:

> (7) Each person who takes part in or organises a demonstration in the designated area is guilty of an offence if—
>
> (a)   he knowingly fails to comply with a condition imposed under subsection (3) which is applicable to him (except where it is varied under section 135), or
>
> (b)   he knows or should have known that the demonstration is carried on otherwise than in accordance with the particulars set out in the authorisation by virtue of subsection (5).

The following statutory defence is provided in s 134(8):

> (8) It is a defence for a person accused of an offence under subsection (7) to show—
>
> (a)   (in a paragraph (a) case) that the failure to comply, or
>
> (b)   (in a paragraph (b) case) that the divergence from the particulars,
>
> arose from circumstances beyond his control, or from something done with the agreement, or by the direction, of a police officer.

The offence under s 134(7) is triable summarily only. The penalty for the offence is, where the offence was in relation to the defendant's capacity as organiser of the demonstration, imprisonment for a term not exceeding 51 weeks, or a fine not exceeding level 4 on the standard scale, or both and, otherwise, a fine not exceeding level 3 on the standard scale. The penalty for inciting another to either:

(a) do anything which would constitute an offence under s 134(7); or

(b) fail to do anything where the failure would constitute such an offence,

is imprisonment for a term not exceeding 51 weeks, or a fine not exceeding level 4 on the standard scale, or both.

6.14.7   Contravening supplementary conditions imposed on authorised demonstrations in the vicinity of Parliament

Under s 135, the senior police officer may give directions to those taking part in or organising the demonstration imposing such additional conditions or varying any such condition already imposed. The 'senior police officer' is the highest ranking officer present at the scene (s 135(5)).

Section 135(3) of the 2005 Act creates the following offence:

(3) A person taking part in or organising the demonstration who knowingly fails to comply with a condition which is applicable to him and which is imposed or varied by a direction under this section is guilty of an offence.

The following statutory defence is provided in s 135(4):

(4) It is a defence for him to show that the failure to comply arose from circumstances beyond his control.

The offence under s 135(3) is triable summarily only. The penalty for the offence is, where the offence was in relation to the defendant's capacity as organiser of the demonstration, imprisonment for a term not exceeding 51 weeks, or a fine not exceeding level 4 on the standard scale, or both and, otherwise, a fine not exceeding level 3 on the standard scale. The penalty for inciting another to either:

(a) do anything which would constitute an offence under s 135(3); or

(b) fail to do anything where the failure would constitute such an offence,

is imprisonment for a term not exceeding 51 weeks' imprisonment, or a fine not exceeding level 4 on the standard scale, or both.

6.15 Bomb hoaxes

An offence under s 51(1) of the Criminal Law Act 1977 is triable either way and is punishable on indictment with a term of seven years' imprisonment, and on summary conviction with a term not exceeding six months' imprisonment, or a fine not exceeding the statutory maximum or both (s 51(4)).

The offence is defined as follows:

(1) A person who—
   (a) places any article in any place whatever, or
   (b) dispatches any article by post, rail or any other means whatever of sending things from one place to another,

with the intention (in either case) of inducing in some other person a belief that it is likely to explode or ignite and thereby cause personal injury or damage to property is guilty of an offence. In this subsection 'article' includes substance.

(2) A person who communicates any information which he knows or believes to be false to another person with the intention of inducing in him or any other person a false belief that a bomb or other thing liable to explode or ignite is present in any place or location whatever is guilty of an offence.

See *Browne* (1984) 6 Cr App R (S) 5; *Dunbar* (1987) 9 Cr App R (S) 393; and *Wilburn* (1992) 13 Cr App R (S) 309.

6.16 Offences in relation to collective trespass or nuisance on land

6.16.1 Powers regarding trespass

Section 61(1)–(3) of the Criminal Justice and Public Order Act 1994 (CJPOA 1994) enables a senior police officer to make a direction for two or more trespassers to leave land.

61.—(1) If the senior police officer present at the scene reasonably believes that two or more persons are trespassing on land and are present there with the common purpose of residing there for any period, that reasonable steps have been taken by or on behalf of the occupier to ask them to leave and—

    (a) that any of those persons has caused damage to the land or to property on the land or used threatening, abusive or insulting words or behaviour towards the occupier, a member of his family or an employee or agent of his, or

    (b) that those persons have between them six or more vehicles on the land,

he may direct those persons, or any of them, to leave the land and to remove any vehicles or other property they have with them on the land.

  (2) Where the persons in question are reasonably believed by the senior police officer to be persons who were not originally trespassers but have become trespassers on the land, the officer must reasonably believe that the other conditions specified in subsection (1) are satisfied after those persons became trespassers before he can exercise the power conferred by that subsection.

  (3) A direction under subsection (1) above, if not communicated to the persons referred to in subsection (1) by the police officer giving the direction, may be communicated to them by any constable at the scene.

The offence under s 61(4) is defined as follows:

  (4) If a person knowing that a direction under subsection (1) above has been given which applies to him—

    (a) fails to leave the land as soon as reasonably practicable, or

    (b) having left again enters the land as a trespasser within the period of three months beginning with the day on which the direction was given,

he commits an offence and is liable on summary conviction to imprisonment for a term not exceeding three months or a fine not exceeding level 4 on the standard scale, or both.

When the Criminal Justice Act 2003, s 280(2) is brought into force, the maximum penalty will be increased to 51 weeks' imprisonment.

The following statutory defence is provided in s 61(6):

  (6) In proceedings for an offence under this section it is a defence for the accused to show—

    (a) that he was not trespassing on the land, or

    (b) that he had a reasonable excuse for failing to leave the land as soon as reasonably practicable or, as the case may be, for again entering the land as a trespasser.

Section 61(9) defines various terms including 'common land', 'occupier', 'trespass' and 'vehicle'.

Section 62A(1)–(3) of the CJPOA 1994 enables the senior police officer present at the scene to make a direction for one or more trespassers who are present on land with one or more vehicles and who are there with the purpose of residing there to leave the land. If the trespasser is on the land with a caravan there must be a suitable pitch available before such a direction can be made (s 62A(2)(e)).

Section 62B creates the following offence:

62B.—(1) A person commits an offence if he knows that a direction under section 62A(1) has been given which applies to him and—

    (a) he fails to leave the relevant land as soon as reasonably practicable; or

    (b) he enters any land in the area of the relevant local authority as a trespasser before the end of the relevant period with the intention of residing there.

  (2) The relevant period is the period of 3 months starting with the day on which the direction is given.

  (3) A person guilty of an offence under this section is liable on summary conviction to imprisonment for a term not exceeding 3 months or a fine not exceeding level 4 on the standard scale or both.

When the Criminal Justice Act 2003, s 280(2) is brought into force, the maximum penalty for this offence will be increased to 51 weeks' imprisonment.

The following statutory defence is provided in 62B(5):

> (5) *In proceedings for an offence under this section it is a defence for the accused to show—*
>
> > (a) *that he was not trespassing on the land in respect of which he is alleged to have committed the offence; or*
> >
> > (b) *that he had a reasonable excuse—*
> >
> > > (i) *for failing to leave the relevant land as soon as reasonably practicable; or*
> > >
> > > (ii) *for entering land in the area of the relevant local authority as a trespasser with the intention of residing there; or*
> >
> > (c) *that, at the time the direction was given, he was under the age of 18 years and was residing with his parent or guardian.*

The provisions apply to common land with the modifications set out in s 62D.

Section 62E defines various terms including 'land', 'occupier', 'trespass' and 'vehicle'.

6.16.2 Powers regarding raves

Section 63(1)– (5) of the CJPOA 1994 enables a police officer of at least the rank of superintendent to give a direction for persons to leave land if two or more of them are preparing for a rave, or ten or more of them are waiting for, or attending a rave.

> 63.—(1) *This section applies to a gathering on land in the open air of 20 or more persons (whether or not trespassers) at which amplified music is played during the night (with or without intermissions) and is such as, by reason of its loudness and duration and the time at which it is played, is likely to cause serious distress to the inhabitants of the locality; and for this purpose—*
>
> > (a) *such a gathering continues during intermissions in the music and, where the gathering extends over several days, throughout the period during which amplified music is played at night (with or without intermissions); and*
> >
> > (b) *'music' includes sounds wholly or predominantly characterised by the emission of a succession of repetitive beats.*
>
> (1A) *This section also applies to a gathering if—*
>
> > (a) *it is a gathering on land of 20 or more persons who are trespassing on the land; and*
> >
> > (b) *it would be a gathering of a kind mentioned in subsection (1) above if it took place on land in the open air.*
>
> (2) *If, as respects any land, a police officer of at least the rank of superintendent reasonably believes that—*
>
> > (a) *two or more persons are making preparations for the holding there of a gathering to which this section applies,*
> >
> > (b) *ten or more persons are waiting for such a gathering to begin there, or*
> >
> > (c) *ten or more persons are attending such a gathering which is in progress,*
> >
> > *he may give a direction that those persons and any other persons who come to prepare or wait for or to attend the gathering are to leave the land and remove any vehicles or other property which they have with them on the land.*
>
> (3) *A direction under subsection (2) above, if not communicated to the persons referred to in subsection (2) by the police officer giving the direction, may be communicated to them by any constable at the scene.*
>
> (4) *Persons shall be treated as having had a direction under subsection (2) above communicated to them if reasonable steps have been taken to bring it to their attention.*
>
> (5) *A direction under subsection (2) above does not apply to an exempt person.*

The offence under s 63(6) is defined as follows:

> *(6) If a person knowing that a direction has been given which applies to him—*
>
> (a) *fails to leave the land as soon as reasonably practicable, or*
>
> (b) *having left again enters the land within the period of 7 days beginning with the day on which the direction was given,*
>
> *he commits an offence and is liable on summary conviction to imprisonment for a term not exceeding three months or a fine not exceeding level 4 on the standard scale, or both.*

When the Criminal Justice Act 2003, s 280(2) is brought into force, the maximum penalty will be increased to 51 weeks' imprisonment.

The following statutory defence is provided in s 63(7):

> *(7) In proceedings for an offence under subsection (6) above it is a defence for the accused to show that he had a reasonable excuse for failing to leave the land as soon as reasonably practicable or, as the case may be, for again entering the land.*

The offence under s 63(7A) is defined as follows:

> *(7A) A person commits an offence if—*
>
> (a) *he knows that a direction under subsection (2) above has been given which applies to him; and*
>
> (b) *he makes preparations for or attends a gathering to which this section applies within the period of 24 hours starting when the direction was given.*
>
> *(7B) A person guilty of an offence under subsection (7A) above is liable on summary conviction to imprisonment for a term not exceeding 3 months or a fine not exceeding level 4 on the standard scale, or both.*

When the Criminal Justice Act 2003, s 280(2) is brought into force, the maximum penalty for this offence will be increased to 51 weeks' imprisonment.

Section 63(9) provides that licensed gatherings are not included in the section and an 'exempt person' is defined in s 63(10) as an occupier, any member of his family, his employee or agent and any person whose home is on the land.

Section 65(1)–(3) enables a police officer in uniform to stop a person on his way to a rave within a radius of five miles of the site of the rave and to direct him not to proceed to the rave.

> 65.—(1) *If a constable in uniform reasonably believes that a person is on his way to a gathering to which section 63 applies in relation to which a direction under section 63(2) is in force, he may, subject to subsections (2) and (3) below—*
>
> (a) *stop that person, and*
>
> (b) *direct him not to proceed in the direction of the gathering.*
>
> (2) *The power conferred by subsection (1) above may only be exercised at a place within 5 miles of the boundary of the site of the gathering.*
>
> (3) *No direction may be given under subsection (1) above to an exempt person.*

The offence under s 65(4) is defined as follows:

> *(4) If a person knowing that a direction under subsection (1) above has been given to him fails to comply with that direction, he commits an offence and is liable on summary conviction to a fine not exceeding level 3 on the standard scale.*

Powers of entry, seizure, retention and charges in respect of seized property are provided by ss 64, 66 and 67.

6.16.3   Aggravated trespass

The offence of aggravated trespass is triable summarily only and carries a maximum penalty of three months' imprisonment, or a fine not exceeding level 4, or both (s 68(3)).

When the Criminal Justice Act 2003, s 280(2) is brought into force, the maximum penalty will be increased to 51 weeks' imprisonment.

It is defined in s 68 of the CJPOA 1994 as follows:

> 68.—(1)   *A person commits the offence of aggravated trespass if he trespasses on land and, in relation to any lawful activity which persons are engaging in or are about to engage in on that or adjoining land, does there anything which is intended by him to have the effect—*
>
> >   (a)   *of intimidating those persons or any of them so as to deter them or any of them from engaging in that activity,*
> >
> >   (b)   *of obstructing that activity, or*
> >
> >   (c)   *of disrupting that activity.*
>
>   (2)   *Activity on any occasion on the part of a person or persons on land is 'lawful' for the purposes of this section if he or they may engage in the activity on the land on that occasion without committing an offence or trespassing on the land.*

Section 69 enables a senior police officer to direct trespassers to leave land where they are present in connection with an offence under s 68.

> 69.—(1)   *If the senior police officer present at the scene reasonably believes—*
>
> >   (a)   *that a person is committing, has committed or intends to commit the offence of aggravated trespass on land; or*
> >
> >   (b)   *that two or more persons are trespassing on land and are present there with the common purpose of intimidating persons so as to deter them from engaging in a lawful activity or of obstructing or disrupting a lawful activity,*
>
>   *he may direct that person or (as the case may be) those persons (or any of them) to leave the land.*
>
>   (2)   *A direction under subsection (1) above, if not communicated to the persons referred to in subsection by the police officer giving the direction, may be communicated to them by any constable at the scene.*

The offence under s 69(3) is defined as follows:

> (3)   *If a person knowing that a direction under subsection (1) above has been given which applies to him—*
>
> >   (a)   *fails to leave the land as soon as practicable, or*
> >
> >   (b)   *having left again enters the land as a trespasser within the period of three months beginning with the day on which the direction was given,*
>
>   *he commits an offence and is liable on summary conviction to imprisonment for a term not exceeding three months or a fine not exceeding level 4 on the standard scale, or both.*

When the Criminal Justice Act 2003, s 280(2) is brought into force, the maximum penalty will be increased to 51 weeks' imprisonment.

The following statutory defence is provided in s 69(4):

> (4)   *In proceedings for an offence under subsection (3) it is a defence for the accused to show—*
>
> >   (a)   *that he was not trespassing on the land, or*
> >
> >   (b)   *that he had a reasonable excuse for failing to leave the land as soon as practicable or, as the case may be, for again entering the land as a trespasser.*

6.16.4 Contravening prohibition of trespassory assembly

Section 14A of the Public Order Act 1986 enables a local authority to make an order prohibiting the holding of trespassory assemblies within a specified district for a period of up to three months.

> 14A.—(1) *If at any time the chief officer of police reasonably believes that an assembly is intended to be held in any district at a place on land to which the public has no right of access or only a limited right of access and that the assembly—*
>
> (a) *is likely to be held without the permission of the occupier of the land or to conduct itself in such a way as to exceed the limits of any permission of his or the limits of the public's right of access, and*
>
> (b) *may result—*
>
> (i) *in serious disruption to the life of the community, or*
>
> (ii) *where the land, or a building or monument on it, is of historical, architectural, archaeological or scientific importance, in significant damage to the land, building or monument,*
>
> *he may apply to the council of the district for an order prohibiting for a specified, period the holding of all trespassory assemblies in the district or a part of it, as specified.*
>
> (2) *On receiving such an application, a council may—*
>
> (a) *in England and Wales, with the consent of the Secretary of State make an order either in the terms of the application or with such modifications as may be approved by the Secretary of State.*

In the City of London and the metropolitan police district, such order can only be made by the Commissioner of Police for the City of London or the Commissioner of Police of the Metropolis, respectively (s 14A(4)). The consent of the Secretary of State is again required.

Section 14B of the Public Order Act 1986 creates three offences which are defined as follows:

> (1) *A person who organises an assembly the holding of which he knows is prohibited by an order under section 14A is guilty of an offence.*
>
> (2) *A person who takes part in an assembly which he knows is prohibited by an order under section 14A is guilty of an offence.*
>
> (3) *In England and Wales, a person who incites another to commit an offence under subsection (2) is guilty of an offence.*

The penalty for each of the offences under s 14B(1) and (3) is imprisonment for a term not exceeding three months or a fine not exceeding level 4 on the standard scale, or both. When the Criminal Justice Act 2003, s 280(2) is brought into force, the maximum penalty for these offences will be increased to 51 weeks' imprisonment. The penalty for the offence under s 14B(2) is a fine not exceeding level 3 on the standard scale.

In *DPP v Jones* [1999] 2 WLR 625, the defendants had taken part in a peaceful, non-obstructive assembly on the highway adjacent to the monument at Stonehenge in respect of which there was in force an order under s 14A. The House of Lords held that the public had a right to use the highway for such reasonable and usual activities, including peaceful assembly, as were consistent with the primary right to use it for passage and repassage, and that a peaceful assembly for a reasonable period that did not unreasonably obstruct the highway was not necessarily unlawful, nor did it necessarily constitute a trespassory assembly. Each case had to be decided in the light of its particular facts, and the right of public assembly could, in certain circumstances, be exercised on the highway, provided that it caused no obstruction to persons passing along the highway and that the tribunal of fact made a finding that it had been a reasonable user.

Section 14C of the Public Order Act 1986 enables a police officer in uniform to stop persons on their way to trespassory assemblies and to direct them not to proceed in that direction.

> *14C.—(1) If a constable in uniform reasonably believes that a person is on his way to an assembly within the area to which an order under section 14A applies which the constable reasonably believes is likely to be an assembly which is prohibited by that order, he may, subject to subsection (2) below—*
>
> *(a) stop that person, and*
>
> *(b) direct him not to proceed in the direction of the assembly.*
>
> *(2) The power conferred by subsection (1) may only be exercised within the area to which the order applies.*

The offence under s 14C is triable summarily only and is punishable with a fine not exceeding level 3 (s 14C(5)).

The offence is defined as follows:

> *(3) A person who fails to comply with a direction under subsection (1) which he knows has been given to him is guilty of an offence.*

6.16.5 Removal of unauthorised campers

Section 77 of the CJPOA 1994 enables a local authority to give a direction for removal of unauthorised campers from land.

> *77.—(1) If it appears to a local authority that persons are for the time being residing in a vehicle or vehicles within that authority's area—*
>
> *(a) on any land forming part of a highway;*
>
> *(b) on any other unoccupied land; or*
>
> *(c) on any occupied land without the consent of the occupier,*
>
> *the authority may give a direction that those persons and any others with them are to leave the land and remove the vehicle or vehicles and any other property they have with them on the land.*
>
> *(2) Notice of a direction under subsection (1) must be served on the persons to whom the direction applies, but it shall be sufficient for this purpose for the direction to specify the land and (except where the direction applies to only one person) to be addressed to all occupants of the vehicles on the land, without naming them.*

The offence under s 77(3) is defined as follows:

> *(3) If a person knowing that a direction under subsection (1) above has been given which applies to him—*
>
> *(a) fails, as soon as practicable, to leave the land or remove from the land any vehicle or other property which is the subject of the direction, or*
>
> *(b) having removed any such vehicle or property again enters the land with a vehicle within the period of three months beginning with the day on which the direction was given,*
>
> *he commits an offence and is liable on summary conviction to a fine not exceeding level 3 on the standard scale.*

Guidance relating to the making of removal directions and to service of notices of directions was provided by the Divisional Court in *Wealden DC, ex p Wales* The Times, 22 September 1995.

Section 78(1)–(3) enables a local authority to apply to a magistrates' court for an order requiring the removal of vehicles or property from the land where a direction has been breached.

78.—(1) *A magistrates' court may, on a complaint made by a local authority, if satisfied that persons and vehicles in which they are residing are present on land within that authority's area in contravention of a direction given under section 77, make an order requiring the removal of any vehicle or other property which is so present on the land and any person residing in it.*

(2) *An order under this section may authorise the local authority to take such steps as are reasonably necessary to ensure that the order is complied with and, in particular, may authorise the authority, by its officers and servants—*

(a) *to enter upon the land specified in the order; and*

(b) *to take, in relation to any vehicle or property to be removed in pursuance of the order, such steps for securing entry and rendering it suitable for removal as may be so specified.*

(3) *The local authority shall not enter upon any occupied land unless they have given to the owner and occupier at least 24 hours' notice of their intention to do so, or unless after reasonable inquiries they are unable to ascertain their names and addresses.*

The offence under s 78(4) is defined as follows:

(4) *A person who wilfully obstructs any person in the exercise of any power conferred on him by an order under this section commits an offence and is liable on summary conviction to a fine not exceeding level 3 on the standard scale.*

Section 78(5) provides that it is not necessary for the names of the occupants of vehicles on the land in question to be named in any summonses sent to them.

6.16.6   Trespassing on a designated site

The offence under s 128 of the Serious Organised Crime and Police Act 2005 is triable summarily. Section 128 defines the offence as follows:

(1) *A person commits an offence if he enters, or is on, any protected site in England and Wales or Northern Ireland as a trespasser.*

(1A) *In this section 'protected site' means—*

(a) *a nuclear site; or*

(b) *a designated site.*

(1B) *In this section 'nuclear site' means—*

(a) *so much of any premises in respect of which a nuclear site licence (within the meaning of the Nuclear Installations Act 1965) is for the time being in force as lies within the outer perimeter of the protection provided for those premises; and*

(b) *so much of any other premises of which premises falling within paragraph (a) form a part as lies within that outer perimeter.*

(1C) *For this purpose—*

(a) *the outer perimeter of the protection provided for any premises is the line of the outermost fences, walls or other obstacles provided or relied on for protecting those premises from intruders; and*

(b) *that line shall be determined on the assumption that every gate, door or other barrier across a way through a fence, wall or other obstacle is closed.*

(2) *A 'designated site' means a site—*

(a) *specified or described (in any way) in an order made by the Secretary of State, and*

(b) *designated for the purposes of this section by the order.*

    (3) The Secretary of State may only designate a site for the purposes of this section if—

        (a) it is comprised in Crown land; or

        (b) it is comprised in land belonging to Her Majesty in Her private capacity or to the immediate heir to the Throne in his private capacity; or

        (c) it appears to the Secretary of State that it is appropriate to designate the site in the interests of national security.

A statutory defence is provided in s 128(4):

    (4) It is a defence for a person charged with an offence under this section to prove that he did not know, and had no reasonable cause to suspect, that the site in relation to which the offence is alleged to have been committed was a protected site.

The penalty for an offence under s 128 is imprisonment for a term not exceeding 51 weeks, or a fine not exceeding level 5 on the standard scale, or both.

    Proceedings may not be brought for an offence under s 128 without the consent of the Attorney-General (s128(6)).

6.17 Further reading

Card, R., *Public Order Law* (Bristol: Jordans, 2000).

Offensive weapons

7.1 Introduction

This chapter deals with some of the more common offences relating to weapons that a junior practitioner is likely to come across in early practice. It does not deal with firearms legislation, which is extensive, and for which reference should be made to textbooks or practitioner works.

7.2 Prevention of Crime Act 1953

Section 1 provides:

> *(1) Any person who without lawful authority or reasonable excuse, the proof whereof shall lie on him, has with him in any public place any offensive weapon shall be guilty of an offence.*

This is an offence that is triable either way, and is punishable on indictment with a term of four years' imprisonment or a fine or both, or on summary conviction with six months' imprisonment or a fine not exceeding the prescribed sum or both. Section 1(2) permits the court on conviction of an offence under s 1 to make an order for the forfeiture or disposal of any weapon in respect of which the offence was committed.

It should be noted that, generally, offences relating to weapons are used to deal with those people who *carry* weapons with them: those who actually *use* a weapon to inflict, say, an assault, are usually charged with the relevant substantive assault charge. A person who, on the spur of the moment, uses a lawfully carried article to attack another is unlikely to have committed an offence under s 1 (although that person is likely to be liable for some form of assault). On this point, see, eg *Jura* [1954] 1 QB 503; *Ohlson v Hylton* [1975] 1 WLR 724; *Bates v Bulman* [1979] 1 WLR 1190; and *Veasey* [1999] Crim LR 158.

7.2.1 'Has with him'

It must be proved that the defendant had the article with him knowingly, although forgetting that the article is in one's possession is not an excuse (*McCalla* (1988) 87 Cr App R 372). However, on the question of whether forgetfulness can amount to reasonable excuse (see **7.2.4**), see *Glidewell* (1999) 163 JP 557.

7.2.2 'Public place'

Public place is defined as including any highway and any other premises or place to which at the material time the public have or are permitted to have access, whether on payment or otherwise (s 1(4)).

7.2.3 'Offensive weapon'

Section 1(4) defines an offensive weapon as:

. . . any article made or adapted for use for causing injury to the person, or intended by the person having it with him for such use by him or by some other person.

The Court of Appeal in *Simpson* (1983) 78 Cr App R 115 explained this as meaning that there were three categories of offensive weapon: articles made for causing injury to the person (often known as weapons offensive *per se*); articles adapted for that purpose; and articles not so made or adapted, but which were carried with an intention to use to cause injury to the person.

The distinction between the first two categories and the third one is important, for in the third category the prosecution is required to prove the accused had the requisite intent to cause injury. In the first two categories, such additional intent is not needed.

Where intent must be proved, it must be shown that the accused had the requisite intent at the time and place specified in the charge. Evidence which shows only that he had the intent at an earlier stage will not be sufficient (see *Allamby* [1974] 1 WLR 1494).

The question of whether an article is offensive *per se* is usually a question of fact for the jury to decide; however, in some cases the judge can take judicial notice that an article is offensive *per se* and direct the jury accordingly. For examples of both types of situation, see *Gibson v Wales* [1983] 1 WLR 393 and *Simpson* (1983) 78 Cr App R 115 (flick knives); *DPP v Hynde* [1998] 1 WLR 1222 (butterfly knives, on similar legislation); *Houghton v Chief Constable of Greater Manchester* (1986) 84 Cr App R 319 (a police truncheon); *Copus v DPP* [1989] Crim LR 577 (a rice flail); *Butler* [1988] Crim LR 696 (a sword stick); and *R* [2008] 1 Cr App R 26 (sand gloves).

Articles adapted for causing injury would include articles such as a deliberately broken bottle. Articles that are not made or adapted for use for causing injury to the person (eg, a baseball bat or sandbag) can still class as offensive weapons if the prosecution can show that the article was carried with the intention of using it to cause injury.

7.2.4 'Lawful authority or reasonable excuse'

If a person has with him an offensive weapon in a public place with lawful authority or reasonable excuse, no offence is committed. The burden of proving lawful authority or reasonable excuse lies with the defendant: it is not for the prosecution to disprove it as part of its case (see **7.3.1**). As with other legal burdens of proof cast on the defence, the standard of proof is on a balance of probabilities. The compatibility of the imposition of the legal burden on the defendant has yet to be considered by the appellate courts. However, it is submitted that it is justified and does not infringe Article 6 of the ECHR.

What constitutes lawful authority or reasonable excuse will depend on the circumstances of each case. Some people are permitted by the nature of their employment to carry offensive weapons at times, a common example being a police officer carrying a truncheon. A more common claim made by a defendant is that of reasonable excuse: carrying a police truncheon as part of a police uniform worn at a fancy dress party may amount to reasonable excuse (*Houghton v Chief Constable of Greater Manchester* (1986) 84 Cr App R 319). A defendant who carried a machete and a catapult in order to kill squirrels to feed wild birds which he kept under licence was held to have reasonable excuse (*Southwell v Chadwick* (1986) 85 Cr App R 235). On whether lack of knowledge that an object is an offensive weapon amounts to a reasonable excuse, see *Densu* [1998] 1 Cr App R 400.

Often the defendant says that he carried the article in self-defence, and claims this to amount to reasonable excuse. A number of cases have considered this point, and the answer is ultimately one of degree. A person who habitually carries a weapon with him on his person or in his vehicle on the off chance that he may be attacked is unlikely to satisfy the test. However, carrying an offensive weapon following an assault which might be repeated may amount to reasonable excuse. See *Evans v Hughes* (1972) 56 Cr App R 813; *Peacock* [1973] Crim LR 639; *Malnik v DPP* [1989] Crim LR 451; and *Archbold* (2007) 171 JP 664.

Mere forgetfulness that one has an article in one's possession cannot of itself provide a reasonable excuse for possession of an offensive weapon but forgetfulness may be relevant as part of a wider set of circumstances relied on as providing a reasonable excuse, depending on the circumstances of the particular case (see *McCalla* (1988) 87 Cr App R 372; *Glidewell* (1999) 163 JP 557; *DPP v Patterson* [2004] EWHC 2744 (Admin); and *Tsap* (2009) 173 JP 4).

7.3 Criminal Justice Act 1988

7.3.1 Section 139

Section 139 of the 1988 Act states:

> (1) *Subject to subsections (4) and (5) below, any person who has an article to which this section applies with him in a public place shall be guilty of an offence.*
>
> (2) *Subject to subsection (3) below, this section applies to any article which has a blade or is sharply pointed except a folding pocketknife.*
>
> (3) *This section applies to a folding pocketknife if the cutting edge of its blade exceeds 3 inches.*

This section creates an offence which is triable either way, and is punishable on indictment with a term of imprisonment of up to four years and/or a fine, and on summary conviction by a term of six months' imprisonment and/or a fine not exceeding the prescribed amount.

Certain articles that are carried may not fall within the ambit of the Prevention of Crime Act 1953, s 1, but may come within the scope of the Criminal Justice Act 1988, s 139, eg a sheath knife for which there is no evidence of the specific intent necessary to make it an offensive weapon.

A folding pocket knife which locks in position when opened does not come within the term 'folding pocketknife' used by the section (*Harris v DPP* (1992) 96 Cr App R 235, followed in *Deegan* [1998] 2 Cr App R 121).

A screwdriver has been held not to be a bladed article within the meaning of s 139 (*Davis* [1998] Crim LR 564).

'Public place' includes any place to which at the material time the public have or are permitted access, whether on payment or otherwise (s 139(7)).

Section 139(4) makes it a defence for the defendant to prove that he had good reason or lawful authority for having the article with him in a public place. This is a legal burden that lies on the defendant. The statutory imposition on the defendant of a legal burden of proof has been the subject of challenge in a number of cases, on the basis that the burden concerned is incompatible with Article 6 of the ECHR. Such challenges have sometimes been successful (see, eg *Lambert* [2002] 2 AC 545 (Misuse of Drugs Act 1971) and *Sheldrake v DPP* [2003] 2 All ER 497 (Road Traffic Act 1988)). However, claims that the legal burden imposed under the Criminal Justice Act, s 139 is incompatible have failed (see *L v DPP* [2003] QB 137 and *Mathews*[2004] QB 690). A failure to leave to the jury the issue of whether self-defence amounted to good reason has resulted in the conviction being quashed (see *Emmanuel* [1998] Crim LR 347).

Section 139(5) additionally provides that, without prejudice to the generality of subsection (4), it shall be a defence for the accused to prove that he had the article for use at work; for religious reasons; or as part of any national costume. For an example of an attempt to rely on the 'use at work' defence, see *Manning* [1998] Crim LR 198.

7.3.2 Section 139A

Section 139A provides an additional triable either way offence of having an article within the meaning of s 139 or an offensive weapon within the meaning of the Prevention of Crime Act 1953, s 1 on school premises. This is subject to the defence of good reason or lawful authority, and to the use at work/religious reasons/national dress defence, as well as an additional one of having the article on the premises for educational purposes. Punishment depends on whether the article comes within s 139, in which case punishment is the same as s 139 itself, or whether it comes within the Prevention of Crime Act 1953, s 1, in which case punishment is the same as s 1.

Section 139B provides search and seizure powers for the police to enter school premises and search people thereon for an article within the meaning of s 139 or an offensive weapon within the meaning of the Prevention of Crime Act 1953. Under s 550AA of the Education Act 1996 and s 85B of the Further and Higher Education Act 1992, members of staff are given the power to search pupils and further education students for weapons.

7.4 Using another to mind a dangerous weapon

The offence of using someone to mind a weapon is indictable only. It is defined in s 28 of the Violent Crime Reduction Act 2006 as follows:

(1) *A person is guilty of an offence if—*

    (a)   *he uses another to look after, hide or transport a dangerous weapon for him; and*

    (b)   *he does so under arrangements or in circumstances that facilitate, or are intended to facilitate, the weapon's being available to him for an unlawful purpose.*

(2) *For the purposes of this section the cases in which a dangerous weapon is to be regarded as available to a person for an unlawful purpose include any case where—*

    (a)   *the weapon is available for him to take possession of it at a time and place; and*

    (b)   *his possession of the weapon at that time and place would constitute, or be likely to involve or to lead to, the commission by him of an offence.*

(3) In this section 'dangerous weapon' means—

(a)   *a firearm other than an air weapon or a component part of, or accessory to, an air weapon; or*

(b)   *a weapon to which section 141 or 141A of the Criminal Justice Act 1988 (c. 33) applies (specified offensive weapons, knives and bladed weapons).*

Sections 141 and sec141A of the Criminal Justice Act (CJA) 1988 create offences in relation to the sale of specified offensive weapons, knives and bladed weapons. Section 141 of the 1988 Act applies to offensive weapons specified by the Secretary of State (for a list of the prohibited weapons see Criminal Justice Act 1988 (Offensive Weapons) Order 2002 (SI 2002/3998)). Section sec141A of the Act applies to any knife, knife blade, razor blade, axe and any other article which has a blade or which is sharply pointed and which is made or adapted for use for causing injury to the person.

Where the dangerous weapon in respect of which the offence was committed is a weapon to which ss 141 or 141A of the CJA 1988 applies, the penalty is imprisonment for a term not exceeding four years or to a fine, or both (s 29(2) of the Violent Crime Reduction Act 2006).

7.5   Other offences

In addition to the commonly used offences under the Prevention of Crime Act 1953 and the Criminal Justice Act 1988, there are a number of other pieces of legislation that seek to restrict the carrying, manufacture, sale, hire, purchase and use of weapons. These include the Restriction of Offensive Weapons Act 1959, ss 141 and 141A of the Criminal Justice Act 1988, the Crossbows Act 1987 and the Knives Act 1997. Reference to practitioner works such as *Archbold* or *Blackstone's Criminal Practice* should be made for details of these offences.

Road traffic offences: general

8.1 Introduction

This chapter deals with the offences of dangerous driving, careless (or inconsiderate) driving, failing to stop after an accident and failing to report an accident. The various offences related to drinking and driving are dealt with in **Chapter 10**. Between them, these offences constitute a representative sample of the road traffic offences likely to confront counsel in early practice. Road traffic offences which involve causing death are not covered in this manual.

The standard reference work for practitioners is Wilkinson, *Road Traffic Offences* (London: Sweet & Maxwell). Section C of *Blackstone's Criminal Practice* is devoted to driving offences.

There is one point which is of general application to road traffic offences, but has particular relevance to dangerous and careless driving. The Highway Code is often used by the courts as a guide to what constitutes safe or careful driving. The position in law is that a failure to observe a provision of the Code does not of itself constitute an offence. Any such failure may, however, be relied upon by any party to civil or criminal proceedings as tending to prove or disprove liability in those proceedings (Road Traffic Act 1988, s 38(7)). In practice, it is common for advocates, and the court, to place reliance upon the Code's provisions in evaluating the evidence in the case.

8.2 Dangerous driving

The offence of dangerous driving is defined in s 2A of the Road Traffic Act (RTA) 1988. It reads as follows:

> 2A.—(1) For the purposes of sections 1 and 2 above a person is to be regarded as driving dangerously if (and, subject to subsection (2) below, only if)—
>
> > (a)   the way he drives falls far below what would be expected of a competent and careful driver, and
> >
> > (b)   it would be obvious to a competent and careful driver that driving in that way would be dangerous.
>
> (2)   A person is also to be regarded as driving dangerously for the purposes of sections 1 and 2 above if it would be obvious to a competent and careful driver that driving the vehicle in its current state would be dangerous.
>
> (3)   In subsections (1) and (2) above 'dangerous' refers to danger either of injury to any person or of serious damage to property; and in determining for the purposes of those subsections what would be expected of, or obvious to, a competent and careful driver in a particular case, regard shall

be had not only to the circumstances of which he could be expected to be aware but also to any
circumstances shown to have been within the knowledge of the accused.

(4) *In determining for the purposes of subsection (2) above the state of a vehicle, regard may be had*
to anything attached to or carried on or in it and to the manner in which it is attached or carried.

The offence of dangerous driving was not in fact an entirely new one. It was on the statute books until 1977, when it was replaced by 'reckless driving'. The offence of reckless driving, which was not statutorily defined, gave rise to voluminous case law as the courts attempted to grapple with the concept of recklessness. In its revived form, the offence of dangerous driving is arguably somewhat more widely drawn than the concept of reckless driving, and is subject to a statutory definition.

The core of that definition is contained in s 2A(1), and it poses two questions in relation to the allegedly dangerous driving:

(a) Did the driving fall far below the standard which would be expected of a competent and careful driver? Clearly, the word upon which the defence will frequently focus in argument is 'far', and its presence in the definition appears to be one of the features which distinguishes this offence from that of careless driving (see **8.3**).

(b) Would it be obvious to that hypothetical competent and careful driver that driving in such a way would be dangerous? The key words in this formulation would seem to be 'obvious' and 'dangerous'. As far as 'dangerous' is concerned, some assistance is provided by the opening words to s 2A(3), which tie the concept to danger of injury to the person or serious damage to property. In view of the fact that the word 'danger' is unqualified, it would seem that danger to any person, even though slight, would suffice, provided that it is not *de minimis*.

The prosecution must prove both elements (a) and (b) above before s 2A(1) is satisfied (*Aitken* v *Lees* (1994) SLT 182).

As can be seen from the wording of s 2A(3), in interpreting s 2A(1) and (2), regard must be had:

• to circumstances of which a competent and careful driver could be expected to be aware; and

• to circumstances which are shown to be within the (actual) knowledge of the accused.

8.2.1 Evidence of dangerous driving

What, then, constitutes evidence of dangerousness to measure against the statutory definition? Obviously, it depends upon the particular facts of the case, and precedents are of little, if any, assistance. Some guidance is available in the Crown Prosecution Service's *Guidance on Prosecuting Cases of Bad Driving*, a summary of which can be found at http://www.cps.gov.uk/legal/p_to_r/road_traffic_offences_guidance_on_prosecuting_cases_of_bad_driving/. It must be stressed, however, that this document provides guidance for police and prosecutors, and is not authoritative as far as the courts are concerned. The *Guidance* gives the following as examples of what is likely to be characterised as dangerous driving:

• racing or competitive driving;

• speed which is particularly inappropriate for the prevailing road or traffic conditions;

- aggressive driving, such as sudden lane changes, cutting into a line of vehicles or driving much too close to the vehicle in front;

- disregard of traffic lights and other road signs, which, on an objective analysis, would appear to be deliberate;

- disregard of warnings from fellow passengers;

- overtaking which could not have been carried out safely;

- driving when knowingly suffering from a medical or physical condition that significantly and dangerously impairs the offender's driving skills, such as having an arm or leg in plaster, or impaired eyesight. It can include the failure to take prescribed medication;

- driving when knowingly deprived of adequate sleep or rest;

- driving a vehicle knowing it has a dangerous defect or is poorly maintained or is dangerously loaded;

- using a hand-held mobile phone or other hand-held electronic equipment whether as a phone or to compose or read text messages when the driver was avoidably and dangerously distracted by that use;

- driving whilst avoidably and dangerously distracted such as whilst reading a newspaper/map, talking to and looking at a passenger, selecting and lighting a cigarette or by adjusting the controls of electronic equipment such as a radio, hands-free mobile phone or satellite navigation equipment;

- failing to have a proper and safe regard for vulnerable road users such as cyclists, motorcyclists, horse riders, the elderly and pedestrians or in the vicinity of a pedestrian crossing, hospital, school or residential home; and

- a brief but obvious danger arising from a seriously dangerous manoeuvre. This covers situations where a driver has made a mistake or an error of judgement that was so substantial that it caused the driving to be dangerous even for only a short time.

8.2.2 Notice of intended prosecution

Dangerous driving, like careless driving, is one of the offences to which s 1 of the Road Traffic Offenders Act (RTOA) 1988 applies. This states:

1.—(1) Subject to section 2 of this Act, a person shall not be convicted of an offence to which this section applies unless—

    (a) he was warned at the time the offence was committed that the question of prosecuting him for some one or other of the offences to which this section applies would be taken into consideration, or

    (b) within 14 days of the commission of the offence a summons . . . or the offence was served on him, or

    (c) within 14 days of the commission of the offence a notice of the intended prosecution specifying the nature of the alleged offence and the time and place where it is alleged to have been committed, was—

        (i) in the case of an offence under section 28 or 29 of the Road Traffic Act 1988 (cycling offences), served on him,

        (ii) in the case of any other offence, served on him or on the person, if any, registered as the keeper of the vehicle at the time of the commission of the offence.

  (1A) A notice required by this section to be served on that person may be served on that person

    (a) by delivering it to him;

    (b) by addressing it to him and leaving it at his last known address;

(c) by sending it by registered post, recorded delivery service or first class post addressed to him at his last known address.

(2) A notice shall be deemed for the purposes of subsection (1)(c) above to have been served on a person if it was sent by registered post or recorded delivery service addressed to him at his last known address, notwithstanding that the notice was returned undelivered or was for any other reason not received by him.

(3) The requirement of subsection (1) above shall in every case be deemed to have been complied with unless and until the contrary is proved.

(4) Schedule 1 to this Act shows the offences to which this section applies.

The offences in respect of which there is an obligation under s 1 include a number of the most common road traffic offences, eg dangerous driving (contrary to the RTA 1988, s 2), careless driving (s 3), leaving a vehicle in a dangerous position (s 22), dangerous cycling (s 28), careless cycling (s 29), failing to comply with traffic directions (s 35) or signs (s 36).

The warning must have been understood by the defendant. In *Gibson v Dalton* [1980] RTR 410, Donaldson LJ (as he then was) put it like this (at 413–14):

The obligation on the prosecutor is to warn the accused, not merely to address a warning to him or to give a warning. The mischief to which this section is directed is clear. It is that motorists are entitled to have it brought to their attention at a relatively early stage there is likely to be a prosecution in order that they may recall and, it may be, record the facts as they occurred at the time…But a warning which does not get through to the accused person is of no value at all.

If, viewing the matter objectively, one would expect that the words addressed to the accused person would have been heard and understood by him, then prima facie he was warned within the meaning of the statute. But it is only a prima facie case. It is open to the defendant to prove, if he can, that he did not understand or hear or appreciate the warning and therefore that he was not warned.

Section 2 of the RTOA 1988, however, lays down certain circumstances in which no notice of intended prosecution is required:

2.—(1) The requirement of section 1(1) of this Act does not apply in relation to an offence if, at the time of the offence or immediately after it, an accident occurs owing to the presence on a road of the vehicle in respect of which the offence was committed.

(2) …

(3) Failure to comply with the requirement of section 1(1) of this Act is not a bar to the conviction of the accused in a case where the court is satisfied—

(a) that neither the name and address of the accused nor the name and address of the registered keeper, if any, could with reasonable diligence have been ascertained in time for a summons, or, as the case may be, a complaint to be served or for a notice to be served or sent in compliance with the requirement, or

(b) that the accused by his own conduct contributed to the failure.

(4) Failure to comply with the requirement of section 1(1) of this Act in relation to an offence is not a bar to the conviction of a person of that offence by virtue of the provision of—

(a) section 24 of this Act, or

(b) any of the enactments mentioned in section 24(6);

but a person is not to be convicted of an offence by virtue of any of those provisions if section 1 applies to the offence with which he was charged and the requirement of section 1(1) was not satisfied in relation to the offence charged.

As can be seen, there is no requirement to warn of an intended prosecution in the case of an accident. As to the meaning of 'accident', see *Currie* [2007] 2 Cr App R 246. If the accident was so trivial that the defendant was unaware of it, however, a notice will still be necessary (*Bentley v Dickinson* [1983] RTR 356).

The rationale was set out by Bingham LJ in *DPP v Pidhajeckvj* [1991] RTR 136:

> The point of a notice is to alert the driver to the risk of prosecution so that he can promptly investigate the facts and prepare his defence. Ordinarily there is no need for such a notice where there has been an accident, because the driver is alerted to the situation and the possibility of proceedings. But there is a need where the driver is unaware of any accident, because then he has nothing to alert him to the possibility of proceedings.

The point which arose in *Pidhajeckvj* was whether a notice was required where the accident was so serious that its effects resulted in amnesia (contrast *Bentley* where it was so trivial that the defendant could not remember it). The Divisional Court in *Pidhajeckvj* held that this situation was distinguishable from that in *Bentley*. Where the defendant could not remember the details after an accident, but it was apparent that one had occurred, the exemption still applied and no notice of intended prosecution was required. As Bingham LJ put it:

> Parliament cannot have intended oral warnings to be given to the unconscious survivors of serious motor accidents, not the giving of written notices to survivors so badly injured as to be unable to read them or understand their effect.

In *Currie* [2007] 2 Cr App R 18, the Court of Appeal held that whether or not there has been an accident is a matter for the judge and not the jury.

In *Myers* [2007] 2 Cr App R 19, it was held that s 2 does not require the offence with which the defendant is charged to have been the cause of the accident because the section attributes the accident to the presence of a vehicle on the road, not to the fact that its driver committed a road traffic offence. However, the court added that the policy of the section requires there to be a sufficient causal link between the offence and the accident for the driver not to need to be warned of the risk of prosecution.

Note that there is a presumption in favour of compliance (see the RTOA 1988, s 1(3)). In other words, the prosecution do not have to prove a warning as part of their case. Hence, if the defence challenge the prosecution on this basis, they bear the burden of proof on a balance of probabilities. This can be a difficult onus to discharge, since it requires evidence from both the driver and the keeper of the vehicle in order to establish that neither of them was served in accordance with the RTOA, s 1(1)(c)(i). The prosecution may of course make an admission that one or other was not served. Once the defence establishes that there was no service, the prosecution can prove that a notice was sent to the last known address by recorded or registered delivery. However, in a case where the prosecution argue that such notice was not necessary because there had been an accident, it is for the prosecution to prove beyond reasonable doubt that an accident had occurred (*Currie* [2007] 2 Cr App R 18).

8.2.3   Alternative verdict

Section 24 of the RTOA 1988 lays down a series of alternative verdicts which can be brought in road traffic cases. The relevant part reads as follows:

> **24.**—*(A1) Where–*
>
> (a)   *a person charged with manslaughter in connection with the driving of a mechanically propelled vehicle by him is found not guilty of that offence, but*
>
> (b)   *the allegations in the indictment amount to or include an allegation of any of the relevant offences,*
>
> *he may be convicted of that offence.*

(A2) For the purposes of subsection (A1) above the following are the relevant offences–

(a)   an offence under section 1 of the Road Traffic Act 1988 (causing death by dangerous driving),

(b)   an offence under section 2 of that Act (dangerous driving),

(c)   an offence under section 3A of that Act (causing death by careless driving when under influence of drink or drugs), and

(d)   an offence under section 35 of the Offences against the Person Act 1861 (furious driving).

(1) Where—

(a)   a person charged with an offence under a provision of the Road Traffic Act 1988 specified in the first column of the Table below (where the general nature of the offences is also indicated) is found not guilty of that offence, but

(b)   the allegations in the indictment or information (or in Scotland complaint) amount to or include an allegation of an offence under one or more of the provisions specified in the corresponding entry in the second column,

he may be convicted of that offence or of one or more of those offences.

Offence charged	Alternative
Section 1 (causing death by dangerous driving)	Section 2 (dangerous driving)
	Section 2B (causing death by careless, or inconsiderate, driving)
	Section 3 (careless, and inconsiderate, driving)
Section 2 (dangerous driving)	Section 3 (careless, and inconsiderate, driving)
Section 2B (causing death by careless, or inconsiderate, driving)	Section 3 (careless, and inconsiderate, driving)
Section 3A (causing death by careless driving when under influence of drink or drugs)	Section 2B (causing death by careless, or inconsiderate, driving)
	Section 3 (careless, and inconsiderate, driving)
	Section 4(1) (driving when unfit to drive through drink or drugs)
	Section 5(1)(a) (driving with excess alcohol in breath, blood or urine)
	Section 7(6) (failing to provide specimen)
	Section 7A(6) (failing to give permission for laboratory test)
Section 4(1) (driving or attempting to drive when unfit to drive through drink or drugs)	Section 4(2) (being in charge of a vehicle when unfit to drive through drink or drugs)
Section 5(1)(a) (driving or attempting to drive with excess alcohol in breath, blood or urine)	Section 5(1)(b) (being in charge of a vehicle with excess alcohol in breath, blood or urine)
Section 28 (dangerous cycling)	Section 29 (careless, and inconsiderate, cycling)

(2) Where the offence with which a person is charged is an offence under section 3A of the Road Traffic Act 1988, subsection (1) above shall not authorise his conviction of any offence of attempting to drive.

(3) Where a person is charged with having committed an offence under section 4(1) or 5(1)(a) of the Road Traffic Act 1988 by driving a vehicle, he may be convicted of having committed an offence under the provision in question by attempting to drive.

(4) Where by virtue of this section a person is convicted before the Crown Court of an offence triable only summarily, the court shall have the same powers and duties as a magistrates' court would have had on convicting him of that offence.

. . .

(6) This section has effect without prejudice to section 6(3) of the Criminal Law Act 1967 (alternative verdicts on trial on indictment) . . . and section 23 of this Act.

As will be apparent, the offence of careless, and inconsiderate, driving is an alternative which the magistrates can find where they decide not to convict the accused of dangerous driving.

8.2.4 Punishment

Dangerous driving is punishable:

- on indictment, with two years' imprisonment, or an unlimited fine or both;
- after summary trial, six months' imprisonment or a fine not exceeding level 5 on the standard scale or both.

There is a minimum disqualification period of 12 months, unless special reasons (see **10.4**) can be established by the defence. Where the driver is disqualified, retesting by way of an extended driving test is mandatory. Endorsement is obligatory in the absence of special reasons (3 to 11 points unless the defendant is disqualified, in which case there is endorsement but without penalty points).

8.2.5 Sentencing guidelines

The Court of Appeal has not issued a definitive guideline judgment in relation to dangerous driving. The following cases are illustrative: *Moore* (1995) 16 Cr App R (S) 536; *Templeton* [1996] 1 Cr App R (S) 380; *Joseph* [2002] 1 Cr App R (S) 74.

The Sentencing Guidelines Council (SGC), in its *Magistrates' Court Sentencing Guidelines*, provides useful guidance on the approach that should be taken in a magistrates' court when sentencing for offences of dangerous driving. Regard may also usefully be had to the SGC's *Guideline on Causing Death by Dangerous Driving* which identifies the following five categories of aggravating factors which, it is submitted, apply equally to offences of dangerous driving:

Awareness of risk

(a) a prolonged, persistent and deliberate course of very bad driving.

Effect of alcohol or drugs

(b) consumption of alcohol above the legal limit;

(c) consumption of alcohol at or below the legal limit where this impaired the offender's ability to drive;

(d) failure to supply a specimen for analysis;

(e) consumption of illegal drugs where this impaired the offender's ability to drive;

(f) consumption of legal drugs or medication where this impaired the offender's ability to drive (including legal medication known to cause drowsiness) where the driver knew, or should have known, about the likelihood of impairment.

Inappropriate speed of vehicle

(g) greatly excessive speed; racing; competitive driving against another vehicle;

(h) driving above the speed limit;

(i) driving at a speed that is inappropriate for the prevailing road or weather conditions;

(j) driving a PSV, HGV or other goods vehicle at a speed that is inappropriate either because of the nature of the vehicle or its load, especially when carrying passengers.

Seriously culpable behaviour of offender

(k) aggressive driving (such as driving much too close to the vehicle in front, persistent inappropriate attempts to overtake, or cutting in after overtaking);

(l) driving while using a hand-held mobile phone;

(m) driving whilst the driver's attention is avoidably distracted, for example by reading or adjusting the controls of electronic equipment such as a radio, hands-free mobile phone or satellite navigation equipment;

(n) driving when knowingly suffering from a medical or physical condition that significantly impairs the offender's driving skills, including failure to take prescribed medication;

(o) driving when knowingly deprived of adequate sleep or rest, especially where commercial concerns had a bearing on the commission of the offence;

(p) driving a poorly maintained or dangerously loaded vehicle, especially where commercial concerns had a bearing on the commission of the offence.

Victim

(q) failing to have proper regard to vulnerable road users.

In *Howells* [2003] 1 Cr App R (S) 61, the Court of Appeal held that for 'road rage' cases of dangerous driving, where no accident nor injury results, and where there is no consumption of alcohol, but where there is ample evidence to suggest furious driving in temper with an intent of causing fear and possible injury, the appropriate sentencing bracket lies between 6 and 12 months.

8.3 Careless driving

Section 3 of the RTA 1988 states:

3. If a person drives a mechanically propelled vehicle on a road or other public place without due care and attention, or without reasonable consideration for other persons using the road or place, he is guilty of an offence.

As will be seen from the statute, the offence is not defined, but it may take one of two forms:

(a) driving without due care and attention. The test is whether the defendant has failed to exercise 'the degree of care and attention which a reasonable prudent driver would exercise' (*Simpson v Peat* [1952] 2 QB 447);

(b) driving without reasonable consideration. The test is whether other road users were inconvenienced by the defendant's inconsiderate driving.

Section 3ZA of the RTA 1988 creates a statutory definition of careless or inconsiderate driving. It provides as follows:

3ZA.—(1)   This section has effect for the purposes of sections 2B and 3 above and section 3A below.

(2)   A person is to be regarded as driving without due care and attention if (and only if) the way he drives falls below what would be expected of a competent and careful driver.

(3)   In determining for the purposes of subsection (2) above what would be expected of a careful and competent driver in a particular case, regard shall be had not only to the circumstances of which he could be expected to be aware but also to any circumstances shown to have been within the knowledge of the accused.

(4)   A person is to be regarded as driving without reasonable consideration for other persons only if those persons are inconvenienced by his driving.

Section 3ZA applies to all offences involving a careless driving element, including causing death by careless, or inconsiderate, driving, and causing death by careless driving when under influence of drink or drugs (s 3ZA(1)). The definition of driving without due care and attention in s 3ZA(2) essentially formalises the interpretation of careless driving already developed under the significant body of road traffic case law, which no doubt will continue to be relied upon to determine what is expected of a competent and careful driver and whether a defendant fell below this standard. Section 3ZA(3) is drafted in very similar terms to s 2A(3) in relation to dangerous driving (see **8.2**).

The Crown Prosecution Service's *Guidance on Prosecuting Cases of Bad Driving* (see **8.2.1** for comment on its status) gives the following as examples of driving that are likely to be regarded as careless driving:

- overtaking on the inside;
- driving inappropriately close to another vehicle;
- inadvertently driving through a red light;
- emerging from a side road into the path of another vehicle;
- tuning a car radio;
- using a hand-held mobile phone or other hand-held electronic equipment when the driver was avoidably distracted by that use; and
- selecting and lighting a cigarette or similar when the driver was avoidably distracted by that use.

It is submitted that the public interest will tend to be against a prosecution for careless driving where:

- the incident is of a type such as frequently occurs at parking places, roundabouts, junctions or in traffic queues, involving minimal carelessness such as momentary inattention or a minor error of judgment; and/or
- only the person at fault suffered injury and damage, if any, which was mainly restricted to the vehicle or property owned by that person.

As far as the second limb of the offence, inconsiderate driving, is concerned, the accused must be shown to have fallen below the standard of a reasonable, prudent and competent driver *and* to have done so without reasonable consideration for others. It follows that a person who drives without reasonable consideration for other road users can be convicted of driving without due care and attention, but the reverse does not necessarily apply. The Crown Prosecution Service *Guidance* suggests that this offence is appropriate when the driving amounts to a clear act of incompetence, selfishness, impatience or aggressiveness. There must, however, also be some inconvenience to other road users, for example, forcing other drivers to move over and/or brake as a consequence (see s 3ZA(4)). The *Guidance* gives the following examples of what is likely to be regarded as inconsiderate driving:

- flashing of lights to force other drivers in front to give way;
- misuse of any lane to avoid queuing or gain some other advantage over other drivers;
- unnecessarily remaining in an overtaking lane;
- unnecessarily slow driving or braking without good cause;
- driving with undipped headlights which dazzle oncoming drivers;
- driving through a puddle causing pedestrians to be splashed;
- driving a bus in such a way as to alarm passengers.

The usual basis on which the prosecution puts its case under s 3, however, is an allegation of careless driving. In determining whether the defendant fell short of the necessary standard, the court must not judge him or her with hindsight. An illustration is provided by *Bristol Crown Court, ex p Jones* [1986] RTR 259. The defendant's lights suddenly failed when he was driving at night. He pulled on to the motorway's hard shoulder and collided with an unlit parked vehicle of which he was unaware. It was held that his behaviour was reasonable, and the offence was not proved.

Where the defendant is unable to explain an accident, the facts of the case may lead to an irresistible inference that it resulted from careless driving. Thus, in *Rabjohns v Burgar* [1971] RTR 234, the defendant's car collided with the wall of a bridge, leaving skid marks on the road. The weather was fine and the road dry. There was no evidence of the involvement of any other vehicle, and no witnesses. The defendant did not give evidence or put forward any explanation. The Divisional Court held that the only conclusion possible on this evidence was that the defendant had driven carelessly.

Where the defendant does put forward an exculpatory explanation, however, it is incumbent on the prosecution to disprove it, provided that it is not fanciful. For example, in *Butty v Davey* [1972] RTR 75, rain had made the road unexpectedly slippery. The defendant's car slid to the wrong side of the road and hit another vehicle. The magistrates found that this did not constitute driving without due care and attention, and their decision was upheld. Similarly, in *Lodwick v Jones* [1983] RTR 273, the defendant put forward the existence of an unexpected icy patch as an explanation for skidding. Again, this was accepted by the justices and it was held that they were entitled to do so.

8.3.1 Procedural matters

By s 24 of the RTOA 1988, a verdict of careless driving is an alternative where dangerous driving is charged (see **8.2.3**). Careless driving is one of those specified offences for which a notice of intended prosecution is usually necessary (see **8.2.2**). But note that by s 2(4) of the RTOA 1988, a failure to warn a suspect of an intended prosecution does not act as a bar to conviction of one of the alternative offences specified in s 24, ie provided that notice has been given in relation to the original offence, the defendant can be convicted of one of the alternatives.

8.3.2 Punishment

Careless driving is a summary offence, punishable by a fine not exceeding level 5 on the standard scale, with discretionary disqualification. Endorsement is obligatory (3 to 9 points), except where there are special reasons.

8.4 Failing to stop/failing to report

This offence is created by s 170 of the RTA 1988:

170. —(1) *This section applies in a case where, owing to the presence of a mechanically propelled vehicle on a road or other public place, an accident occurs by which—*

(a) *personal injury is caused to a person other than the driver of that mechanically propelled vehicle, or*

(b) *damage is caused—*

(i) *to a vehicle other than that mechanically propelled vehicle or a trailer drawn by that mechanically propelled vehicle, or*

(ii) *to an animal other than an animal in or on that mechanically propelled vehicle or a trailer drawn by that mechanically propelled vehicle, or*

(iii) *to any other property constructed on, fixed to, growing in or otherwise forming part of the land on which the road in question is situated or land adjacent to such land.*

(2) *The driver of the mechanically propelled vehicle must stop and, if required to do so by any person having reasonable grounds for so requiring, give his name and address and also the name and address of the owner and the identification marks of the vehicle.*

(3) *If for any reason the driver of the mechanically propelled vehicle does not give his name and address under subsection (2) above, he must report the accident.*

(4) *A person who fails to comply with subsection (2) or (3) above is guilty of an offence.*

(5) *If, in a case where this section applies by virtue of subsection (1)(a) above, the driver of a motor vehicle does not at the time of the accident produce such a certificate of insurance or security, or other evidence, as is mentioned in section 165(2)(a) of this Act—*

(a) *to a constable, or*

(b) *to some person who, having reasonable grounds for so doing has required him to produce it, the driver must report the accident and produce such a certificate or other evidence.*

This subsection does not apply to the driver of an invalid carriage.

(6) *To comply with a duty under this section to report an accident or to produce such a certificate of insurance or security, or other evidence, as is mentioned in section 165(2)(a) of this Act, the driver—*

(a) *must do so at a police station or to a constable, and*

(b) *must do so as soon as is reasonably practicable and, in any case, within twenty-four hours of the occurrence of the accident.*

(7) *A person who fails to comply with a duty under subsection (5) above is guilty of an offence, but he shall not be convicted by reason only of a failure to produce a certificate or other evidence if, within seven days after the occurrence of the accident, the certificate or other evidence is produced at a police station that was specified by him at the time when the accident was reported.*

(8) *In this section 'animal' means horse, cattle, ass, mule, sheep, pig, goat or dog.*

By s 170(2), then, the driver of a vehicle involved in an accident which falls within the definition laid down in s 170(1), must stop and, if reasonably required to do so, give appropriate details. If the driver does not give his or her name and address, then he or she must report the accident to the police as soon as possible and, in any event, within 24 hours of the accident (s 170(3)).

A contravention of s170 is a summary offence, punishable by up to six months' imprisonment or a fine not exceeding level 5 on the standard scale or both. It carries discretionary disqualification, and obligatory endorsement (5 to 10 points), subject to special reasons (see **10.4**).

9

Drink driving offences

9.1 Introduction

Alcohol is a major cause of road accidents. One in five drivers killed in road accidents have levels of alcohol which are over the legal limit. The seriousness with which the problem of drink driving is viewed is reflected not only by the range of offences created in the Road Traffic Acts (driving with excess alcohol, failure to provide a specimen for analysis etc) but also by the very severe penalties imposed for those offences (see **Chapter 10**).

9.2 Prescribed limits

Under the drink driving provisions, drink means an alcoholic drink and drugs can refer to medicines as well as prohibited drugs and substances which affect the control of the body (eg *Bradford v Wilson* [1993] Crim LR 482, toluene inhaled when glue sniffing). The prescribed limits are 35 microgrammes (μg) of alcohol in 100 ml of breath, or 80 mg of alcohol in 100 ml of blood or 107 mg of alcohol in 100 ml of urine. This level can be achieved by a man drinking about $3^1/_2$ to 5 units within an hour and a woman drinking about $2^1/_2$ to 4 units within an hour. (A unit of alcohol is approximately equal to a half-pint of ordinary beer, lager or cider, or a single measure of spirits (whisky, vodka, gin, bacardi, etc) or a glass of wine or small glass of sherry.) There is no sure way of telling how much an individual can drink before reaching this limit. It varies with each person, depending on weight, age, sex, whether the person has just eaten and the sort of drinks which have been consumed. These factors may also affect the rate of absorption of alcohol into the blood. Most of the alcohol drunk is rapidly absorbed into the bloodstream. Nearly all the alcohol has to be burnt up by the liver, the rest is disposed of either in sweat or urine. Only time can remove the alcohol from the bloodstream. In an average-sized man, it may be broken down at the rate of about one unit per hour.

9.3 Specimen tests

9.3.1 Preliminary tests

There is no restriction on random stopping of motorists but a request for a preliminary test can be made only if one or more of the conditions in s 6(2) to (5) are satisfied (*Chief*

Constable of Gwent v Dash [1986] RTR 41), ie that the officer suspects that a person has been driving with alcohol or a drug in his body or whilst under the influence of a drug, has committed a traffic offence or has been involved in an accident. Section 6E enables a constable to enter any place to carry out a preliminary test where an accident has occurred. Where the person is suspected of having alcohol above the prescribed limit in his body the officer will administer a roadside breath test, which is a preliminary test involving the driver inflating a small bag by blowing into it (see RTA 1988, s 6A). The bag has to be inflated by a single breath and there should be no smoking immediately before or during the test as this may affect the result. In addition, 20 minutes ought to have elapsed between the last drink of alcohol and the use of the device. This also relates to other aromatic drinks and mouth sprays. In *DPP v Kay* [1999] RTR 109, the Divisional Court held that the failure of officers to ask questions such as when the defendant had last drank or smoked did not invalidate the roadside breath test or the subsequent arrest. The Home Office has warned that the operation of breath test devices may be affected by police radio equipment operating within inches of the devices. Where the suspect may have drugs in his body or may be unfit to drive through drink or drugs the officer may administer a preliminary drug test (see RTA 1988, s 6C) or a preliminary impairment test (see RTA 1988, s 6B). If the suspect fails a preliminary test he may be arrested and an evidential specimen may be taken. The evidential specimen, which will usually be taken at the police station but may also be taken at a hospital, will form the basis of any subsequent prosecution.

9.3.2   Failure to co-operate with a preliminary test

Under the RTA 1988, s 6(6), failure without reasonable excuse to co-operate with a preliminary test when required to do so by a police constable is an offence. Before the court can convict of the s 6(6) offence, there must be some evidence that the statutory conditions in s 6(2) to (5) are met (see **9.3.1** above). The constable's suspicions may arise after the defendant has been stopped. Although the absence of a reasonable cause may invalidate an arrest, it will not invalidate the subsequent procedure (*DPP v Godwin* [1991] RTR 303). The court may always, of course, exercise its discretion to exclude the evidence under PACE 1984, s 78.

The offence under s 6(6) is triable summarily and is punishable by a fine not exceeding level 3 on the standard scale, a discretionary disqualification and obligatory endorsement with 4 penalty points. See the Sentencing Guidelines Council's *Magistrates' Courts Sentencing Guidelines* for guidance as to how the court should approach the size of the fine to be imposed.

9.3.3   Evidential specimens

There are three types of specimen which may be adduced as evidence against a defendant: breath, blood and urine. The provision of these evidential specimens is governed by RTA 1988, s 7. The most common specimen is one of breath and must be taken on an approved device. Section 7 requires that two samples be taken. The lower of the two readings is the one that the prosecution will rely on in determining whether a prosecution can be founded. The machine provides a printout, a copy of which is given to the driver, and this printout then forms part of the admissible evidence against the defendant.

Where the lower reading is not more than $50\mu g$ of alcohol in 100 ml of breath, the person providing the sample may request that it should be replaced by a blood or urine sample (s 8(2)). Although the accused can express a preference for a particular sample, the choice will be made by the officer (see *DPP v Warren* [1993] RTR 58 and RTA 1988, s 7(4)).

Where the machine is broken or unavailable or the suspected offence may be due to a drug rather than alcohol, or there are medical reasons for not requiring a sample of breath, the police constable will offer the driver the chance to provide a blood specimen or a urine sample. The choice of whether to provide a blood or urine sample is again that of the police officer and not the driver (RTA 1988, s 7(4)).

The only right of the defendant to object to giving blood and to give urine instead will be for medical reasons to be determined by the medical practitioner or registered health care professional (s7(4A)). In *Epping Justices, ex p Quy* [1998] RTR 158, the Divisional Court held that a fear of needles was capable of being a medical reason. In that case, the officer should have asked further questions and/or called a medical practitioner. A specimen of blood must be taken with the accused's consent and by a medical practitioner (RTA 1988, s 11(4)).

In all cases, the officer must warn the accused that failure to provide the specimen of breath, blood or urine is an offence that may render the accused liable to prosecution and also carries the penalty of disqualification (s 7(7)). Failure to give the warning renders the results of the test inadmissible (*Murray v DPP* [1993] Crim LR 968).

The breath test machines operate a self-check system to indicate that they are operating accurately but challenges to the reliability of devices are sometimes made. In *DPP v Spurrier* [2000] RTR 60, the Divisional Court held that it was not always necessary for magistrates to hear expert evidence to rebut the presumption of reliability of a Lion Intoximeter (the predecessor of the Lion Intoxilyser) when the defendant's evidence of consumption was contradicted by the device. The defendant had not driven erratically, was not unsteady on her feet and her eyes were not glazed but she produced a reading of 143 mg (four times over the limit). She claimed to have consumed two cans of lager and a significant proportion of a bottle of whisky, 12 hours previously. Accepting her evidence, the justices concluded that the Lion Intoximeter could not have been reliable and that there was no need to call evidence on that point.

9.3.4 Failure to provide an evidential specimen

What constitutes failure is a question of fact. Failure includes a refusal and also includes a conditional agreement (eg, only allowing blood to be taken from an inappropriate part of the body, *Solesbury v Pugh* [1969] 2 All ER 1171). A refusal may be implied from conduct. In *Smyth v DPP* [1996] RTR 59, the defendant said 'no' when asked to provide a specimen, but within five seconds said that he wanted to change his mind. He was convicted by the magistrates. The Queen's Bench Division, allowing his appeal and concluding he had not refused to provide a specimen, said that the tribunal should have had regard to all the defendant's words and conduct.

It is a defence for the defendant to have a reasonable excuse for not providing a specimen. The issue of reasonable excuse has to be raised by the defendant; the burden is on the prosecution to disprove it beyond reasonable doubt. In *Lennard* [1973] 1 WLR 483, it was stated per Lawton LJ that no excuse could be reasonable unless the person from whom the specimen was required is physically or mentally unable to provide a specimen or the provision of the specimen would entail a substantial risk to health. A common reason that is advanced is a fear of needles. In *Harding* [1974] RTR 325, the court noted that no fear short of a phobia recognised by medical science to be as strong and inhibiting as, for instance, claustrophobia, can be allowed to excuse failure to provide a specimen for a laboratory test, and in most, if not all, cases where the fear of providing it is claimed to be invincible the claim will have to be supported by medical evidence.

An inability to understand what is being said owing to a limited grasp of English may be a reasonable excuse (*Chief Constable of Avon and Somerset v Singh* [1988] RTR 107). In *Harling* [1970] RTR 441, a reasonable excuse was said to exist where the defendant lost confidence in the doctor's ability after the doctor had made three unsuccessful attempts to take blood.

Cases in which the defence of reasonable excuse have failed are *Sykes v White* [1983] RTR 419 (dislike of blood not amounting to a phobia); *DPP v Fountain* [1988] Crim LR 123 (fear of contracting AIDS through the use of needles, but compare *DeFreitas v DPP* [1993] RTR 98, a genuine but unreasonable phobia of contracting AIDS was found to be a reasonable excuse); *Woolman v Lenton* [1985] Crim LR 516 (difficulty in blowing through the nose); *Daniels v DPP* [1992] RTR 140 (a belief that no offence had been committed); *DPP v Coyle* The Times, 20 July 1995 (motorist not told of necessity to provide required specimen within a total of three minutes, see also *Cosgrove v DPP* The Times, 29 March 1996); *Thomas v DPP* [1991] RTR 292 (a previous unlawful arrest was not relevant to the subsequent procedures and could not amount to a reasonable excuse, see also *Matto v Wolverhampton Crown Court* [1987] RTR 337).

In *DPP v Varley* [1999] Crim LR 753, the defendant asked for legal advice before he would agree to the breath test procedure. The sergeant said that he was not prepared to wait for the duty solicitor. The magistrates concluded that the defendant had a reasonable excuse and acquitted him. The Divisional Court held that those facts were not capable of amounting to a reasonable excuse; generally, a reasonable excuse existed when a defendant was mentally or physically unable to provide a specimen.

Where the specimen is required to ascertain ability to drive, or the proportion of alcohol at the time the accused was driving, or attempting to drive, the offence is punishable with six months' imprisonment or a fine not exceeding level 5 on the standard scale, or both, and obligatory disqualification and endorsement. Endorsement carries 3 to 11 penalty points. In all other cases, it is three months' imprisonment, discretionary disqualification or 10 penalty points. See the Sentencing Guidelines Council's *Magistrates' Courts Sentencing Guidelines* which indicate that where there is evidence of serious impairment and deliberate refusal or failure to provide a specimen then the appropriate starting point is a 12-week custodial sentence. Where the defendant was only 'in charge' of a vehicle, a custodial sentence will be unlikely other than in the most serious cases.

9.3.5 Protection for hospital patients

If the accused is in hospital as a patient, there can be no requirement to provide a specimen unless the medical practitioner in charge of the case has been notified and the specimen is provided at the hospital. If the medical practitioner decides that the provision of a specimen or the warning required under s 7(7) would be prejudicial to the proper care and treatment of the patient, then the requirement must not be made (s 9).

9.3.6   Failure to give permission for analysis of a specimen

Section 7A of the 1988 Act authorises a constable to request a medical practitioner to take a specimen of blood from a person who has been involved in an accident and is incapable of giving valid consent (ie, the person is unconscious). However, while a person is at a hospital as a patient, no specimen of blood shall be taken from him under s 7A if the medical practitioner in immediate charge of his case objects under s 9 (see **9.3.5** above). Any specimen taken shall not be subjected to a laboratory test, unless the person from whom it was taken has given his permission (s 7A(4)). While a person is at a hospital as a patient, he shall not be required to give his permission for a laboratory test of a specimen if the medical practitioner in immediate charge of his case objects under s 9. It is an offence for a person, without reasonable excuse, to fail to give permission (s 7A(6)).

Where the test would be for ascertaining ability to drive, or the proportion of alcohol at the time the offender was driving, or attempting to drive, the offence is punishable with six months' imprisonment or a fine not exceeding level 5 on the standard scale, or both, and obligatory disqualification. Endorsement carries 3 to 11 points. In all other cases, it is three months' imprisonment or a fine not exceeding level 4 on the standard scale, or both, discretionary disqualification or 10 penalty points.

9.4   Driving, attempting to drive or being in charge of a vehicle when unfit

Under the RTA 1988, s 4, it is an offence to drive, to attempt to drive, or to be in charge of a mechanically propelled vehicle on a road or other public place when under the influence of drink or drugs. The relevant parts read as follows:

4.—(1)   A person who, when driving or attempting to drive a mechanically propelled vehicle on a road or other public place, is unfit to drive through drink or drugs is guilty of an offence.

(2)   Without prejudice to subsection (1) above, a person who, when in charge of a mechanically propelled vehicle which is on a road or other public place, is unfit to drive through drink or drugs is guilty of an offence.

(3)   For the purposes of subsection (2) above, a person shall be deemed not to have been in charge of a mechanically propelled vehicle if he proves that at the material time the circumstances were such that there was no likelihood of his driving it so long as he remained unfit to drive through drink or drugs.

(4)   The court may, in determining whether there was such a likelihood as is mentioned in subsection (3) above, disregard any injury to him and any damage to the vehicle.

(5)   For the purposes of this section, a person shall be taken to be unfit to drive if his ability to drive properly is for the time being impaired.

The essence of driving is the use of the driver's controls to direct the movement of the vehicle (*McDonagh* [1974] QB 48). However, in *Planton v DPP* [2002] RTR 9, the defendant was in the driver's seat of his vehicle, with the engine running and the vehicle lights on. He failed a breath test and was convicted. He appealed on the ground that the vehicle was stationary and therefore he was not 'driving'. The court found that he was driving, much the same as if he had been waiting for traffic lights to change. Being in charge is a wide concept, see *DPP v Watkins* [1989] QB 821. The owner or a person who has recently driven the vehicle would be in charge, unless he or she has put the vehicle in someone else's charge or unless there was no realistic possibility of resuming control of the vehicle. It is a question of fact and degree if someone is in charge, see *DPP v Watkins* [1989] QB 821.

'Road' is defined in s 192 as 'any highway and any other road to which the public has access'. The other public place need not be a road but must be a place to which the public has access, eg a car park.

Evidence of unfitness may be provided by specimen sample of blood/breath/urine. Opinion evidence may also be received of the defendant's state (eg, eyes glazed, speech slurred, unsteady on feet, etc) but not of whether or not the defendant was fit to drive (*Davies* [1962] 3 All ER 97). In *Leethams v DPP* (1999) RTR 29, officers gave evidence that the defendant's eyes were red, his speech slurred and slow. He admitted smoking a cannabis cigarette some hours earlier. The blood sample showed no alcohol but cannabis consumption some time before the sample. (The effect of cannabis begins immediately after use, rises to a maximum after 20 minutes and disperses after two to four hours.) The Divisional Court held that despite lack of evidence from a doctor, the officers had proved the case by the evidence of the appellant's driving, his appearance, behaviour and admission.

The offence under s 4(1) is punishable with six months' imprisonment or a fine not exceeding level 5 on the standard scale or both, and obligatory endorsement and disqualification. Where penalty points are endorsed, the range is 3 to 11 points. The offence under s 4(2) is punishable with three months' imprisonment or a fine not exceeding level 4 on the standard scale or both, and discretionary disqualification. Endorsement is obligatory and carries 10 penalty points. See the Sentencing Guidelines Council's *Magistrates' Courts Sentencing Guidelines* which indicate that for cases involving a high level of impairment and one or more aggravating factors, the starting point is a 12-week custodial sentence. The aggravating factors are poor road or weather conditions, carrying passengers, driving for hire or reward, large goods vehicle and nature of driving. Only the most serious cases of being 'in charge' whilst unfit should attract a custodial penalty.

9.5 Driving or being in charge above the prescribed limit

The offence of driving, attempting to drive or being in charge when over the prescribed limit is dealt with in s 5:

5.—(1) If a person—

    (a) drives or attempts to drive a motor vehicle on a road or other public place, or

    (b) is in charge of a motor vehicle on a road or other public place, after consuming so much alcohol that the proportion of it in his breath, blood or urine exceeds the prescribed limit he is guilty of an offence.

  (2) It is a defence for a person charged with an offence under subsection (1)(b) above to prove that at the time he is alleged to have committed the offence the circumstances were such that there was no likelihood of his driving the vehicle whilst the proportion of alcohol in his breath, blood or urine remained likely to exceed the prescribed limit.

  (3) The court may, in determining whether there was such a likelihood as is mentioned in subsection (2) above, disregard any injury to him and any damage to the vehicle.

In *DPP v H* [1998] RTR 200, it was affirmed that driving with excess alcohol was an offence of strict liability, so that *mens rea* was not an issue and the defence of insanity was not available.

The prosecution are entitled to do a back-calculation to show that at the time of driving, attempting to drive or being in charge, the alcohol in the driver's breath was in excess of the prescribed amount. In *Gumbley v Cunningham* [1988] QB 170, the appellant was involved in a fatal accident before midnight. He gave a specimen of blood with a reading of 59 Bg at 3.35 am the following morning. The prosecution adduced evidence of a calculation showing that a person with the appellant's age and physical characteristics would eliminate blood alcohol at the rate of 10 to 25μg per hour and therefore his blood alcohol level at the time of the accident would have been between 120 and 130μg of alcohol per 100 ml of blood. This means that where a specimen contains less than the legal limit, but it can be shown by back-calculation that the driver had excess alcohol at the time of the offence then a conviction will follow. Mann J said, 'those who drive whilst above the prescribed limits cannot necessarily escape punishment because of the lapse of time'. He further stressed that:

> ...the prosecution should not seek to rely on evidence of back-calculation save where that evidence is easily understood and clearly persuasive of the presence of excess alcohol at the time when a defendant was driving. Moreover, justices must be very careful especially where there is conflicting evidence not to convict unless, upon the scientific and other evidence which they find it safe to rely on, they are sure an excess of alcohol was in the defendant's body when he was actually driving as charged.

9.5.1   The hip-flask defence

Where the defendant wishes to claim that a post-driving drink took him over the limit (the hip-flask defence), the burden of proof lies on him to show that on a balance of probabilities. The court is entitled to assume that the alcohol level at the time of driving was not less than that at the time of the test (RTOA 1988, s 15(2)). This statutory assumption will not be made if the defendant proves that he consumed alcohol after he stopped driving, attempting to drive or being in charge and before he provided a specimen, and that had he not done so the proportion of alcohol in his breath/blood/urine would not have exceeded the prescribed limit. See *DPP v Williams* [1989] Crim LR 382.

9.5.2   No likelihood of driving

Under s 5(2), it is a defence to an offence of being 'in charge' for a person to prove that there was no likelihood of him driving whilst the proportion of alcohol in his blood/breath or urine remained likely to exceed the prescribed limit. A similar defence is afforded under s 4(3), where the allegation relates to being unfit through drink or drugs.

The s 5(2) defence potentially conflicted with the presumption of innocence guaranteed by Article 6 of the ECHR, insofar as it placed the legal burden on the defendant. However, in *Sheldrake v DPP* [2005] 1 AC 264, the House of Lords held that the imposition of the legal burden on a defendant under s 5(2) did not infringe Article 6 as the imposition of a legal burden upon the defendant did not go beyond what was necessary and reasonable, and was not in any way arbitrary. Thus, under s 5(2), it is for the defendant to show, on the balance of probabilities, that there was no likelihood of him driving the vehicle of which he was in charge.

9.5.3 Laced drinks

It is not a defence to the charge but the fact that drinks may have been laced may be put forward as a special reason for not disqualifying or endorsing. The defendant would have to show that he or she had been misled by a third party and would be expected to have made some enquiry about what he or she was drinking. The person lacing the drinks may be convicted of procuring a person to commit an offence under the RTA 1988, s 5. See *Attorney-General's Reference (No 1 of 1975)* [1975] QB 773.

9.5.4 Sentencing

The offence under s 5(1)(a) is punishable with six months' imprisonment or a fine not exceeding level 5 on the standard scale, or both, and obligatory disqualification and endorsement. Where penalty points are endorsed, the range is 3 to 11 points. The offence under s 5(1)(b) is punishable with three months' imprisonment or a fine not exceeding level 4 on the standard scale, or both, and discretionary disqualification. Endorsement carries 10 penalty points.

The Sentencing Guidelines Council's *Magistrates' Courts Sentencing Guidelines* state that those driving with more than $120\mu g$ in 100 ml of breath (ie, over three times the limit) should be considered for a custodial sentence. Aggravating features identified by the Sentencing Guidelines Council include: poor road or weather conditions, carrying passengers, driving for hire or reward, large goods vehicle and nature of driving. The Guidelines indicate that only in the most serious cases should offences of being 'in charge' result in a custodial sentence.

9.6 Cycling when under the influence of drink or drugs

Section 30 of the RTA 1988 states:

A person who, when riding a cycle on a road or other public place, is unfit through drink or drugs (that is to say, is under the influence of drink or a drug to such an extent as to be incapable of having proper control of the cycle) is guilty of an offence.

The offence covers riding a bicycle, tricycle or other cycle having four or more wheels, but not being a motor vehicle, on a road. The offence is committed on public highways as well as footways. The police cannot require the cyclist to provide a specimen of breath, blood or urine but if one is provided it may be used in a prosecution.

The offence is summary only and punishable by a fine not exceeding level 3 on the standard scale.

9.7 Procedure and sentence

Most motoring offences are summary only offences and are brought to court by way of charge and requisition, but in most drink driving cases the motorist will have been charged at the police station and bailed to appear at the magistrates' court. As the drink driving offences carry punishment of disqualification, which cannot be ordered in the defendant's absence, the offences cannot be dealt with by way of postal written pleas of guilty.

Public funding is rarely given in road traffic cases, but the criteria set out in Access to Justice Act 1999, Sch 3, para 5(2), for considering the grant of a representation order may be satisfied in some drink driving cases.

Road traffic offences: penalties

10.1 Introduction

The distinctive penalties for road traffic offences are endorsement and disqualification from driving. It is common for the court to impose a fine for a driving offence, although in appropriate cases, a custodial or community sentence might be imposed. This chapter concentrates on endorsement and disqualification.

10.2 Endorsement

An endorsement involves entering details of the conviction on the offender's driving licence. If the endorsement is obligatory, then the court must cause it to be carried out. It is 'part of the penalty'. The matters to be endorsed include the convicting court, the dates of offence, conviction and sentence, the particulars of offence and the sentence imposed.

Under the Road Traffic Offenders Act (RTOA) 1988, s 97A, 'driving record' is a record held by the Secretary of State designed for endorsements. Under RTOA 1988, s 44(3A), the details of a conviction for an offence committed by persons who are not holders of a British driving licence are endorsed on the driving record. Section 10 of the Road Safety Act 2006, which is not yet in force, will amend the RTOA 1988 with the effect that endorsements for all drivers will be made on a defendant's 'driving record' rather than his driving licence.

10.2.1 Expiry of the endorsement

An endorsement remains on the defendant's licence until he or she can apply for a clean one, surrendering the one which has been endorsed and paying an administrative fee. Application for a clean licence can be made:

- after 11 years from the date of conviction for an excess alcohol offence;
- after 4 years from the date of conviction where the defendant was disqualified, or the offence is one of dangerous driving;
- after 4 years from the date of the offence in other cases.

10.2.2 Production of licence

The defendant is under an obligation to produce a driving licence when convicted of an offence involving endorsement. It is an offence to fail to do so. If the defendant is unable to produce a licence, then the court will lack vital information in determining sentence. It may therefore decide to adjourn for the licence to be produced, or a printout of the defendant's driving record to be produced from the DVLA, so as to establish any previous endorsements. When it does come to sentence the offender, the court may take into account any endorsements, including old ones which are no longer effective for 'totting up' purposes (see **10.3.1.2**).

10.2.3 Penalty points

The framework for the imposition of penalty points is set out in the RTOA 1988, s 28:

28.—(1) (1) *Where a person is convicted of an offence involving obligatory endorsement, then, subject to the following provisions of this section, the number of penalty points to be attributed to the offence is—*

    (a) *the number shown in relation to the offence in the last column of Part I or Part II of schedule 2 to this Act, or*

    (b) *where a range of numbers is shown, a number within that range.*

  (2) *Where a person is convicted of an offence committed by aiding, abetting, counselling or procuring, or inciting to the commission of, an offence involving obligatory disqualification, then, subject to the following provisions of this section, the number of penalty points to be attributed to the offence is 10.*

  (3) *For the purposes of [sections 57(5), 57A(6), 77(5) and 77A(8)]3 of this Act, the number of penalty points to be attributed to an offence is—*

    (a) *where both a range of numbers and a number followed by the words "(fixed penalty)" is shown in the last column of Part 1 of Schedule 2 to this Act in relation to the offence, that number,*

    (b) *where a range of numbers followed by the words "or appropriate penalty points (fixed penalty)" is shown there in relation to the offence, the appropriate number of penalty points for the offence, and*

    (c) *where only a range of numbers is shown there in relation to the offence, the lowest number in the range.*

  (3A) *For the purposes of subsection (3)(b) above the appropriate number of penalty points for an offence is such number of penalty points as the Secretary of State may by order made by statutory instrument prescribe.*

  (3B) *An order made under subsection (3A) above in relation to an offence may make provision for the appropriate number of penalty points for the offence to be different depending on the circumstances, including (in particular)—*

    (a) *the nature of the contravention or failure constituting the offence,*

    (b) *how serious it is,*

    (c) *the area, or sort of place, where it takes place, and*

    (d) *whether the offender appears to have committed any offence or offences of a description specified in the order during a period so specified.*

(4) *Where a person is convicted (whether on the same occasion or not) of two or more offences committed on the same occasion and involving obligatory endorsement, the total number of penalty points to be attributed to them is the number or highest number that would be attributed on a conviction of one of them (so that if the convictions are on different occasions the number of penalty points to be attributed to the offences on the later occasion or occasions shall be restricted accordingly).*

(5) *In a case where (apart from this subsection) subsection (4) above would apply to two or more offences, the court may if it thinks fit determine that that subsection shall not apply to the offences (or, where three or more offences are concerned, to any one or more of them).*

(6) *Where a court makes such a determination it shall state its reasons in open court and, if it is a magistrates' court ... shall cause them to be entered in the register ... of its proceedings.*

The penalty points applicable to those offences which carry them are set out in the RTOA 1988, Sch 2, extracts from which are set out below.

For most offences carrying penalty points, the number of points is fixed, eg 3 points for failing to comply with a traffic sign (by jumping a red light, for instance). Other offences have a range, from which the sentencer can select the most appropriate, eg 3 to 6 points for speeding.

What if the defendant is convicted of two or more offences on the same occasion, and both carry penalty points? Say, for example, that the defendant is convicted of careless driving (for which a range of 3 to 9 points is laid down) and driving without insurance (6 to 8 points). Assume further that the episode of careless driving took place while the defendant was uninsured. The situation used to be that the court had to decide which of the offences committed on the same occasion was the more serious, and fix the appropriate number of points for that offence. It could not then impose any extra points for the other offence(s) (*Johnson v Finbow* [1983] 1 WLR 879).

The position is now governed by the RTOA 1988, s 28(5). The court can now, if it thinks fit, impose penalty points for more than one offence committed on the same occasion. In the example given above, that would mean that the court could, for example, impose 9 points for the careless driving, and an additional 6 points for the driving without insurance, thus triggering off a penalty points disqualification (see **10.3.1.2**). The normal practice, however, is still to impose penalty points only for the most serious offence. If the court wishes to exercise its powers under s 28(5), it must state its reasons in open court and they must be put on the register.

When the Road Safety Act 2006, s 34 is brought into force, it will insert new ss 30A, 30B, 30C and 30D into the RTOA 1988. These new provisions will enable courts to offer persons convicted of the offences of careless and inconsiderate driving, failing to comply with traffic signs or speeding, the opportunity to undertake a retraining course in certain circumstances where the driver is not to be disqualified but is to have his licence endorsed with penalty points. Where a person successfully completes a course, 3 points (or fewer if the court endorsed fewer) relating to the conviction will cease to be taken into consideration for the purposes of the 'totting-up' provisions (see **10.3.1.2** below).

ROAD TRAFFIC OFFENDERS ACT 1988 SCHEDULE 2 (EXTRACTS)
PROSECUTION AND PUNISHMENT OF OFFENCES
PART I
OFFENCES UNDER THE TRAFFIC ACTS

(1) Provision creating offence	(2) General nature of offence	(3) Mode of prosecution	(4) Punishment	(5) Disqualification	(6) Endorsement	(7) Penalty points
Offences under the Road Traffic Regulation Act 1984						
RTRA section 16(1)	Contravention of temporary prohibition or restriction.	Summarily.	Level 3 on the standard scale.	Discretionary if committed in respect of a speed restriction.	Obligatory if committed in respect of a speed restriction.	3–6 or 3 (fixed penalty).
RTRA section 17(4)	Use of special road contrary to scheme or regulations.	Summarily.	Level 4 on the standard scale.	Discretionary if committed in respect of a motor vehicle otherwise than by unlawfully stopping or allowing the vehicle to remain at rest on a part of a special road on which vehicles are in certain circumstances permitted to remain at rest.	Obligatory if committed as mentioned in the entry in column 5.	3–6 or 3 (fixed penalty if committed in respect of a speed restriction, 3 in any other case.
RTRA section 25(5)	Contravention of pedestrian crossing regulations.	Summarily.	Level 3 on the standard scale.	Discretionary if committed in respect of a motor vehicle.	Obligatory if committed in respect of a motor vehicle.	3
RTRA section 28(3)	Not stopping at school crossing	Summarily.	Level 3 on the standard scale.	Discretionary if committed in respect of a motor vehicle.	Obligatory if committed in respect of a motor vehicle.	3
RTRA section 29(3)	Contravention of order relating to street playground.	Summarily.	Level 3 on the standard scale.	Discretionary if committed in respect of a motor vehicle.	Obligatory if committed in respect of a motor vehicle.	2
RTRA section 89(1)	Exceeding speed limit.	Summarily.	Level 3 on the standard scale.	Discretionary.	Obligatory.	3–6 or 3 (fixed penalty).
Offences under the Road Traffic Act 1988						
RTA section 1	Causing death by dangerous driving.	On indictment.	14 years.	Obligatory.	Obligatory.	3–11
RTA section 2	Dangerous driving.	(a) Summarily.	(a) 6 months or the statutory maximum or both.	Obligatory.	Obligatory.	3–11
		(b) On indictment.	(b) 2 years or a fine or both.			
RTA section 2B	Causing death by careless, or inconsiderate, driving.	(a) Summarily.	(a) 12 months or the statutory maximum or both.	Obligatory.	Obligatory.	3–11
		(b) On indictment.	(b) 5 years or a fine or both.			
RTA section 3	Careless, and inconsiderate, driving.	Summarily.	Level 5 on the standard scale.	Discretionary.	Obligatory.	3–9
RTA section 3A	Causing death by careless driving when under influence of drink or drugs.	On indictment.	14 years or a fine or both.	Obligatory.	Obligatory.	3–11

(1) Provision creating offence	(2) General nature of offence	(3) Mode of prosecution	(4) Punishment	(5) Disqualification	(6) Endorsement	(7) Penalty points
RTA section 3ZB	Causing death by driving: unlicensed, disqualified or uninsured.	(a) Summarily.	(a) 12 months or the statutory maximum or both. (b) 2 years or a fine or both.	Obligatory.	Obligatory.	3–11
RTA section 4(1)	Driving or attempting to drive when unfit to drive through drink or drugs.	Summarily.	6 months or level 5 on the standard scale or both.	Obligatory.	Obligatory.	3–11
RTA section 4(2)	Being in charge of a mechanically propelled vehicle when unfit to drive through drink or drugs.	Summarily.	3 months or level 4 on the standard scale or both.	Discretionary.	Obligatory.	10
RTA section 5(1)(a)	Driving or attempting to drive with excess alcohol in breath, blood or urine.	Summarily.	6 months or level 5 on the standard scale or both.	Obligatory.	Obligatory.	3–11
RTA section 5(1)(b)	Being in charge of a mechanically propelled vehicle with excess alcohol in breath blood or urine.	Summarily.	3 months or level 4 on the standard scale or both.	Discretionary	Obligatory.	10
RTA section 6	Failing to co-operate with a preliminary test.	Summarily.	Level 3 on the standard scale.	Discretionary.	Obligatory.	4
RTA section 7	Failing to provide specimen for analysis or laboratory test.	Summarily.	(a) Where the specimen was required to ascertain ability to drive or proportion of alcohol at the time offender was driving or attempting to drive, 6 months *or* level 5 on the standard scale or both. (b) In any other case, 3 months or level 4 on the standard scale or both.	(a) Obligatory in case mentioned in column 4(a). (b) Discretionary in any other case.	Obligatory.	(a) 3–11 in case mentioned in column 4(a). (b) 10 in any case.
RTA section 7A	Failing to allow specimen to be subjected to laboratory test.	Summarily.	(a) Where the test would be for ascertaining ability to drive or proportion of alcohol at the time offender was driving or attempting to drive, 6 months or level 5 on the standard scale or both. (b) In any other case, 3 months or level 4 on the standard scale or both.	(a) Obligatory in the case mentioned in column 4(a). (b) Discretionary in any other case.	Obligatory.	3–11, in case mentioned in column 4(a). 10 in any other case.

(1) Provision creating offence	(2) General nature of offence	(3) Mode of prosecution	(4) Punishment	(5) Disqualification	(6) Endorsement	(7) Penalty points
RTA section 12	Motor racing and speed trials on public ways.	Summarily.	Level 4 on the standard scale.	Obligatory.	Obligatory.	3–11
RTA section 22	Leaving vehicles in dangerous positions.	Summarily.	Level 3 on the standard scale.	Discretionary if committed in respect of a motor vehicle.	Obligatory if commited in respect of a motor vehicle.	3
RTA section 22A	Causing danger to road users.	(a) Summarily.	(a) 6 months or the statutory maximum or both.			
		(b) On indictment.	(b) 7 years or a fine or both.			
RTA section 23	Carrying passenger on motorcycle contrary to section 23.	Summarily.	Level 3 on the standard scale.	Discretionary.	Obligatory.	3
RTA section 35	Failing to comply with traffic directions.	Summarily.	Level 3 on the standard scale.	Discretionary, if committed in respect of a motor vehicle by failure to comply with a direction of a constable or traffic warden.	Obligatory if committed as described in column 5.	3
RTA section 36	Failing to comply with traffic signs.	Summarily.	Level 3 on the standard scale.	Discretionary, if committed in respect of a motor vehicle by failure to comply with an indication given by a sign specified for the purpose of this paragraph in regulations under RTA section 36.	Obligatory if committed as described in column 5.	3
RTA section 40A	Using vehicle in dangerous condition, etc.	Summarily.	(a) Level 5 on the standard scale if committed in respect of a goods vehicle or a vehicle adapted to carry more than eight passengers.	(a) Obligatory if committed within three years of a previous conviction of the offender under section 40A.	Obligatory.	3
			(b) Level 4 on the standard scale in any other case.	(b) Discretionary in any other case.		
RTA section 41A	Breach of requirement as to brakes, steering-gear or tyres.	Summarily.	(a) Level 5 on the standard scale if committed in respect of a goods vehicle or a vehicle adapted to carry more than eight passengers.	Discretionary.	Obligatory.	3
			(b) Level 4 on the standard scale in any other case.			
RTA section 87(1)	Driving otherwise than in accordance with a licence.	Summarily.	Level 3 on the standard scale.	Discretionary in a case where the offender's driving would not have been in accordance with any licence that could have been granted to him.	Obligatory in the case mentioned in column 5.	3–6

(1) Provision creating offence	(2) General nature of offence	(3) Mode of prosecution	(4) Punishment	(5) Disqualification	(6) Endorsement	(7) Penalty points
RTA section 92(10)	Driving after making false declaration as to physical fitness.	Summarily.	Level 4 on the standard scale.	Discretionary.	Obligatory.	3–6
RTA section 93(3)	Failure to deliver revoked licence and counterpart to Secretary of State.	Summarily.	Level 3 on the standard scale.			
RTA section 94(3)	Failure of notify Secretary of State of onset of, or deterioration in, relevant or prospective disability.	Summarily.	Level 3 on the standard scale.			
RTA section 94(3A)	Driving after such a failure.	Summarily.	Level 3 on the standard scale.	Discretionary.	Obligatory.	3–6
RTA section 94A	Driving after refusal of licence under section 92(3) or revocation under section 93 or service of a notice under section 99C or 109B.	Summarily.	6 months or level 5 on the standard scale or both.	Discretionary.	Obligatory.	3–6
RTA section 96	Driving with uncorrected defective eyesight, or refusing to submit to test of eyesight.	Summarily	Level 3 on the standard scale.	Discretionary	Obligatory.	3
RTA section 99(5)	Driving licence holder failing to surrender licence and counterpart.	Summarily.	Level 3 on the standard scale.			
RTA section 103(1)(a)	Obtaining driving licence while disqualified.	Summarily.	Level 3 on the standard scale.			
RTA section 103(1)(b)	Driving while disqualified.	Summarily.	6 months or level 5 on the standard scale or both.	Discretionary.	Obligatory.	6
RTA section 143	Using motor vehicle while uninsured or unsecured against third party risks.	Summarily.	Level 5 on the standard scale.	Discretionary.	Obligatory.	6–8
RTA section 163	Failing to stop motor vehicle or cycle when required by constable.	Summarily.	(a) Level 5 on the standard scale if committed by a person driving a mechanically propelled vehicle. (b) Level 3 on the standard scale if committed by a person riding a cycle.			

(1) Provision creating offence	(2) General nature of offence	(3) Mode of prosecution	(4) Punishment	(5) Disqualification	(6) Endorsement	(7) Penalty points
RTA section 170(4)	Failing to stop after accident and give particulars or report accident.	Summarily.	6 months or level 5 on the standard scale or both.	Discretionary.	Obligatory.	5–10
RTA section 170(7)	involving injury to another, to produce evidence of insurance or security or to report accident.	Summarily.	Level 3 on the standard scale.			
RTA section 171	Failure by owner of motor vehicle to give police information for verifying compliance with requirement of compulsory insurance or security.	Summarily.	Level 4 on the standard scale.			
RTA section 172	Failure of person keeping vehicle and others to give police information as to identity of driver, etc., in the case of certain offences.	Summarily.	Level 3 on the standard scale.	Discretionary if committed otherwise than by virtue of subsection (5) or (11).	Obligatory if committed otherwise than By virtue of subsection (5) or (11).	6

10.3   Disqualification

All orders of disqualification from driving run from the moment they are pronounced (*Meese* [1973] 1 WLR 675 (CA)). In that case, the trial judge ordered that the two periods of disqualification which he was imposing should run consecutively. The Court of Appeal held that such a sentence was unlawful, since the start of the second period would be postponed. They must run concurrently.

Disqualification can be for any period—even life. But a life disqualification is extremely rare. The danger which the appellate courts have seen with very long periods of disqualification (eg, ten years) is that they may shut the defendant out of a substantial number of jobs, and create an incentive to disregard the law.

10.3.1   Categories of disqualification

There are three categories of disqualification: obligatory; penalty points; and discretionary. The succeeding paragraphs deal with each in turn.

10.3.1.1   Obligatory

Where an offence carries obligatory disqualification, there must be an order of disqualification unless there are special reasons (see **10.4**).

As far as the minimum period for which the court must disqualify is concerned:

(a) the minimum is usually 12 months;

(b) for certain of the most serious offences (manslaughter, causing death by dangerous driving, and causing death by careless driving while under the influence of drink or drugs), there is a longer minimum of two years;

(c) a minimum of two years must be imposed when the defendant has been disqualified for 56 days or more at least twice in the three years preceding the commission of the offence in question; and

(d) there is a special minimum sentence of three years' disqualification under RTOA 1988, s 34(3) where the defendant is convicted of an alcohol-related offence which was committed within ten years of the date of conviction of an earlier alcohol-related offence.

10.3.1.2 Penalty points

This applies where the defendant 'tots up' 12 or more points within three years (RTOA 1988, s 29). Such a 'totter' is then disqualified for a minimum of six months, in the absence of clearly defined 'mitigating grounds'.

The penalty points to be taken into account are:

(a) any for the offence(s) of which the defendant is now convicted (disregarding any for which the court disqualifies); and

(b) any ordered to be endorsed on a previous occasion for an offence *committed* in the preceding three years.

The law used to be that, if the defendant was disqualified, the slate was wiped clean and he or she started again to tot up towards 12. Now, there is no general rule that the slate will be wiped clean once there is disqualification. The rule is that all penalty points remain until there is a penalty points disqualification, whereupon they are wiped off.

The court may decide not to impose a penalty points disqualification (or impose a shorter one than six months) if there are mitigating grounds. When the term is applied to a 'totter', then it has a restricted meaning. Certain factors may not be mitigating grounds by virtue of the RTOA 1988, s 35(4), ie:

• any circumstances that are alleged to make the offence(s) not a serious one;

• hardship, other than exceptional hardship;

• any circumstances taken into account as mitigating grounds in the preceding three years.

Frequently, 'exceptional hardship' is argued in relation to the offender's employment. The court might take into account the following factors, together with any others which appear from the facts:

• whether the offender requires a licence to drive as a necessary part of the job;

• whether he or she needs to drive in order to get to work;

• the distances to be travelled to work;

• the availability of public transport;

- the hours required by the job (eg, are they at a time when public transport is available);

- the offender's age and health; any other means of transport available;

- any particular hardship caused to the offender's family by the loss of the job or reduced wages;

- any employees dependent on the offender's ability to drive.

10.3.1.3   Discretionary

Where an offence carries discretionary disqualification, the court can disqualify for the offence where it imposes less than 12 points.

10.3.1.4   Probationary period

Every driver who qualified on or after 1 June 1997 is subject to a probationary period of two years, beginning with the day on which he or she qualified (Road Traffic (New Drivers) Act 1995). A driver who acquires six or more penalty points during that probationary period, will have his or her licence revoked and must undergo retesting before a full driving licence can once again be issued.

10.3.2   Ending disqualification

In the normal course of events, the disqualification will end once the period laid down by the court expires. Prior to that, the offender can apply for his or her licence back before the period of disqualification ends, provided that a certain period of time has elapsed. That period is:

- at least two years in any event;

- half the period of disqualification if the period ordered is between four and ten years;

- five years if the disqualification is for ten years or more.

10.3.3   Order for retest

There is, however, provision for the sentencing court to lay down that the offender must pass a driving test before the disqualification comes to an end. Whilst such an order is within the court's discretion, it should not be imposed on a punitive basis, but in order to protect the safety of other road users, eg because of the age, infirmity or lack of experience of the offender, or the nature of the offence (*Guilfoyle* [1973] 2 All ER 844). Retests are now compulsory when the court disqualifies for manslaughter or for dangerous driving (whether it causes death or not): RTOA 1988, s 36.

10.4   Special reasons

As mentioned above, where disqualification is obligatory, the court must disqualify unless there are 'special reasons'. A similar rule applies where endorsement is obligatory.

Where special reasons are necessary, these must relate to the offence, and not to the circumstances of the offender. As it was put in *Whittal v Kirby* [1947] KB 194:

A 'special reason' within the exception is one which is special to the facts of the particular case, that is, special to the facts which constitute the offence. It is, in other words, a mitigating or extenuating circumstance, not amounting in law to a defence to the charge, yet directly connected with the commission of the offence, and one which the court ought properly to take into consideration when imposing punishment. A circumstance peculiar to the offender as distinguished from the offence is not a 'special reason' within the exception.

Frequently, special reasons are put forward where the defendant alleges that his or her drink was laced. Guidance has now been laid down in *DPP v O'Connor* [1992] RTR 66 as to what constitutes special reasons in these circumstances. The defence must show on the balance of probabilities:

- that the defendant's drink had been laced;
- that the defendant did not know or suspect that it had been laced;
- that, if the defendant had not taken the laced drink, his or her alcohol level would not have exceeded the prescribed limit.

Another series of cases relates to drink driving in an emergency. In *Chatters v Burke* [1986] 1 WLR 1321, the court laid down seven matters which the justices ought to take into account in such cases:

First of all they should consider how far the vehicle was in fact driven; secondly, in what manner it was driven; thirdly, what was the state of the vehicle; fourthly, whether it was the intention of the driver to drive any further; fifthly, the prevailing conditions with regard to the road and the traffic upon it; sixthly, whether there was any possibility of danger by contact with other road users; and finally, what was the reason for the vehicle being driven at all.

The argument that there are special reasons is not, however, confined to drink driving cases. For example, it also has application to a speeding case (*Police Prosecutor v Humphreys* [1970] Crim LR 234).

The defendant can argue that there are special reasons not to impose penalty points as well as not to disqualify.

Part III

A case to prepare

11

Introduction to the sample brief

This chapter introduces the papers for a criminal case (reproduced in **Chapter 12**) which are intended to provide you with the opportunity to make use of some of the skills which are required of a barrister in criminal practice. The issues which are involved are ones which ought to be familiar by the time you have reached this part of the manual. From time to time, however, you will find it helpful to make reference to some of the other manuals in this series, eg the *Opinion Writing Manual*, the *Advocacy Manual* and the *Conference Skills Manual*.

The case is one where there are a number of co-defendants, who are charged with offences of violence and offences against public order. There are issues relating to identification, alibi, severance of the indictment, admissibility and the overall strengths and weaknesses of the prosecution case. You need to address the question of advising on plea and on sentence. The set of papers includes a questionnaire which has to be filled in before the Plea and Case Management Hearing, so that you have to consider whether it can be filled in on the information which you have to hand, or whether more details are needed (eg, from the client in conference) before you are able to do so. Considering the questionnaire will give you the opportunity to become familiar with a document which a barrister in criminal practice is frequently required to complete. The guidance notes that are published with the questionnaire are included to assist you. In addition, the papers include a copy of a custody record, which is a fertile source of information for both sides in a criminal trial, and needs careful consideration as you advise and prepare for trial. There are copies of other documents in common use, such as a crime report.

In making use of this set of papers, it is suggested that you should proceed as follows:

- use the papers as an exercise in writing an Advice on Evidence;
- use them to draft a Defence Statement;
- use them to complete the Plea and Case Management Questionnaire;
- then use them to prepare for a conference with the client;
- finally, use them to prepare for the advocacy tasks involved in a trial.

Each of these suggestions is considered in more detail in the succeeding sections.

11.1 Advice on evidence

The papers take the form of a brief received by counsel, with instructions to provide an Advice on Evidence for the defendant John Hanson. Your initial use of the papers ought, therefore, to be as an exercise in writing an Advice on Evidence in a criminal case. Prior to doing so, you should read through **Chapter 2** of the *Opinion Writing Manual*, which deals with this task. You may also find it helpful to take a look at **Chapter 14** in the *Case Preparation Manual*. (*You should avoid looking at the sample Advice which is printed at the end of this Manual. If you do so, it will obviously destroy much of the value in doing the Advice as an exercise.*)

Once you have refreshed your memory as to the steps involved in writing an Advice on Evidence in a criminal case, you should be ready to start. In order to make sure that you manage your time effectively, and to ensure that you do not become too remote from the situation in practice, it is suggested that you work against the clock, and that you do not allow yourself more than six hours to produce the Advice, including any legal research which you need to do.

Having started the clock, you might read through the papers once, quickly, in order to get the general sense. Second and third readings are then likely to be necessary in order to be able to analyse the evidence and form an initial judgement on the points which need to be dealt with in the Advice. As you read the papers for the second or third time, you might compile a chronology, a list of issues, a schedule of the various descriptions of the defendants in whom you are particularly interested. You should also begin to make a list of the points on which your instructing solicitors need to take action, the documents which you need to see and the missing pieces of information.

Having gone through the papers several times in this way, you are in a position to make a plan of your Advice. Consider how the various points which you need to cover should be dealt with and the logical order in which you should present them. You can then write your Advice, keeping an eye on the clock so that you do not produce something which is unrealistic in terms of length and degree of detail.

Once your Advice is completed, and you have taken a pause in order to recover, look at the sample Advice, which is printed in **Chapter 13**. (*This should be the first time that you have glanced at it!*)

Consider your Advice against the sample. Bear in mind that it is a sample and not a model. Your version may be superior, at least in certain respects, to what is printed. But wherever you reach a different conclusion from the sample, you should consider which is preferable, and why. Think also about the form in which the sample is written and compare it with yours in order to gain some constructive feedback.

11.2 Defence Statement

Your solicitors have also instructed you to draft a Defence Statement (sometimes referred to as a 'Defence Case Statement'). This is not an uncommon request by solicitors and, despite some initial concerns about potential professional conduct issues that might arise, the Bar Council has said that it is appropriate for counsel to draft such documents as long as they have sufficient instructions to do so.

A Defence Statement is a mandatory requirement in proceedings in the Crown Court and should be served within 14 days of the date upon which the prosecution has complied with, or purported to comply with, the duty of primary or initial disclosure.

A Defence Statement must comply with the requirements of the Criminal Procedure and Investigations Act 1996, s 6A and the Court of Appeal's guidance in *Disclosure: A Protocol for the Control and Management of Unused Material in the Crown Court*. The Protocol was, *inter alia*, an attempt to change the approach that had usually been taken to Defence Statements. The Protocol states that, in the past, the Defence Statement was often little more than an assertion that the defendant was not guilty. This was often because defence lawyers were reluctant to divulge the details of their defence in advance of trial. The Protocol stresses that there must be a complete change in culture. Judges will now expect to see Defence Statements that contain a clear and detailed exposition of the issues of fact and law in the case, and should examine the Defence Statement with care to ensure that it complies with the formalities required by the Criminal Procedure and Investigations Act 1996. For the full text of the Protocol, see *Blackstone's Criminal Practice.*

Once you have written your advice, you should draft your Defence Statement. Now that you are familiar with the issues in the case, this should not take very long. You should be able to draft a Defence Statement within an hour at the very most. There is no prescribed way of setting out a Defence Statement. However, aim to make your draft easy for the judge to read and digest. It may be useful to structure the Defence Statement around the requirements in s 6A of the 1996 Act, using each requirement as a separate heading. For example, you could include sections headed 'Nature of the defence', 'Matters of fact on which the defendant takes issue with the prosecution', etc.

When you have completed your Defence Statement, consider the Defence Statement printed in **Chapter 13** and compare yours with the sample. Again, bear in mind that it is a sample and not a model. Yours may be better. What is important is that where yours differs, you identify which is better and why.

11.3 Plea and Case Management Questionnaire

A Plea and Case Management Questionnaire must be completed for every contested case in the Crown Court. It is therefore a document that counsel will frequently have to consider and any experience you have of doing so before you are instructed to appear at your first Plea and Case Management Hearing is invaluable.

At this stage, you do not have all the information you need to enable to fully complete this form but you have sufficient information to complete most of it. The guidance notes are included with your brief in order to assist you filling in the form.

11.4 Preparing for conference

The next task which you might undertake with the *Hanson* papers is preparation for conference. It is not giving away any deep secret to suggest that part of the advice which you are likely to provide is that there should be a conference with the client. In preparing for this task, you may work in parallel with a friend or colleague, with each of you working separately, and then comparing your conclusions.

In any event, you will find it helpful before using the papers in this way to read the relevant sections of the *Conference Skills Manual*—in particular **Chapter 5**. You will need to consider, among other matters, the information which you need to obtain from your client, and how best to obtain it; and the advice which needs to be given, for example on plea and likely sentence if convicted. Having prepared and produced a working plan for the conference, compare notes with the friend or colleague who has been performing the same task.

11.5   Preparing for trial

The papers can be used again to prepare for trial. Again, you might wish to work in parallel with someone on this task. It would be sensible if the two of you worked out the answers which you have been given in the imaginary conference referred to in **11.2**. This will then give you a basis for preparation for trial, ie you prepare on the assumption that the client has given you certain answers to the questions which you asked in conference.

As to the areas which need preparation, it is suggested that you deal with each of the areas described in the following paragraphs.

11.5.1   Closing speech

It actually makes a lot of sense to prepare your closing speech before preparing the matters which you have to deal with during the course of the trial.

Your closing speech ought to be your interpretation of the points which arise in trial. If you are able to make certain realistic assumptions about what is likely to emerge during the trial, preparing your closing speech first gives the rest of your preparation a clear focus. Obviously, if the trial actually took place, the speech would need to be rewritten at intervals during its course, in order to ensure that it was based, not on assumptions, but on the evidence which in fact emerged.

11.5.2   Submissions

From the time that you prepared to write your Advice on Evidence, it will have been apparent that there would be disputes about the admissibility of certain pieces of evidence. You need to consider how you will present the argument in relation to these points of admissibility. In doing so, you are likely to find **Chapter 39** of the *Advocacy Manual* of assistance. Similarly, you should consider whether you are at all likely to be making a submission of no case to answer on behalf of your client(s). If so, prepare a framework, using **Chapter 40** of the *Advocacy Manual* to remind yourself of the process involved.

11.5.3   Cross-examination

There are two areas of cross-examination which you must prepare. First, there are the prosecution witnesses, both police and civilian. The themes and arguments which you intend to develop in your closing speech will determine the course of cross-examination here to some extent. Your cross-examination will also be affected by the instructions which you have received in the brief and those which are obtained in conference.

Second, you must consider any co-defendants who stand trial with your client. If they appear on the indictment before your client, you will have to cross-examine them before your client gives evidence.

In addition, consider the points to keep in mind in preparing any cross-examination (see **Chapter 22** of the *Advocacy Manual*).

11.5.4   Examination in chief

One of the most important tasks in preparing for trial as defence counsel is to consider the impression your client would make as a witness. Will it be necessary for your client to give evidence? If it is, then prepare to examine him in chief, using **Chapter 21** of the *Advocacy Manual* as a reminder of the steps you need to take.

11.5.5 Comparing notes

Once you have dealt with each of the advocacy tasks which you are likely to face, discuss your approach with your friend or colleague and compare notes.

11.6 The papers in *R v Hanson and others*

You can now read the brief contained in **Chapter 12**, and start preparing the Advice on Evidence. (*Remember not to look at the sample Advice in* **Chapter 13** *until you have finished.*)

R v Hanson and others

Contents

<u>IN THE CROWN COURT SITTING AT OXTON</u>
<u>T0155/09</u>

BETWEEN:

R

–and–

JOHN HANSON & Others

INSTRUCTIONS TO COUNSEL

Messrs. Archer & Balcombe
Centenary House,
Bray Street,
Oxton. OT5 16MM

<u>Solicitors for the Defendants</u>

<u>IN THE CROWN COURT SITTING AT OXTON</u>   T0155/09
BETWEEN:

R

–v–

JOHN HANSON and Others

INSTRUCTIONS TO COUNSEL

Counsel has herewith:
1. Copy Indictment.
2. Statements of prosecution witnesses.
3. Interviews of Mr Spring & Mr Hanson.
4. Custody records.
5. Unused material.
6. Previous convictions of Mr Spring and Mr Hanson.
7. Proof of Evidence of Mr Hanson.

Counsel is instructed on behalf of the Defendant, John Hanson, who is charged with Violent Disorder, Causing Grievous Bodily Harm with intent to resist arrest of Nicholas Spring and Attempted Robbery.

The facts of this case are set out in the various documents and Instructing Solicitors do not intend to repeat them herein. All defendants were sent for trial on 17th July.

The other defendants are represented by Messrs Glidewell and Speed. They have informed us that Sean Baker and Martin Thompson will plead guilty to Violent Disorder whilst Louis Bucknell, Simon Bratt and Anthony Mead will plead guilty to Affray. The CPS have indicated that these pleas are acceptable. Nicholas Spring intends to plead not guilty to all the charges he faces.

Counsel is asked to advise generally on evidence and plea.

Counsel is also requested to complete the questionnaire for the Plea and Case Management Hearing, which is to be held on 21st August 2009 and to draft a defence case statement for both defendants.

21 July 2009

The Crown Court	Plea and Case Management Hearing

Advocates Questionnaire

Parties must complete this form.

This form is to be used at all Crown Court Centres, without local variation.

There is an electronic version of the form which contains answer boxes that expand. The form is at:
http://www.hmcourts-service.gov.uk/HMCSCourtFinder

Case No   D1   [   ]

Date of trial   [   ]

Fixed   ☐
Warned   ☐

1

Date of PCMH	PTI URN
[ ]	[ ]
Judge	Estimated length of trial
[ ]	[ ]

2   **Parties' details**

	Parties name	Age	Remand status	CTL expires	Advocate at PCMH	Trial advocate (if known)
P			████████████			
D1			C ☐ B ☐			

3   **Contact details**

3.1   Parties

P   Office

Name	Phone
Email	

Advocate

Name	Phone
Email	

D1   Solicitor

Name	Phone
Email	

Advocate

Name	Phone
Email	

3.2

Case progression officers

P

Name	Phone
Email	

D1

Name	Phone
Email	

Court

Name	Phone
Email	

4   Which orders made at the magistrates' court have not been complied with?

5

D1   Has the defendant been advised that he or she will receive credit for a guilty plea?   ☐ No ☐ Yes

6

D1   Has the defendant been warned that the case may proceed in his or her absence?   ☐ No ☐ Yes

7   What plea(s) is/are the defendant(s) offering?

D1

8   Should the case be referred to the Resident Judge for a trial judge to be allocated?   ☐ No ☐ Yes

9   Give details of any issues relating to the fitness to plead or to stand trial.

D1

10

10.1   Has the prosecution made statutory disclosure?

P

D1

10.2   Has a defence statement been served?

D1

_____

10.3   Does it comply with the statutory requirements?

P

_____

10.4   If not clear from the defence statement, what are the real issues?

D1

_____

10.5
D1   Has/will the defence made/make an application in writing under
        section 8 of the Criminal Procedure and Investigations Act 1996?   ☐ No ☐ Yes

11   What further evidence is to be served by the prosecution?
         By when is it reasonably practicable to serve this?

P

_____

12
12.1   Give details of any expert evidence likely to be relied upon, including
        why it is required and by when it is reasonably practicable to serve this.

P

_____

D1

_____

12.2   Is a note of agreement/disagreement required?

_____

13
13.1
D1   Has the defence completed the Witness List (see **36**)?   ☐ No ☐ Yes

13.2   Is any witness summons necessary?

13.3
  D1   Is a timetable for the calling of witnesses required (see **30**)?   ☐ No   ☐ Yes

14

14.1
  D1   Is a certificate for a litigator sought?   ☐ No   ☐ Yes

14.2   If **Yes**, why and for how long?
  D1

For 15 to 35, answer the relevant questions only

15   Admissions, schedules etc.

What matters can usefully be admitted or put into schedules, diagrams, visual aids etc.?

---

16   Case summary

  P   Is it proposed to serve a case summary or note of opening?   ☐ No   ☐ Yes

17   Special measures

17.1   Give details of any special measures application to be made.

17.2

Can any order be made now?   ☐ No   ☐ Yes

17.3   What other arrangements are needed for any young/vulnerable/intimidated witness?

┌───┐
│   │
│   │
│   │
└───┘

18   Young defendants

Are any arrangements needed for any young defendant?

D1
┌───┐
│   │
│   │
└───┘

19   Reporting restrictions

State type and grounds of any reporting restriction sought.

P
┌───┐
│   │
│   │
└───┘

D1
┌───┐
│   │
│   │
└───┘

20   Third party material

20.1   What third party material is sought, from whom, and why?

P
┌───┐
│   │
│   │
│   │
└───┘

D1
┌───┐
│   │
│   │
│   │
└───┘

20.2   If the material can be obtained without a court order, by whom and by when?

P
┌───┐
│   │
│   │
│   │
└───┘

D1
┌───┐
│   │
│   │
│   │
└───┘

20.3   Should any person adversely affected by an order be notified?

┌───┐
│   │
│   │
│   │
└───┘

21   Defendant's interview(s)

21.1   Is there an issue in relation to the accuracy of
the transcript/admissibility of the defendant's interview?

D1

21.2   What proposals are made for any editing required?

D1

21.3   What proposals are made to summarise the interview(s)?

D1

22   Video Evidence

22.1   Is there video evidence of any young/vulnerable/intimidated witness yet to be served?

22.2   Has each video been transcribed?

22.3   Is there an issue in relation to the accuracy/admissibility/quality of any video or transcript?

23   Witness interview(s)

23.1   Are there any videos/audio tapes of witness interviews which,
if they meet the disclosure test, are yet to be disclosed as unused material?

23.2   If so, is any application made for that video/audio tape to be
transcribed and, if so, why?

24   CCTV evidence

24.1   Are there any outstanding issues in relation to service disclosure of CCTV footage?
If the material is in the possession of a third party, complete 20 instead.

24.2   Is an edited version to be served/used?

25   Electronic equipment

25.1   Give details of any special equipment (e.g. CCTV, live link, audio recordings, DVD)
required in the trial courtroom.

P

D1

25.2   Is the evidence in its present form compatible with the equipment in court?

26   Cross-examination on sexual history

If an application has not already been made, does the defence intend to make
an application under section 41 of the Youth Justice and Criminal Evidence Act 1999
to cross-examine a witness about his or her sexual history?

D1

27   Bad character

Are any directions necessary in relation to bad character applications?
Are there any further applications?

P

D1

[blank box]

28   Hearsay

Are any directions necessary in relation to hearsay applications?
Are there to be any further applications?

P

[blank box]

D1

[blank box]

29   Admissibility and legal issues

What points on admissibility/other legal issues are to be taken?
Is it necessary for any to be resolved before trial?

P

[blank box]

D1

[blank box]

30   Timetable of trial

Are there matters which need to be determined on the day of trial, which
may affect the timetable of trial?
If so, when will (1) the jury and (2) the witnesses be required?

P

[blank box]

31   Public interest immunity

Is any 'on notice' public interest immunity application to be made?

P

32   Jury bundle

What proposals do the prosecution make for a jury bundle?

P

33   Concurrent family proceedings

Give details of any concurrent family proceedings.

34   Other special arrangements

Give details of any special arrangements (e.g., interpreter, intermediary,
wheelchair access, hearing loop system) needed for anyone attending the trial.

35   Linked criminal proceedings

Are there other criminal proceedings against the defendant or otherwise linked?

36   Witness List

The defence should indicate here which prosecution witnesses are required to give evidence at trial. The attendance of any witness is subject to the judge's direction.

Name of witness	Page No.	Type of witness: *Provide specific details of the type of witness. For example: eye witness, police officer, firearms expert, continuity*	Required by

PLEA AND CASE MANAGEMENT HEARING FORM:

<u>GUIDANCE NOTES</u>

How to use the form

The parties should complete only one form for each case. **The form should be used in every Crown Court centre, without any local exception or variation**.

The form may be completed in manuscript or electronically.

Questions 1 to 14 must be answered in every case. Questions 15–35 need only be answered if they are relevant.

The advocate may be asked by the court to expand upon or explain an entry, or to account for the absence of an entry, where one is required. The judge will record on the template any orders made and, if practicable, issue a copy to the parties before the hearing ends. The parties must obtain a copy of that record and comply with the orders made by the date given.

Accessing the form

The current version of the form is available on the Court Service web-site at http://www.hmcourts-service.gov.uk/HMCSCourtFinder. Please note that the form will be updated from time to time. When you open the file, a box will appear with the options of disabling or enabling macros. Choosing "enable macros" will produce a fully operational e-form. Choosing "disable macros" may cause some of the functions to be lost, including the option of altering the number of defendants or using a screen reader.

Next will appear the box giving the option of a screen reader. This is software which translates text into speech.

The next box asks for the number of defendants in the case. This can be altered later by clicking on "Add Def" in the toolbar at the top of the screen.

Once this question has been answered, the form that is produced is ready for completion.

The space available to answer any question expands to accommodate the text inserted. The Tab button can be used to jump to the next box. Alternatively, the arrow keys will move the cursor backwards or forwards.

Transmitting the form

If you complete the form on the screen, it can still be printed off and used in hard copy. Alternatively, it can be emailed; the process for this differs depending on whether Outlook is available.

In order to send the form by email, click on the "e-mail" button on the toolbar at the top of the screen and follow the instructions. If the document is to be emailed using Outlook, that programme must be open at the time. Following the instructions will produce an e-mail window with the form attached. If Outlook is not used, the file must be saved and can then be attached in the usual way.

The need for an effective PCMH

The public, and all those concerned in or affected by a criminal case, have a right to expect that the business of the courts will be conducted fairly but also efficiently and effectively. Delays cost money and adversely impact on the quality of justice. The Plea and Case Management Hearing offers the best, and often the only, opportunity for the judge properly and effectively to manage the case before it is listed for trial. Other hearings – formerly called 'mentions'– are expensive and should actively be discouraged; nearly everything formerly done at a 'mention' can – and should – be done in some other way (usually by telephone or on paper or by an exchange of email, as permitted by CrimPR 3.5(2)(d)). An effective PCMH is therefore vital.

Advocates should attend the hearing fully prepared to deal with the issues that are likely to arise, and the listing officer should consider reasonable requests to list the PCMH to enable trial counsel to attend.

Since an effective PCMH can only take place after the defence have had a proper opportunity to consider the papers, it is suggested that at least four weeks should elapse between the service and listing of the PCMH.

The short guidance given here is intended to be followed in every case but, of course, it is not possible to cover exhaustively all the situations which may be relevant to achieving an effective PCMH. See also Consolidated Criminal Practice Direction (CCPD) IV.41, Management of Cases to be Heard in the Crown Court; V.56 Case Management in Magistrates' Courts and Criminal Case Management Framework (available on-line at www.cjsonline.gov.uk/framework).

Contents of the form

Date of trial and custody time limits

The date of trial should normally be fixed at the PCMH (or before). Any application to extend the Custody Time Limit is best dealt with at the PCMH, when the reasons for fixing a case beyond the time limits will be clear; otherwise there will be the avoidable expense of another hearing.

1,2 and 3 details of case and parties

This section must be fully completed. The parties must be able to contact one another as must case progression officers and the court. Any change in the details must immediately be notified to the other parties and to the court. See CrimPR 3.4.

4 Compliance with the directions given by magistrates' courts

The standard/specific directions given by magistrates' courts should be complied with (CrimPR 3.5(3)). The court will need to know which orders have not been complied with, and why.

5 Credit for guilty plea

Defendants are entitled to be given the advice that credit is given for guilty pleas and the earlier the plea is entered, the greater is the credit given. The judge needs to know that this advice has been given.

6 Trial in absence

Defendants need to be warned that if they waive their right to attend, the trial may proceed in their absence. No one can engineer an adjournment simply by absconding. Those who claim to be ill must support that claim by medical evidence to the effect that they are unfit to attend their trial; it is unlikely that a medical certificate merely suggesting that they are unfit to work will be sufficient. See CCPD , I.13; CrimPR 3.8(2)(a).

7 The pleas which the defendant is offering

Recording in writing pleas offered to alternative offences which the prosecution are initially unwilling to accept will be advantageous to the defendant if the prosecution subsequently changes its position. In such circumstances, it will be easier for a defendant to claim maximum credit if that offer has been recorded. Pleas offered to counts on the indictment must similarly be recorded before credit is claimed.

8 Allocation of the case

Most courts have a system to identify before the PCMH those cases which require allocation to a particular judge; this question is intended to seek out those cases which have been missed.

9 Fitness to plead

This is self explanatory but the judge will need assistance to fix a timetable for the service of experts' reports and for the issue to be tried.

10 Disclosure and defence statement

The parties must identify any outstanding disclosure points. The defence must serve a detailed defence statement setting out the issues in the trial; any failure to do so may be the subject of adverse comment at the trial and the judge may issue a warning to this effect, under section 11(3) of the Criminal Procedure and Investigations Act 1996. Pending service of a defence statement, question 10.4 allows the defence to give some notification of the defence. The practice of appending long 'shopping lists' to vague and unspecific defence statements has no legal foundation; any application for further disclosure should be made by way of formal application under section 8 of the Criminal Procedure and Investigations Act 1996 (as amended). The judge will expect reference to and compliance with the Disclosure Protocol: A Protocol for the Control and Management of Unused Material in the Crown Court.

11 and 12 Timetable of further evidence and expert evidence

Advocates should have available proper information as to what remains to be served, together with a realistic timetable for compliance. Parties should be prepared to provide realistic time estimates and not rely on a standard time period of, for example, 28 days if this has little bearing on the true amount of time likely to be required. The court needs detailed and accurate information as to when the evidence will be available. These enquiries should be made before the hearing. Failure to do so is likely to cause unnecessary adjournments. Consideration should be given to CrimPR 33.5 and whether (now or later) the experts should be asked to confer to identify the real areas of dispute.

13 Witness list (see also 36)

The mere fact of warning a witness to attend may cause him or her anxiety. Furthermore, the warning of witnesses is time consuming and expensive. The court may decline to order the attendance of witnesses unless their presence is really necessary. Consideration should therefore also be given to those witnesses in respect of whom a summons is required. See CrimPR Part 28 for rules on witness summonses. Thought should always be given to the staggering of witnesses to eliminate or reduce waiting times. The witnesses' availability must be known at the PCMH to ensure that the trial date is convenient.

14 Certificate for a litigator

Attendance by a litigator is not a matter of right and should always be justified by reference to the facts of the particular case.

15 Admissions

Properly drafted admissions can save a great deal of court time and proposals should be made in most cases.

16 Case Summary

Case Summaries should have been provided before the PCMH in all Class 1 cases and in any other case of complexity, but they may be needed in other cases as well.

17 Special measures

In accordance with CrimPR Part 29, special measures applications should have been made by the parties and considered by the court before the PCMH, but this question serves to remind advocates and judges of any outstanding applications.

18 Young and other vulnerable defendants

The needs of young and other vulnerable defendants must be identified in advance of the trial so that the necessary arrangements can be made. See CCPD III.30.

19 Reporting restrictions

Reporting restrictions need to be carefully considered and balanced against the rights of the press and other interested parties. The judge is likely to require assistance before making any order. See CCPD I.3.

20 Third party material and applications to produce documents

Such applications must comply with CrimPR Part 28. Careful thought needs to go into identifying the witness to be served, the material sought and the reason that it is said to be relevant to an issue in the case. Any person whose right of confidentiality might be adversely affected must also be identified and information provided as to how and by whom they are to be notified, how they are to be permitted to make representations and when and by whom any rulings are to be made. It is important that such applications are made no later than the PCMH to avoid adjournments at a later stage arising out of delayed applications.

21 Defendant's interviews

Inaccuracies within transcriptions and likely submissions as to admissibility must be identified. Furthermore, the police may interview suspects at length, producing bundles of transcripts, the volume of which may make them unsuitable to put before a jury. The parties must consider producing summaries. The production of the first draft is primarily the responsibility of the advocate for the prosecution. If practicable, interviews should be available in electronic form, so that editing, pagination and copying can be done without delay. Further guidance is given in CCPD IV.43.

22 Video evidence

These four questions, each of which raises a separate point, are self explanatory but failure to address them is a frequent source of adjournments. Accuracy, admissibility and quality are not the same. Errors of transcription or material on the tape that is indistinct or unclear, or which is alleged to be inadmissible, must be dealt with at PCMH. Editing takes time. It should not be done on the morning of the trial or the day beforehand. Only if these issues are addressed in advance can child witnesses be called as soon as they arrive at court. It is unacceptable to prolong the anxiety of vulnerable witnesses simply because these issues have not been resolved at PCMH. These matters are already addressed in the Supplementary Pre-trial Checklist for Cases Involving Young Witnesses. See also CrimPR Part 29 for rules on special measures directions; and CCPD IV.40.

23 Witness interviews

The issues raised in this question differ from those raised in question 22. There is a growing practice of recording interviews with witnesses before setting out their evidence in a written witness statement. If this is done, then, subject to the disclosure test, the video or audio recording should be disclosed as unused material. The prosecution advocate therefore needs to know if any witness was interviewed in this way (which may not be clear from the papers served). It will normally suffice for the video or audio recording itself to be disclosed. Transcripts are expensive and any claim for a transcript needs to be justified.

24 and 25 CCTV and electronic equipment

The prosecution only have duties to consider disclosure of CCTV footage in their possession. If the defence seek footage from third parties, it is for them to do so, rather than the prosecution. Furthermore, much CCTV footage is in a format (e.g. multiplex) which is unsuitable for showing in court without adaptation or editing. This must be sorted out before the trial. Many courts have simple VHS video and DVD playback facilities and the parties must ensure that the material which they want to play is compatible with the court equipment (if not, they must provide their own).

26 Cross-examination on sexual history

Section 41 of the Youth Justice and Criminal Evidence Act 1999 enacts an important principle and compliance with its requirements is vital to ensure that those who complain that they are victims of rape (and other sexual offences) receive the protection which the law affords to them. In accordance with CrimPR Part 36, applications should be made and considered – by the trial judge if possible – at or before the PCMH. Applications made on the day of the trial are strongly to be discouraged.

27 and 28 Bad character and hearsay

CrimPR 34.5 and 35.6 provide for detailed applications to be made in the prescribed forms. Questions 27 and 28 therefore only seek to identify any outstanding issues (or potential future applications).

29 Admissibility and legal issues

Issues of admissibility and legal issues should, where possible, be identified before the trial, so that the parties can exchange skeleton arguments and the judge can properly prepare for the hearing. See also section 7 of the Criminal Justice Act 1987; and sections 31 and 40 of the Criminal Procedure and Investigations Act 1996.

30 Timetable of the trial

If there are to be preliminary points taken, then consideration must be given to when a jury will be required and arrangements made to stagger the attendance of witnesses. No one should be asked to attend for a 10.30am start only to find that there is a lengthy legal argument before the case can even be opened. See CrimPR 3.10, which deals with, amongst other things, timetabling and witness arrangements.

31 PII claims

If a claim is to be made on notice, then the necessary arrangements must be made. See CrimPR Part 25.

32 Jury bundle

If a jury bundle will be needed at the trial, then its content will need to be agreed before the trial. Any outstanding issues need to be identified.

33 Concurrent family proceedings

It is important to identify those cases where there are concurrent family proceedings, so that the Designated Family Judge can be alerted.

34 Special arrangements

Any requirements for an interpreter or for those with a disability must be identified in advance, so that proper arrangements can be made. See CrimPR 10.5(1)(h) and 12.1(1)(e).

35 Linked criminal proceedings

These need to be identified, if possible with the court reference numbers.

TEMPLATE FOR ORDERS MADE AT PLEA AND CASE MANAGEMENT HEARING

*delete as appropriate

PCMH question	Description of order/ work required	Order made
	Trial date [*fixed for] [*warned for week commencing]	
1	Estimated length of hearing	
9	The defence to serve expert evidence (fitness to plead)	
9	The prosecution to serve expert evidence in response (fitness to plead)	
10	The defence to serve any Defence Statement by	
10	Was a warning given that inferences may be drawn from failure to comply?	
10	The prosecution to make further disclosure by	
10	The defence to make any application under section 8 CPIA for disclosure by	
11	The prosecution to serve further evidence by	
12	The prosecution to serve expert evidence by	
12	The defence to serve any expert evidence on which they rely by	
13	Defence to serve a list of witnesses required at trial by	
13	Record any ruling that the judge has made that the attendance of any witness on that list is not required'.	
14	Certificate for litigator granted for [*the first day] [*the whole trial]	
15	Prosecution to serve schedule of facts for agreement by	
16	Prosecution to serve case summary or note of opening by	
17	Prosecution to apply for special measures directions by	
17	Defence to apply for special measures directions by	
19	Reporting restrictions made in terms attached	
20	Prosecution to seek disclosure of third party material by	
20	Defence to seek disclosure of third party material by	
20	Person adversely affected [being] to be notified by	
21	Defence to notify editing required of defendant's interview by	
21	Prosecution to respond to same by	
21	Prosecution to prepare summaries for agreement by	
22	Prosecution to serve video tape of vulnerable witness by	
22	Prosecution to serve [*transcript][*summary] of evidence by	
22	Defence to notify editing required of defendant's interview by	
22	Prosecution to respond to same by	
23	Prosecution to serve tapes of witness interviews by	
23	Prosecution to transcribe tapes of witness interviews by	
24	Prosecution to serve or disclose CCTV footage by	
24	Prosecution to serve edited version of CCTV footage by	
25	Prosecution to confirm that court equipment compatible with tape by	
26	Defence to serve application to cross-examine on sexual history by	
27	Prosecution to serve further bad character application by	
27	Defence to serve further bad character application by	
28	Prosecution to serve further hearsay application by	
28	Defence to serve further hearsay application by	
29	Defence to serve skeleton argument on legal points to be taken by	
29	Prosecution to respond by	
	*Other orders	
	*	
	*	

Judge's signature ………………………………..Date…………………………

INDICTMENT

No. T0155/09

THE CROWN COURT AT OXTON

THE QUEEN—v–NICHOLAS SPRING, JOHN HANSON, MARTIN THOMPSON, SEAN BAKER, LOUIS BUCKNELL, SIMON BRATT and ANTHONY MEAD

are charged as follows:

Count 1

STATEMENT OF OFFENCE

VIOLENT DISORDER, Contrary to Section 2(1) of the Public Order Act 1986.

PARTICULARS OF OFFENCE

NICHOLAS SPRING, JOHN HANSON, MARTIN THOMPSON, SEAN BAKER, LOUIS BUCKNELL, SIMON BRATT and ANTHONY MEAD on the 11th day of July 2009, being present together with each other and with other persons unknown used or threatened unlawful violence and their conduct (taken together) was such as would cause a person of reasonable firmness present at the scene to fear for his personal safety.

Count 2

STATEMENT OF OFFENCE

CAUSING GRIEVOUS BODILY HARM WITH INTENT, Contrary to Section 18 of the Offences Against the Person Act 1861.

PARTICULARS OF OFFENCE

NICHOLAS SPRING, JOHN HANSON, MARTIN THOMPSON, SEAN BAKER, LOUIS BUCKNELL, SIMON BRATT and ANTHONY MEAD on the 11th day of July 2009 unlawfully caused grievous bodily harm to Martin Kemp with intent to resist or prevent the lawful apprehension or detainer of the said Nicholas Spring.

Count 3

STATEMENT OF OFFENCE

ATTEMPTED ROBBERY, Contrary to Section 1(1) of the Criminal Attempts Act 1981.

PARTICULARS OF OFFENCE

JOHN HANSON, on the 11th day of July 2009 at Kelly's Off-Licence, Crewkerne Street, Upton attempted to rob Michael Kelly of the contents of a cash till.

OFFENCES ADDED UNDER SECTION 40 of the CRIMINAL JUSTICE ACT 1988

STATEMENT OF OFFENCE

DRIVING WHILST UNFIT THROUGH DRINK OR DRUGS, Contrary to Section 4(1) of the Road Traffic Act 1988.

PARTICULARS OF OFFENCE

JOHN HANSON, on 11th day of July 2009 at Upton in the county of Downshire drove a motor vehicle on a road or other public place, namely the junction of Upton Road and Lymehurst Road, whilst unfit through drink or drugs.

<u>WITNESS STATEMENT</u>

Statement of   Stephen Jordan PC 303 . . . .

Age if under 21   . . . .

This statement (consisting of ⊥ pages each signed by me) is true to the best of my knowledge and belief and I make it knowing that, if it is tendered in evidence, I shall be liable to prosecution if I have wilfully stated in it anything which I know to be false or do not believe to be true.

Dated the 13ᵗʰ day of July   2009

Signature: . . . . S. Jordan . . . .

I am a PC in the Downshire Constabulary currently stationed at Upton. I am currently assigned to 'Homebeat' duties on the Abbey Estate. On the 11th July 2009 I went with other officers to an incident on the Abbey Estate.

We arrived at about 3.35 pm. On arrival I saw that PC 37 was being led to a vehicle by PC 211. Both of them appeared to be dishevelled and PC 37 was bleeding profusely from the nose area. A number of youths appeared to be dispersing from the area, some of them were being chased by other officers. As I am familiar with the estate and the people living there I was able to identify 2 men, who got into a blue Vauxhall parked at the rear of Fountains House, as Tony Mead and Simon Bratt. Tony Mead was wearing blue jeans and a yellow shirt. I was able to identify him easily as he has a shaved head and is 6 3. I only saw the back of Simon Bratt but I have arrested him on a number of occasions and he is well known to me. He was wearing a denim jacket and jeans. There were other people in the car but I was unable to identify any of them. I am unable to say who was driving the car. I then assisted other officers in dispersing the crowd and removing prisoners to Upton police station.

On the 12th July at 6.15 am with other officers I went to 27 Fountains House where I arrested Simon Bratt for an offence of violent disorder. He was cautioned at 6.20 am and made no reply. Also at 27 Fountains House were Kieran Bratt, Tony Mead and Louis Bucknell. They were also arrested for violent disorder and taken to Upton police station.

Signed: S. Jordan

Signature witnessed by: R. Parry

WITNESS STATEMENT

Statement of   Raymond Parry PC 211 . . . .

Age if under 21   . . . .

This statement (consisting of 1 pages each signed by me) is true to the best of my knowledge and belief and I make it knowing that, if it is tendered in evidence, I shall be liable to prosecution if I have wilfully stated in it anything which I know to be false or do not believe to be true.

Dated the 13th day of July   2009

Signature: . . . . *R. Parry* . . . .

I am a PC in the Downshire Constabulary currently stationed at Upton. On the 11th July 2009 I was operating a single manned mobile unit when I was called to an incident on the Abbey Estate at about 3.20 pm.

When I arrived I saw PC 37 struggling with a youth I now know to be Nick Spring. Spring was behaving in a very aggressive and violent manner and PC 37 was acting merely to restrain him. Gathered around them was a group of about 15 youths. There were also a number of bystanders, some with children. The children, in particular, appeared to be scared about what was going on. I parked my vehicle some 30 yards away and immediately radioed for back-up and then got out of my vehicle to assist PC 37. When I got to the edge of the group I shouted out for them to stop and attempted to force my way through to assist PC 37. At this I was immediately set on by a number of youths including one whom I know as Sean Baker. These youths started to punch and kick me. I resisted and attempted to arrest the group but as I was about to tell them they were under arrest I was pulled to the ground and pinioned. One of them, who I now know to be Kieran Bratt spat at me and said 'shut up copper or we'll kick the shit out of you'. At that stage the largest of the youths who were attacking me sat on my legs and groin whilst Bratt with another youth called Louis Bucknell knelt on my shoulders and pinioned my arms. I was extremely frightened at this stage and fearful for my life and safety.

I had been on the ground for a minute or two and was attempting to get up when I heard the sound of police sirens. The youths then let go. I got to my feet and went to see if PC 37 was alright. He was covered with blood which seemed to come from his nose area. I assisted him to his feet and to waiting police transport.

Of the youths I remember Bucknell was wearing a purple tie-dye T shirt with white trousers and black trainers. Baker was wearing a brown bomber type jacket with black jeans and trainers and a baseball cap. Bratt, who was about 5′ 9″ with collar length hair and bad acne, was wearing a denim jacket and jeans with white trainers and a white T shirt.

Signed: *R. Parry*.

Signature witnessed by: S. Jordan

<u>WITNESS STATEMENT</u>

Statement of   Martin Kemp PC 37 . . . .

Age if under 21   . . . .

This statement (consisting of 2 pages each signed by me) is true to the best of my knowledge and belief and I make it knowing that, if it is tendered in evidence, I shall be liable to prosecution if I have wilfully stated in it anything which I know to be false or do not believe to be true.

Dated the 14th day of   July 2009

Signature: . . . . *M Kemp* . . . .

I am a Police Officer. On 11th July 2009 I commenced duty at 8 am as a car response driver. At about 3.20 pm. I was called to a domestic incident at Augustinian Close on the Abbey Estate, Upton. I was single manned at this time. On arriving at Augustinian Close a member of the public directed me to the rear of Fountains House where I saw a man I know to be Nicholas Spring. He was speaking to a girl with long fair hair who he identified as his girlfriend. He was shouting at her that she was not having her car keys because she had been drinking. It was obvious to me that they had both been drinking. I asked where she had to go and she said that she lived in Lymehurst. I stated that was not a problem and if she went to my police car I would ensure that she got home and could collect her car and keys when she was sober.

During this conversation Spring was joined by 3 other males, one of whom I knew as Sean Baker. The other two were not known to me. All 4 men were white. Of the 2 others the first who I shall call (1) was about 6 foot tall with a blue denim jacket, blue shirt, blue jeans and white trainers. He had dark cropped hair and tattoos on his wrists. The other man (2) was 5 10, also with dark cropped hair. He was wearing a brown jacket with black jeans and white trainers. He had a light coloured shirt on but I do not recall if it was white or grey. Both men appeared to be in their early twenties.

Spring didn't say much at this stage and after I had arranged transport for the girl everyone seemed happy. I then walked the girl across to my police car. The four men had walked in the direction of the phone box at the far end of the Close. I reached the police vehicle and as I did I heard a loud bang. I turned to see Spring and the others and could clearly hear Spring shouting that his girl was 'going off with a fucking pig'. I walked towards them and they walked towards me. As I got close to them Spring raised his fists and pushed them towards my face in a 'boxer like' pose. I pushed his hands away and he called me a 'fucking wanker'. I then decided to arrest him for an offence under section 4 of the Public Order Act 1986. I put my left hand on his right shoulder and said 'you are under arrest'. At this point Spring threw a punch at my head with his left fist. The punch missed but he then threw further punches at me which connected with my upper body. I then grabbed hold of him and wrestled him to the ground. In doing so I lost the grip on my radio which fell a few feet away. Whilst I was wrestling with Spring I attempted to reach my radio to call for assistance but he shouted out 'don't let him get it' and man 2 kicked it away so that I could not possibly reach it. We continued to struggle with Spring throwing punches. By this stage the original group had been joined by a number of others from Fountains House who formed a ring about me. At this stage I was on top of Spring. Man 1 then came up and with his right foot and kicked me on the left thigh. Spring shouted 'get the bastard off me'. I shouted back 'anyone who tries will get nicked'.

Spring continued to struggle and shout. My watch had come off my wrist and there was some money on the floor. The money was not mine. Male 2 then picked up the money whilst another youth took the watch. I was restraining Spring and had my hands on his shoulders whilst I was attempting to restrain him from kicking me by holding his legs with my knees. At this stage Spring shouted at the group and in particular at man 2 'Get him off me, kick the bastard in the face or you're out of my house and back on the fucking street'. Man 2 appeared to do nothing and Spring shouted out again 'you're a fucking wanker'. Spring then managed to get his arms free again and punched out hitting me in the chest, body, back and head. I pinned his arms with my hands and told him he was lucky that I wasn't going to hit him back. At this point I looked up and man 2 was standing right in front of me and kicked me in the face. It was quite a deliberate kick as I am sure that he paused before doing it. I lost my grip on Spring and felt a rain of kicks from a number of quarters. One of those kicking me was Sean Baker. Man 1 was also kicking me. I was pushed off Spring by the force of the blows.

At this point Spring managed to get free and I then heard a police siren and the group began to scatter. Other officers then arrived. I saw Spring, Baker and man 1, who I now know as Martin Thompson, being arrested as were a number of others. However I did not see man 2.

I sustained injuries to my face and body and was admitted to Upton District Hospital where they diagnosed a broken nose and fairly extensive bruising.

Signed: *M Kemp*

Signature witnessed by: *G.G. Hartley*

<u>WITNESS STATEMENT</u>

Statement of   Charlotte Robinson PC 7 . . . .

Age if under 21   . . . .

This statement (consisting of 1 pages each signed by me) is true to the best of my knowledge and belief and I make it knowing that, if it is tendered in evidence, I shall be liable to prosecution if I have wilfully stated in it anything which I know to be false or do not believe to be true.

Dated the 14th day of July 2009

Signature: . . . . C Robinson . . . .

I am PC 7 of the Downshire Constabulary currently stationed at Upton. At 15.43 hrs on 11th July 2009 I was on duty in full police uniform in a marked police vehicle in company with police sergeant Church when as a result of information received we attended Augustinian Close on the Abbey Estate.

On arrival I saw a number of youths dispersing from outside Fountains House with PC 37 Kemp lying in the road. About 20 feet away from him PC 211 was getting up from the ground. I stopped the vehicle and ran up to PC Kemp. As I did so he shouted 'get the one in the brown jacket he's just kicked me'. I saw a male running up the slope by the side of Fountains House about 30 yards away. He was with but slightly ahead of a youth I know as Sean Baker. At this stage PC Kemp shouted out 'Get Baker as well he kicked me too'. I gave chase and managed to catch Baker but the man in the brown jacket had run to a blue Cavalier parked at the rear of Fountains House. He got into the driver's door and 2 others got in the car and it drove away. I was able to see the number plate and remember the first part of the registration as CLP but as I was in the process of arresting Sean Baker I was unable to make a full mental note of the number of the car.

I managed to restrain Baker who was struggling and then arrested him for assault on PC Kemp. I handcuffed him and cautioned him and he replied 'I can't hear you'. I then placed him in the rear of a marked police van and he was subsequently conveyed to Upton police station arriving at 16.07 hours when he was taken in front of the custody sergeant.

Signed: C Robinson

Signature witnessed by: G.G. Hartley

<u>WITNESS STATEMENT</u>

Statement of   Ronald Keith PC 375 . . . .

Age if under 21   . . . .

This statement (consisting of 1 pages each signed by me) is true to the best of my knowledge and belief and I make it knowing that, if it is tendered in evidence, I shall be liable to prosecution if I have wilfully stated in it anything which I know to be false or do not believe to be true.

Dated the   12th   day of   July   2009

Signature: . . . . . . *RKeith* . . . .

On the 11th July 2009 I was on duty with PC 63 Raymond Tarry in a marked police vehicle. At about 19.30 hours we were outside Tesco's on the Upton Road when I noticed a metallic blue Vauxhall Cavalier registration number CLY 853X. This vehicle was being driven by a single white male and was driving very slowly and in an erratic manner. As a result of information that we had received earlier and because of the way that the vehicle was being driven I decided to stop the vehicle. This we did about 300 yards past Tescos at the junction of the Upton and Lymehurst roads.

I approached the vehicle and spoke to the driver who I now know as John Hanson. I leant in to the open window of the car, seized the keys and asked him to get out. He was very unsteady on his feet and disorientated. After he got out he collapsed on to the ground. I then arrested him on suspicion of driving a motor vehicle whilst under the influence of drugs and on suspicion of attempted robbery and cautioned him. I do not think that he understood the caution. Together with PC Tarry I then handcuffed him and called for police transport. He was then conveyed to Upton police station where the facts were related to the custody sergeant.

At the time of his arrest he was wearing a brown sports coat, black trousers and trainers.

Signed: *RKeith*

Signature witnessed by: *BBlake.*

WITNESS STATEMENT

Statement of   P. Waller PS 8 ....

Age if under 21   ....

This statement (consisting of **1** pages each signed by me) is true to the best of my knowledge and belief and I make it knowing that, if it is tendered in evidence, I shall be liable to prosecution if I have wilfully stated in it anything which I know to be false or do not believe to be true.

Dated the   12th day of   July   2009

Signature: .... *P Waller* ....

On the 11th July 2009 at 19.45 hours I was the custody sergeant at Upton Police Station. At that time PC 375 and PC 63 brought a John Hanson into the custody area. I then opened a custody record on the CJS computer and the number 5OBC/00317/09 was allocated to the record.

Mr Hanson was unable to stand properly and was obviously disorientated. His eyes were glazed and his breath smelt of intoxicating liquor. I formed the view that he was intoxicated. PC 375 related the facts to me and as a result of what had happened during the afternoon on the 11th July, the facts of which were known to me, I then arrested him on suspicion of an offence of violent disorder and told him that he was being detained for the breathalyser procedure to be conducted and that in addition he was under arrest on suspicion of robbery. I cautioned him to which he then replied 'I only tried to rob the place'. This was contemporaneously recorded on form 439 M and 441N and attached to the custody record.

I then commenced the breathalyser procedure but after a short period it was apparent that Mr Hanson was unable to understand what was going on and I then had him placed in cell 11 and the FME was called. At this stage I was unable to give him his rights as he was intoxicated. On her arrival at 21.13 a specimen of blood was taken from Mr Hanson. The FME, Dr Craig also carried out a number of tests on Mr Hanson in my presence in the detention room. I then arrested Mr Hanson for an offence of driving a motor vehicle on a road whilst unfit to drive through drink or drugs and further cautioned him to which he made no reply.

I produce the custody record, marked as exhibit PW/1.

Signed: *P Waller*

Signature witnessed by: *R Keith*

WITNESS STATEMENT

Statement of   Nuala Carroll . . . .

Age if under 21   19 . . . .

This statement (consisting of 1 pages each signed by me) is true to the best of my knowledge and belief and I make it knowing that, if it is tendered in evidence, I shall be liable to prosecution if I have wilfully stated in it anything which I know to be false or do not believe to be true.

Dated the   14th   day of   July   2009

Signature: . . . Nuala Carroll . . . .

I am the above named. I live with my sister, Michelle Davison in Jervaulx House on the Abbey Estate in Upton. I have just finished studying for my 'A' levels at Upton College and hope to go on to a degree course in Portsmouth in September.

On 11th July 2009 I was at home when my sister came in and asked me to telephone the police. Before I did this I looked out of the window of the flat and saw Nick Spring and his girlfriend arguing, it looked to me as if Nick had hit her as she was clutching her face and crying hysterically. I telephoned the police and a car arrived about 5 minutes later with one police officer in it. I could see that Nick was with a number of other men. I didn't recognise any of them except that I remember one was wearing a brown type bomber jacket. When the policeman arrived there was a bit of noise and then it seemed to go quiet and I went to make some tea in the kitchen which overlooks the other side of Jervaulx House.

A few minutes after I heard a loud bang. I carried on making the tea but then after a few more minutes I heard shouting and screaming. I went to the window and saw 2 police officers being set on by a number of men. Some of them I recognised as coming from Fountains House opposite. The first police officer to arrive, who was a very large man appeared to be sitting on Nick, I heard him shouting out 'get the fuck off me' and 'you're strangling me'. The second officer to arrive, who was much smaller than the first officer and was quite slight, was being held back and hit by 3 men from Fountains House, including one I recognised as Sean Baker. I also think I recognised John Hanson in the crowd that had gathered around. I can't remember what he was wearing. He just seemed to be on the edge of the fight. I know John from the pub in Upton where I used to work as a part-time bar maid, he has only just come out of prison.

The fight seemed to go on for ages and while it was going on a number of people seemed to get involved and there were a number of people watching. I kept on watching but it was difficult to see all the time although I could hear a lot of threats and swearing. Towards the end of the incident, just before more police officers arrived I saw a man come out of the crowd and deliberately kick the first officer in the face. It made a sickening dull thud and must have been very painful. Then others started to kick and push him and Nick got free, stood up and went to talk with his girlfriend who was standing close by. At this stage a number of other policemen arrived and everybody scattered. I saw Sean Baker being arrested and Martin Thompson and Nick Spring. I don't really recall what clothes were worn by whom or what their footwear was.

I am willing to attend court and give evidence.

Signed: Nuala Carroll

Signature witnessed by: C Robinson

WITNESS STATEMENT

Statement of   Paula Anne Ryan . . . .

Age if under 21   . . . .

This statement (consisting of pages each signed by me) is true to the best of my knowledge and belief and I make it knowing that, if it is tendered in evidence, I shall be liable to prosecution if I have wilfully stated in it anything which I know to be false or do not believe to be true.

Dated the   14th   day of   July   2009

Signature: D A Ryan . . . .

I am Paula Anne Ryan and I live on the Abbey Estate, Upton at an address known to police.

At about 3.40 pm on the 11th July 2009 I was walking along Augustinian Close coming from Bishop Montford School. I had my 5-year-old son, Thomas, with me and I was pushing my daughter Siobhan in a push chair.

As I came round the corner from the road which leads to the school I heard loud shouts from several male voices. I could see 2 men lying on the road just outside Fountains House. I immediately saw that one of the men was a police officer who was restraining a man on the tarmac. The man was lying on his back and the police officer was holding his arms and lying half across the man's chest.

I recognised the man as Nick Spring who I have known for 4 years or so, but only on a casual basis. He was shouting very loudly things like 'get off me', 'bastard, get off you bastard' and a barrage of foul language like that. I did not hear the police officer say anything. Nick was kicking violently with his legs and struggling to escape from the officer.

At that time I saw a number of men immediately next to the policeman and Nick. A handful of onlookers had gathered, including a number of youths from Fountains House. There were 2 men in particular close to the policeman, one was Sean Baker, the other was a man I have seen before but not recently. He was wearing a short jacket, I can't remember the colour. He had his hair short cropped and had dark trousers and white trainers on. I'm not sure that I would recognise the man again. Sean was wearing white trainers as well.

Nick was struggling very violently. I saw him break free a couple of times and the officer would grab him. Each time Nick would lash out at him, punching out with clenched fists and kicking out in a crazed and determined manner, trying with all his effort to punch the policeman in the head and face as hard as he could. The police officer's face was red where he had been punched, although I could see no blood. As Nick was flailing away the police officer bent forward to duck the punches and at the same time grabbed Nick around the waist and pushed him to the ground. Nick landed on his back and the policeman landed squarely on Nick's front. Sean and the other man carried on standing next to the policeman. They were swearing and saying things like 'get off him or you're dead' and other threats. The crowd was also noisy. During the fight another officer arrived. I don't know where he came from but some of the youths were struggling with him to prevent him from assisting his colleague. I then saw a girl come up to where Nick and the policeman were and tried to pull Nick off the policeman.

Nick shrugged the girl off and continued to kick and punch in a violent manner. It was obvious nothing was going to stop him.

At that stage a whole load of other police officers arrived and a number of the crowd, including Nick and Sean were arrested. I did not see the man in the dark jacket again but I lost sight of a lot of what was going on because of the number of police and onlookers although I did have a clear and uninterrupted view of the incident which lasted for at least 5 to 10 minutes. I have a clear recollection of how red the police officer's face had turned from being repeatedly punched by Nick Spring.

I am willing to attend court and give evidence.

Signed: *D A Ryan*

Signature witnessed by: *C Robinson*

WITNESS STATEMENT

Statement of   Michele Martine Davison . . . .

Age if under 21   19 . . . .

This statement (consisting of **1** pages each signed by me) is true to the best of my knowledge and belief and I make it knowing that, if it is tendered in evidence, I shall be liable to prosecution if I have wilfully stated in it anything which I know to be false or do not believe to be true.

Dated the   14th day of   July   2009

Signature: . . . .*Michele Davison*. . . . .

I live with my husband, 11-month-old son and sister Nuala at an address known to the police.

At about 3.15 pm on 11th July 2009 I noticed an incident outside Fountains House, which is opposite Jervaulx House, involving Nick Spring and his girlfriend. Because I was concerned I asked Nuala to telephone the police when I got back to my flat. After a while a police car arrived and later I saw Nick's girlfriend go with the police officer to his car. At the same time Nick and a number of other men walked down to the phone kiosk at the bottom of the close. Nick was with Sean Baker and Martin Thompson and another man who I don't know. I can't really remember what they were wearing but Martin had a dark jacket on and the other man was wearing white trainers. As they got to the kiosk I saw Nick kick the glass in the kiosk and there was a loud bang as if it had smashed.

The policeman left Nick's girlfriend and walked towards the kiosk. Nick walked towards him with his friends just behind. I then heard Nick say 'he pushed me' pointing behind him with his thumb. At that stage Nick began to turn as if to walk away and the policeman took hold of his right arm. At that they began to struggle and were having a scuffle in the middle of the road. They both fell to the ground, the officer managing to sit on top of Nick and pinning his arms to the ground. After a while a number of other youths came out of Fountains House and joined Nick's friends who were gathered round the officer. Nick was struggling violently and kicking and lashing out at the officer. At one stage I saw one of the group kick the officer's radio away and there was a lot of shouting and swearing and abuse but I couldn't understand what was being said.

After a while another police officer arrived and he was set on by some of the youths from Fountains House. They were trying to stop him interfering with Nick Spring. I saw the girl get out of the car and go up to the group. I then saw one of the group, I think it was the male with the white trainers, approach the policeman who was restraining Nick and with great force kicked the officer directly in the face. The blow was with such force that the policeman's head went back and he lost his grip on Nick. Then a number of the group started to punch and kick the officer. At that time the other officer was being restrained near the edge of the group. I can't be sure but I think he was on the ground, my main attention was directed towards the first officer who had arrived.

I had already phoned the police during the fight but I became so incensed at their behaviour that I left and phoned again. When I came back I saw that a number of other officers had arrived and the group had dispersed and were being chased by the police. A number of people were arrested and taken away by the police.

I am willing to attend court and give evidence.

Signed: *Michele Dawson*

Signature witnessed by: *C Robinson*

WITNESS STATEMENT

Statement of   Robert Lloyd-Jones . . . .

Age if under 21   . . . . Occupation: Dental Practitioner

This statement (consisting of 1 pages each signed by me) is true to the best of my knowledge and belief and I make it knowing that, if it is tendered in evidence, I shall be liable to prosecution if I have wilfully stated in it anything which I know to be false or do not believe to be true.

Dated the 17th day of July 2009

Signature: *Rlloyd-Jones* . . . .

I am a registered Dental Practitioner and my qualifications are: BDS 1977.

On the 17th July 2009 I examined Martin Kemp and found him to be suffering from psychological trauma associated with dental trauma.

On examination the upper right first central incisor was fractured at its distar incisal edge. This has been repaired by an incisal alisecthed restoration but in the long term may become non vital and need further treatment.

There was a fractured filling at the lower right first permanent premolar which was repaired with a routine filling.

There was extensive bruising to the sockets of the upper right molar teeth which was eased and improved by reshaping the occular fillings.

1. The injury to the upper right first central incisor was probably caused by minor trauma (physical force).

2. The fractured filling and the bruising of the sockets of the upper molar teeth may have been caused by stress related to a traumatic incident.

Signed: *Rlloyd-Jones*

Signature witnessed by: *G Jordan*

<u>WITNESS STATEMENT</u>

Statement of   Richard Purkiss BSc...

Age if under 21   ....

This statement (consisting of 1 pages each signed by me) is true to the best of my knowledge and belief and I make it knowing that, if it is tendered in evidence, I shall be liable to prosecution if I have wilfully stated in it anything which I know to be false or do not believe to be true.

Dated the   10th   day of   August   2009

Signature: ....APurkiss...

I am a forensic scientist employed by the Downshire Constabulary. On the 2nd August 2009 I took receipt of exhibit CC/1 a blood specimen labelled John Hanson. I tested the specimen and found it to contain not less than 103 milligrams of alcohol per 100 millilitres of blood.

Signed: APurkiss

Signature witnessed by: S.T. Harcourt

WITNESS STATEMENT

Statement of   Charlotte Craig. Forensic Medical Examiner........................

Age if under 21   ....

This statement (consisting of **1** pages each signed by me) is true to the best of my knowledge and belief and I make it knowing that, if it is tendered in evidence, I shall be liable to prosecution if I have wilfully stated in it anything which I know to be false or do not believe to be true.

Dated the   11th   day of   July   2009

Signature: ...*Charlotte Craig*...

On the 11th July 2009 I was called to Upton Police Station arriving at 21.09 hours. I then examined a man identified to me as John Hanson. I conducted a number of tests on Mr Hanson and as a result of my examination I formed the view that he was drunk and unfit to drive a motor vehicle. He was then asked to provide a specimen of blood which I took from him. I then divided the specimen into two parts labelled CC/JH/1 (container no. 01765) and CC/JH/2 (01766). In my presence Mr Hanson was offered the second container which he refused.

Signed: *Charlotte Craig*

Signature witnessed by: P C H Mansell

<u>WITNESS STATEMENT</u>

Statement of   Michael Kelly ....

Age if under 21   ....

This statement (consisting of **1** pages each signed by me) is true to the best of my knowledge and belief and I make it knowing that, if it is tendered in evidence, I shall be liable to prosecution if I have wilfully stated in it anything which I know to be false or do not believe to be true.

Dated the   12th day of   July   2009

Signature: .....*Michael Kelly*..

I am the owner of Kelly's off-licence in Crewkerne Street, I live in a flat over the shop with my family. On 11th July 2009 at about 6.25 pm. I was at the till when a man burst into the shop. He was white, about 25, 5′ 10″ and had close cropped dark hair. He was wearing a brown jacket, blue shirt, jeans and white trainers. When he came into the shop he was waving his arms around and shouting. As he came up to the till he pulled his jacket over his face and rushed around the side of the counter shouting 'This is a stick up. Get on the floor'. He didn't have any weapon. The shop is well lit having a large front window and the lights were on. I am certain I would be able to recognise him again.

I started to go down on the floor and he pushed me on the neck. As I got to the floor he shouted at me again to open the till. As I turned to open the till I intended to grab him around the waist or the legs but Francis came running across and pushed him over me and into a display by the front window. I got up and as Francis appeared to be dealing with matters I decided the best thing was to ring the police. The male was shouting all the time this was going on and thrashing around. I tried to keep an eye on what was going on. I saw the male strike Francis on the nose and he then got up charged at me and shouted 'Ring the fucking police and you're dead'. He pushed me over again and ran out of the shop. Francis chased after him and I carried on contacting the police.

I am willing to attend court.

Signed: *Michael Kelly*

Signature witnessed by: *R Keith*

<u>WITNESS STATEMENT</u>

Statement of   Francis Kelly7 . . . .

Age if under 21   . . . .

This statement (consisting of **1** pages each signed by me) is true to the best of my knowledge and belief and I make it knowing that, if it is tendered in evidence, I shall be liable to prosecution if I have wilfully stated in it anything which I know to be false or do not believe to be true.

Dated the   12th   day of   July   2009

Signature: . . . . . *Francis Kelly* . . . .

I am the above named and live at the address overleaf. I am employed by my brother Michael at his off-licence in Crewkerne Street. On 11th July 2009 I was in the shop in the store room at the back of the shop when at about 6.25 pm. I heard a man shouting at Michael to get on the floor. I went to the door of the stock room and saw a man about 25–30, 6′ tall with a blue jacket, black jeans and trainers pushing Michael by the neck. The shop is well lit and the lights were on. I would recognise him again. As he was pushing Michael he also started to hit him and he was screaming at him to open the till. I couldn't see if he was armed or had a weapon but as he had his back to me I ran at him and pushed him over Michael into a display near the window.

After he had fallen into the display I leaped on him and we started to fight. He was obviously drunk and struggled very violently. The next thing I knew he had punched me in the face and caused me to loosen my grip on him. With that he got up and ran over to Michael who was at the telephone. He shouted out 'Call the police and you're fucking dead' and then ran out of the shop colliding with a customer who was coming through the door.

I was dazed but managed to run after him and chased him part of the way down the street to the junction with Crown Street. As I got to the corner I saw him getting into a metallic blue Vauxhall Cavalier which drove down Crown Street in the direction of the Old Market Place. I did not see any one else in the vehicle and I did not manage to take the registration number of the car although I think it was 'Y' registered.

I would be willing to attend court.

Signed: *Francis Kelly*

Signature witnessed by: *R Keith*

DOWNSHIRE CONSTABULARY   Form MG15(T)
RECORD OF TAPE RECORDED INTERVIEW

Person interviewed	Nicholas SPRING	Police Exhibit No TH1
Place of interview	UPTON POLICE STATION	Number of pages 3
Date of interview	11.07.09	
Time commenced	20.03	**Time concluded** 20.24
Duration of interview	21 MINS	**Tape Reference no's** 101124
Interviewing Officer(s)	WPC 7 ROBINSON	
Other persons present	DC 431 COLE, Mr J ARCHER (SOLICITOR)	

Tape counter times	Person speaking	Text
001		INTRODUCTION TO INTERVIEW. CAUTIONED
054		WPC ROBINSON explained that SPRING had been arrested at 3.30 pm following an incident at the Abbey Estate involving SPRING and others.
0410		General discussion about the estate and who lived with SPRING including SEAN BAKER, MARTIN THOMPSON, ANTHONY MEAD AND JOHN HANSON.
0715	ROBINSON	Nick, why did you assault PC KEMP?
	SPRING	I didn't, he assaulted me. I went to speak to him after he shouted out to me, when Charlie was about to get in his car. We met in the road and he put his hand up and grabbed my arm ...
	COLE	Which arm?
	SPRING	My right one. I pushed him away and he grabbed me round the neck and pulled me to the ground.
		WPC Robinson then reads the first half of PC Kemp's statement.
	ROBINSON	You were clearly told you were under arrest but you were looking for a fight as your girlfriend was going off with PC Kemp.
	SPRING	No. KEMP is enormous you'd have to be fucking mad to fight him ...
1020	COLE	But you did Nick, didn't you.
	SPRING	No, I defended myself, he was strangling me.
	ROBINSON	Who else was there?
	SPRING	The BAKERS, LOUIS BUCKNALL, TONY, JOHN, ...
	ROBINSON	JOHN who?
	SPRING	HANSON.
	ROBINSON	You said earlier that he was living with you
	SPRING	Yes
	ROBINSON	In the fight PC KEMP was kicked in the face. He is seriously injured. Who kicked him?
	SPRING	JOHN.
	ROBINSON	But you told him to.
	SPRING	Never. I'm asthmatic, KEMP was strangling me, I couldn't breathe and I just shouted to get off, to get him off ...
1215	ROBINSON	Reads remainder of PC KEMP'S statement. You told HANSON to kick him in the face.

	SPRING	I didn't. HANSON kicked him in the face. He hates KEMP because he got him sent down last time. I just wanted KEMP to stop throttling me so I asked for help.
	ROBINSON	You threatened to put him out on the street.
1500	SPRING	That's rubbish, HANSON could always go and live in another squat or with his Mum or girlfriend, he didn't have to stay with me.

Further questions and discussion about the fight. SPRING Stated that he was too pre-occupied with what was going on with PC KEMP to notice anything else. He agreed that HANSON had kicked the radio away. He also stated that a number of the others appeared to have kicked or punched PC KEMP but denied that he encouraged them in any way.

INTERVIEW CONCLUDES 20.24 HOURS.

DOWNSHIRE CONSTABULARY   Form MG15(T)
RECORD OF TAPE RECORDED INTERVIEW

Person interviewed	John HANSON	Police Exhibit No TH1
Place of interview	UPTON POLICE STATION	Number of pages 3
Date of interview	12.07.09	
Time commenced	20.07	**Time concluded** 12.45
Duration of interview	38 MINS	**Tape Reference no's** 101137
Interviewing Officer(s)	WPC 7 ROBINSON	
Other persons present	DC 431 COLE, Mr J ARCHER (SOLICITOR)	

Tape counter times	Person Speaking	Text
001		INTRODUCTION TO INTERVIEW. CAUTIONED
024		WPC ROBINSON explained that HANSON had been arrested at 19.30 hours by police on suspicion of an assault at Kelly's off-licence.
0350		Discussion regarding what HANSON had been doing prior to the incident. He stated that he had been drinking throughout the day. He'd been to 3 pubs, the last being the Ratcatcher. He cannot remember anything after the Ratcatcher. He was drinking cider and might have had some lager and whisky. He cannot remember going into Kelly's and was not aware until told by an Inspector during his detention.
0900		WPC Robinson read excerpts from Mr F Kelly's statement but HANSON could still not remember. Discussion of injuries received, he stated he had a cut wrist and a sore neck and shoulder.
1100		Discussion regarding statement by Mr Kelly.
1415	WPC 7	So you can't remember any of that?
	HANSON	No, not at all, no.
1530		WPC Robinson showed HANSON the custody record where the Custody Sergeant had written his reply when being booked in. HANSON could not remember saying 'All I tried to do was rob the place'.
1850		DC Cole asked HANSON to describe his clothing and self.
	HANSON	About 5'11", dark hair.
	COLE	Brown wouldn't you say.
	HANSON	Brown, darkish anyway, I'm wearing a brown jacket, blue denim shirt, black denim jeans, white trainers. Green brown eyes.
	COLE	Darkish skinned?
	HANSON	No.
	COLE	With cropped hair.
	HANSON	Close cut, not cropped.
	COLE	Well I'd say cropped.
	HANSON	That's for you.
2000	SOLICITOR	That can be determined, you've taken his photo.
	COLE	Yes. You know Nick Spring?
	HANSON	Yes.
	COLE	And you've been staying with him at Fountains House?
	HANSON	Yes, for about the last week.

	COLE	Since you were released from prison.
		Yesterday afternoon there was an incident on the Abbey Estate involving Spring. Where were you at 3.30 yesterday?
	HANSON	I think I was in the 'Coach' with VICKY BRYANT.
		Discussion regarding Vicky Bryant and where she lives.
2215	COLE	What about the car you were driving. Is that yours?
	HANSON	What car?
	COLE	Come off it John, the one you were driving when you were nicked.
	HANSON	I can't drive.
	COLE	That's what the arresting officer said.
	HANSON	I've had enough of this.
	ROBINSON	Whose car is it CLP 853Y a blue Cavalier.
	HANSON	It's not mine, I don't have a car.
	ROBINSON	You were driving it, whose is it?
	HANSON	I've had enough, I don't feel well.
	ROBINSON	You look fine to me. Whose is it?
	HANSON	No comment. I want to speak to Mr Archer.
	Tape off.	
2500	SOLICITOR	My client finds your manner aggressive. He is unwell and is currently being treated by his GP. On legal advice he does not wish to answer any further questions at this stage.
2515		Further matters put to HANSON who declines to comment.
2900		Interview terminated.

DOWNSHIRE CONSTABULARY

C.R. No.   7651/05

Division   A   **Date**   14th July 2009

Antecedents of: (full name)   John Hanson

Committed from   Upton   **Magistrates' Court on**   17th July 2009

For trial/sentence at   Upton Crown   Court

for offence(s) of   Grievous Bodily Harm with intent, Violent Disorder, Robbery

---

Date and place of birth: 12.04.85, Temple Newsome   **Age:** 24 years

Date of first entry into U.K.: n/a   **Nationality:** British

Date of arrest: 11.07.09, Remanded in custody   **In custody/on bail:** In custody

Education: 1996–2001 Bishop Cross School, Disbury Bridge.
            2001–2002 Upton Technical College

Main employments since leaving school

2002–2005	Royal Artillery Bombadier		
2005–2007	Unemployed		
2008	Sherratts Furniture	Labourer	Dismissed for theft
2009	Unemployed		

Present employment: (Show date of commencement, capacity in which employed, net salary/wage and employer's assessment.)

Hanson is unemployed and in receipt of income support. Amount not disclosed.

At the time of his arrest he was a single man living with friends at 27 Fountains House, Abbot's Down, Abbey Estate, Upton, Downshire.

Hanson does not hold a firearms/shotgun certificate.

At time of the offence Hanson was on licence from Portsmouth Prison. He was released on 28.06.09 having served 2 months of a 4 month sentence for ABH, theft and kindred offences.

List of previous convictions attached:

Offences against the person: 1	Theft and kindred offences:	11
Offences against property: 3	Public Order offences:	2
Fraud and kindred offences: 0	Others:	0

If recently fined state whether paid or not: None traced

Date of last release from custodial sentence: 28.06.09

Names of co-prisoners (if dealt with elsewhere, give details):

<u>DOWNSHIRE CONSTABULARY</u>

PREVIOUS CONVICTIONS

Convictions recorded against: John Hanson   CRO No: 7651/05
Charged in name of: John Hanson   *Denotes spent conviction

Date	Court	Offence(s) (with details of any offence)	Sentence	Date of Release
12.05.05	Driffield Mags	Theft × 3	CSO 100 hours	
		Taking without consent	CSO 100 hours	
		Criminal Damage	£135.00 compensation	
18.10.05	Alderley Mags	Theft × 2	6 months Young Offenders Institution	
		S. 4 Public Order Act	2 months Y.O.	
		Breach CSO	6 months Y.O. concurrent	18.01.03
11.6.06	Upton Crown Court	Deception × 3	Probation 2 years	
31.08.07	Upton Crown Court	Aggravated vehicle Taking	6 months' Imprisonment L/E Disqualified 1 year	30.11.05
		Affray	4 months' imp concurrent	
		Making off without Payment	2 months' imp Concurrent	
29.06.09	Driffield Mags	Actual Bodily Harm	4 months' imprisonment	28.06.06

DOWNSHIRE CONSTABULARY

C.R. No. ___3741/06___

Division ___A___ **Date** ___14th July 2009___

Antecedents of: (full name) ___Nicholas Spring___

Committed from ___Upton___ **Magistrates' Court on** ___17th July 2009___

For trial/sentence at ___Upton Crown___ **Court**

for offence(s) of ___Grievous Bodily Harm with intent, Violent Disorder___

Date and place of birth: 21.06.88, Driffield   **Age:** 21 years

Date of first entry into U.K.: n/a   **Nationality:** British

Date of arrest: 11.07.09, Remanded on bail   **In custody/on bail:** on bail

Education: 1997–2004 Upton Comprehensive
                    2004–2006 Upton Technical College

Main employments since leaving school

2004–2007   Various periods of unemployment with casual labouring jobs
2007–2008   Floral Garden Centre.

Present employment: (Show date of commencement, capacity in which employed, net salary/wage and employer's assessment.)

Spring works as a labourer at the Floral Garden Centre, Driffield, earning £160 a week gross, £133.95 net.

At the time of his arrest he was a single man living at 27 Fountains House, Abbot's Down, Abbey Estate, Upton, Downshire.

Spring does not hold a firearms/shotgun certificate.

List of previous convictions attached:

Offences against the person: 0	**Theft and kindred offences:** 2
Offences against property: 1	**Public Order offences:** 1
Fraud and kindred offences: 0	**Others:** 0

If recently fined state whether paid or not: None traced

Date of last release from custodial sentence: n/a

Names of co-prisoners (if dealt with elsewhere, give details):

DOWNSHIRE CONSTABULARY

PREVIOUS CONVICTIONS

Convictions recorded against: Nicholas Spring   CRO No: 3741/06
Charged in name of: Nicholas Spring   *Denotes spent conviction

Date	Court	Offence(s) (with details of any offence)	Sentence	Date of Release
15.06.06	Upton Mags	Theft	Conditional Discharge 12 months	
17.12.06		Taking vehicle Without consent	CSO 60 hours	
		Criminal Damage	CSO 60 hours concurrent	
		Breach of Conditional Discharge	CSO 60 hours Concurrent	
31.08.08	Upton Crown Court	Affray	Community Order 12 months	

STATEMENT OF JOHN HANSON

I, John Hanson, of HMP Ardington, will say as follows:

I am currently on remand at HMP Ardington and have been since the 11th July. I left full time education in 2002 when I was 17. I had 6 GCSEs and I decided because things were not good at home to join the army. I served in the army for 3 years including a period in Afghanistan where I witnessed a number of very traumatic incidents. As a result I have felt far from well since then. In particular I had been prescribed Prozac from about May by the prison doctors. I am not sure if this led to my loss of memory on the 11th July. It may also explain why I behaved as I am alleged to have behaved in the off-licence. I discovered that the bottle of Prozac which I had contained 4 less tablets than it should. I have never been warned against taking Prozac and alcohol together although I now understand that mixing the two can be dangerous.

On the 11th July I was living at 27 Fountains House on the Abbey estate in Upton. I had only been released from prison two weeks before from a sentence of 4 months' imprisonment imposed by Driffield Magistrates on the 29th April. I was living with Nick Spring at Fountains House but my girlfriend, Vicky Bryant, had offered me a place at her house at 13 Onyx Close, Upton and I was due to move there on the 12th. I was also able to live with my Mother in Driffield but because of the events which led to my imprisonment in April I was not anxious to move there. I have known Nick since 2007 and we were co-defendants in the charge that led to me being imprisoned in August of 2007. I was at that time working for Sherratts furniture as a labourer but lost my job, not because of theft, but because I was imprisoned.

On the 11th July I received some money (£850) from an inheritance and I decided to celebrate. The Cavalier is Vicky Bryant's. I had borrowed it the day before to get back from Vicky's place. I left Fountains House about 10 am and collected the cheque from Chapmans (the solicitors in Upton) and then arranged to get some money from the bank. I had left the car and the keys at Fountains House. I left the bank at about 12.30 pm and went straight to The Three Bells in Bow Avenue, Upton. It is my local and I am well known by the staff and many of the regulars there. I was there until about 2.30–3.00 pm when I left and went to the Coach and Horses where I met up with Vicky Bryant and some of her friends. The Coach and Horses is also in Bow Road and is only a five-minute walk from the Three Bells. I also saw one or two other people I knew in the pub. I left there and went to the Ratcatcher in Upton High Street. I can't remember how much I had had to drink by this time but I know it was a lot. When I got to the Ratcatcher it was about 4 pm Tony a bloke who was also staying with Nick came in with Louis Bucknell, Simon Bratt, Kieran Bratt and a load of others. I could see that he had the keys to the Cavalier. They were all drunk or stoned. We had a row about him driving it and I took the keys back. They all then left. I was pretty drunk by this time and until I woke in the Police Station that is about all I can remember.

I have no recollection of going back to the Abbey Estate. I have spoken to Vicky and she is sure that I was with her at about 3 o'clock. I left her and went to the 'Rat' to meet a friend of mine called Frank. I owed him £50 and had arranged to pay him back. As far as I know I did but I haven't seen him since and although Vicky and some of my friends have been trying to find him it may not be easy as he is a 'traveller'.

I do not dispute that I was in Kelly's off-licence and I understand that I am on the in-store video. I would like advice on my plea as I have, once again, no recollection of what took place there and no recollection of what I am alleged to have said to the custody sergeant at Upton Police station.

CUSTODY RECORD Police & Criminal Evidence Act 1984

Police Station   Force/Station reference

ARREST	DETAINEE

ARREST

Comments made: YES/~~NO~~

Where arrested: Upton Road in Lymehurst Road

Arrested by:
Name: Keith
Rank/No: 375   Station: Upton
Time of arrest: 1932 Date: 11.7.09
Time of arrival at Station: 1943 Date: 11.7.09

DETENTION AUTHORISED

Attempted robbery

To obtain evidence by questioning

Comments made: YES/~~NO~~
Name: P Waller   Rank/No: P58

Signature: P Waller   Time: Date: 11.7.09

DETAINEE

Surname: Hanson
Forenames: John
Address: 27 Fountains House
Abbey Estate
Upton

Occupation: Unemployed
Age: 24   Date of Birth: 12.4.85
Place of Birth: Newton Abbot
Height: 5'11'   Sex: M
Ethnic Appearance: Caucasian
Nationality: British

Officer in case
Name: Cole
Rank/No: DC

Officer opening record
Name: Waller
Rank/No: P58

Signature: P Waller

PRISONERS RIGHTS

1. A notice setting out my rights has been read to me and I have also been provided with a written notice setting out my entitlements whilst in custody.

   Signature: John Hanson   Time: 1945 Date: 11.7.09

   Notices of the detained persons rights and entitlements have been read to me and I have received a copy of each. I have been informed of the Grounds for the detention of the detained person.

   Appropriate Adult   n/a   Signature   Time: Date:

2. I DO require somebody to be informed of my arrest.

   Signature: John Hanson   Time: 1945 Date: 11.7.09

   Nominated Person: V Bryant
   Address/Contact no:

3. I DO require a solicitor as soon as practicable.

   Signature: John Hanson   Time: 1945 Date: 11.7.09

   Nominated Solicitor: D. Sol.

   Appropriate Adult: n/a   Signature: Time: Date:

MEDICAL DETAILS

Are you currently:– Receiving medication
Suffering any illness/injury
Suffering any infirmity

Remarks:–   Intoxicated

(FormCustody) 04/04/1995

CUSTODY RECORD (Property) Police & Criminal Evidence Act 1984

Police Station Upton   Force/Stn ref SOBE/00317/09 Date: 11·7·09

Detained Person Surname: Hanson

Forenames: John

Property retained by Police: re value, prevent harm/damage, interfere with evidence or effect an escape			
Description: Bottle Prozac tablets	Qty: 1	Value: N/K	Seal: 00356113
Description: Lighter	Qty: 1	Value:	Seal: ,,
Description: Belt	Qty:	Value:	Seal: ,,
Description: Wallet + various corresp	Qty:	Value:	Seal: ,,
Description: £75 (7×10, 1×5) notes	Qty:	Value:	Seal: ,,
Description: £4·36 (3×1, 2×50 + change)	Qty:	Value:	Seal: ,,

Property retained by Person at own risk

Description: Qty: Value:

   1   Packet B + H cigs

   1   comb (plastic)

The above is a true record. Property retained by me is at my own risk.

Signature of detainee	Signature of Custody Officer *P Waller*	Name: WALLER P Rank/No: 585
Refused to sign	Signature of Witness *K Simpson*	Name: SIMPSON K Rank/No: PC 171

I have received all property listed above, subject to any variation shown in the custody record log.

Signature of person receiving	Signature of witness	Name: Rank/No:

Detainee searched by

Signature *K Simpson*	Name: SIMPSON K Rank/No: PC 171

(FrmPtyCus1) Ver 1 Feb 95

RECORD OF PERSONAL PROPERTY

Sub-Divisional Custody No. SOBE.l0o3l7l09

RECORD OF PERSONAL PROPERTY		RECORD OF PERSONAL PROPERTY CONTINUED	
Denominations of Notes	**Cash Totals**		
10×7 : 5×1	Notes £ 75		
	£ Coin £ 4		
	Silver £ 20		
	Bronze . 16		
	TOTAL £ 79-36		
Item	**Other Property**		
1	Prozac tablets	Searched by (sign) *Kinger* .	
2	Lighter	Items ....3.+.6........................	
3	Cigarettes	I wish to retain the above items at my own risk	
4	Wallet + coins	Signature ....Refused...................	
5	Belt	Seal No. 0035611B	
6	Comb (plastic)	Officer Sealing (sign) *Kinger* .	
		Witness (sign) *P Walter*	
		Property Locker No. 7	
		PROPERTY SUBJECT OF CHARGE	
		None	
		Property Seal No.	
		Officer Sealing (Sign)	
		Witness (Sign)	
		Special Property Reg. No.	

DOWNSHIRE CONSTABULARY

Detainee's Name: John Hanson

Any comments made after reasons for arrest given:

> ' I only tried to rob the place '

Any comments made after grounds for detention explained:

Any reasons given for not requiring legal advice:

Signed: *P Ulculler*   Rank/No: P 58

DOWNSHIRE CONSTABULARY

CONTINUATION OF CUSTODY RECORD

Page No.	5

Last review of detention conducted at .....1945.....

Sub-Divisional Custody No. ...SQBF./...QO.3.17/...09.........

Name .....HANSON.....

Date	Time	Full details of any action/occurrence involving detained person (include full particulars of all visitors/officers) Individual entries need not be restricted to one line All entries to be signed by the writer	Signature
11.7.09	1945	Fit + well. Detention authorised.	PS8
	1955	To cell (8). Check every 15 mins due to state of dp.	"
	2010	Checked in cell; asleep.	"
	2025	ditto	"
	2040	ditto	"
	2055	ditto	"
	2110	Checked in cell; asleep. Woken for ex by RME. Blood with consent. Concluded 2119. On arrest suspect stated in response to caution 'I only tried to rob the place'. Pillaller	PS8
	2125	Awake. In cell. Refreshment + tea provided.	"
	2140	Awake drinking tea.	"
	2155	Asleep	"
	2210	ditto	"
	2225	Wakened to check alright	"
	2240	Asleep	
	2255	Asleep.	
	23:10	Asleep:- To be checked every 30 mins.	PS34
	23:40	"	"
12/7/09	00:10	Asleep	"
	00:40	"	"
	01:10	"	"
	01:45	Further detention authorised to obtain evidence by questioning. Review at 07:45. Check every hour.	"

DOWNSHIRE CONSTABULARY

CONTINUATION OF CUSTODY RECORD

| | Page No. | 6 |

| Last review of detention conducted at .....0.14.5.... | Sub-Divisional Custody No. ....SOBE./.00.317./.09......... |
| | Name ......HANSON............ |

Date	Time	Full details of any action/occurrence involving detained person (include full particulars of all visitors/officers) Individual entries need not be restricted to one line All entries to be signed by the writer	Signature
12/7/09	02:45	Asleep	PS34
	03:45	Awake. Provided with tea + light.	PS34
	04·45	Asleep.	"
	05:45	Asleep.	"
	06:45	Asleep.	"
	0730	Review. Further detention authorised. Breakfast provided and light for cigs	PS15
	0845	Awake, wishes to see D/solicitor	PS15
	0915	Duty Sol unavailable	PS15
	0935	D. Sol phoned. Unavailable until 1100 am	PS15
	0947	Phone enquiry from V Bryant. Access to DIP refused.	PS15
	1133	D/Sol (Mr Archer) arrives in custody area. DIP to solicitors for consultation.	PS15
	1145	Back to cell 5 pending interview	PS15
	1200	Out of cell for interview.	PS15
	1257	Interview concluded, back to cell 7	PS15
	1310	Out of cell. Charged. Bail refused. To MC for 2 pm hearing	PS15

Custody Record No: SOBE/00317/09

Station: Upton

**DOWNSHIRE POLICE
CHARGE SHEET**

CUSTODY RECORD

PERSON CHARGED: John Hanson

ADDRESS 22 Fountain's House, Abbey Estate, Upton

PLACE/DATE OF BIRTH Newton Abbot/12.4.85 OCCUPATION Unemployed

You are charged with the offence shown below.
You do not have to say anything. But it may harm your defence if you do not mention <u>now</u> something which you later rely on in court. Anything you do say may be given in evidence.

OF61019

1) On the 11th July being present with Nicholas Spring Martin Thompson, Sean Baker, Louis Bucknell, Simon Bratt and Anthony Mead used unlawful violence and this conduct (taken together) was such as would cause a person of reasonable firmness present at the scene to fear for his personal safety, contrary to section 2(1) of the Public Order Act 1986.

Reply: None

Officer in case: D.C. Cole
Station: Upton

Date Charged: 12th July 2009

Signature of person charging: Richard Cole

Signature of Officer accepting charge: Peter Maxwell.

Legal Aid forms served by:
Notices served:

Bail: Refused

DOWNSHIRE CONSTABULARY

Full Name John Hanson	Custody No SO3E / 00317 / 09

CONTINUATION OF CHARGES

You are charged with the offence(s) shown below. You do not have to say anything. But it may harm your defence if you do not mention now something which you later rely on in court. Anything you do say may be given in evidence.

2) On 11th July 2009 at Augustian Grove, Abbey Estate, Upton, unlawfully and maliciously caused grievous bodily harm to PC37 Martin Kemp with intent to cause grievous bodily harm, contrary to s. 18 of the Offences Against the Person Act 1861.

3) On the 11th July, attempted to rob Kelly's off-licence, contrary to s. 1(1) of the Criminal Attempts Act 1981.

4) On the 11th July 2009 at Upton Road junction with Lymehurst Road, drove a motor vehicle whist unfit through drink and drugs, contrary to s. 4(1) of the Road Traffic Act 1988.

Continuation Sheet   Yes   No

Reply (if any) ....
.... Time/Date...13. 10/12:7:09..
Signed (Person reading charge) ...Richard Cole........... Rank/No....DC 341.................
Signed (Custody Officer) ...Peter Maxwell................... Rank/No....DSIS.....................

Officer in Case: Name ...R. Cole..... Rank/No ..DC431.......... Station ....Upton................

DOWNSHIRE CONSTABULARY
CRIME COMPLAINT/REPORT

Upton

M. F. No. ...1263...............

Area ..(Abbey Estate) Sub. Div ...6............... Div.....F8.............
(Where Committed)

C. R. No. ...1054...............

SEE NOTES FOR GUIDANCE ON COVER

H.Q.'s USE ONLY	

CRIME COMPLAINT

1. OFFENCE AS REPORTED .....G.B.H..........
2. REF (TIME AND DATE REPORTED) ...1538......... TO WHOM REPORTED ....
3. NAME AND ADDRESS OF PERSON REPORTING ...Not given. Report.......... from telephone box on Abbey Estate. TEL. NO. —
4. ACTION TAKEN AND BY WHOM ...Vehicles despatched..............

H.Q. use only
H.Q. Classification ....

CRIME REPORT

5. NAME/ADDRESS OF INJURED PERSON ...Martin Kemp PC 37...... ....c/o Upton Police Station......... TEL. NO. — AGE .29.
6. PLACE, TIME, DAY, DATE OF OFFENCE ....1530. Abbey Estate.......... ....Augustian Close........ 11 July 2009......
   MAP REF: ....C6...
7. INJURY TO VICTIM. FATAL ...... SERIOUS ✓. SLIGHT ...... THREATS .... NONE .... TYPE OF WEAPON USED ......Foot...........
8. TYPE OF PREMISES (NOTE 1) .....Abbey Estate...............
9. METHOD (NOTE 2) ....
   Police officer investigating report of fight (see
   CR 1052) set upon by youths. Initial telephone
   report supplemented by officers who attended
   scene and victim who was attacked by N. Spring
   and then kicked in the face by suspect wearing blue
   jacket and jeans and white trainers
10. OFFENCE DETECTED YES/NO ....
11. DESCRIPTION OF SUSPECT OR VEHICLE USED ...Suspect decamped..... ...in blue Vauxhall...............

STOLEN		RECOVERED	
£	p	£	p

12. PROPERTY STOLEN/DAMAGED (NOTE 3)

   .....1 police radio. Value.....
   ...not known......................

TOTAL

13. ENQUIRY TYPE   NEIGH. WATCH AREA   PRIMARY INVESTIGATOR

Child Abuse		Yes	✓	Uniform	✓
Domestic Violence		No		C.I.D.	
Other	✓				

Sample advice and defence statement in *R v Hanson and others*

IN THE CROWN COURT SITTING AT OXTON   T0155/09

REGINA

v

JOHN HANSON

and

OTHERS

ADVICE ON EVIDENCE

1. John Hanson is charged with Violent Disorder contrary to s 2 of the Public Order Act 1986, Causing Grievous Bodily Harm with Intent to Resist Arrest contrary to s 18 of the Offences Against the Person Act 1861, Attempted Robbery contrary to s 1(1) of the Criminal Attempts Act 1981 and Driving Whilst Unfit Through Drink or Drugs contrary to s 4(1) of the Road Traffic Act 1988. On the 17th July Mr Hanson was sent to the Oxton Crown Court to stand trial and his Plea and Case Management Hearing is listed for the 21st August. I am asked to advise John Hanson, on evidence and plea.

The alleged offences

2. The charges of violent disorder and assault arise from an incident on the Abbey Estate, in which a police officer, PC Kemp, sustained a number of quite serious injuries. The prosecution case is that after the officer had attempted to mediate between Mr Spring and his girlfriend, he was punched by Mr Spring. While he was in the process of arresting Mr Spring, PC Kemp was set upon by a group of young men and was repeatedly kicked by his assailants. John Hanson is alleged to have kicked the officer's radio away from him and kicked him in the face. The crowd dispersed when a number of other officers arrived and arrested several of the participants, including Mr Spring.

3. As far as the charge of attempted robbery is concerned, this arises from an incident at an off-licence in which a man, said to be John Hanson, burst in, pulled his jacket over his face and demanded that the owner open the till and give him money. The would-be robber was frustrated by the entry of the owner's brother, whom he punched before escaping. No weapon was involved. Mr Hanson was arrested while he was in

a car about an hour later, apparently on the basis that he and the car answered the description given by the witnesses at the off-licence.

Summary

4. In summary, Mr Hanson's instructions suggest a plea of not guilty on all counts, with the exception of the driving charge. There are defects and discrepancies in the evidence against him, such that his chances of an acquittal on the violent disorder and assault charges are good. Until more information has been received regarding the attempted robbery, it is difficult to evaluate his chances on that count. There are a number of steps which need to be taken by instructing solicitors in the next few days to prepare for trial, and these are set out in paragraph 21.

5. A draft defence statement has been prepared and is appended to this advice. Please note that the defence statement should not be served on the CPS or the court until the CPS have complied with their duties of disclosure. Following service of the unused material schedule the defence statement should be amended to include any unused material sought.

Misjoinder

6. It would be in Mr Hanson's interests for the charges of attempted robbery and driving while unfit to be separated from those arising from the attack on PC Kemp. The counts in question do not appear to arise from the same facts, nor are they part of a series of offences of the same or similar character. Therefore, they do not meet the requirements of Crim PR, r.14.2(3). I would advise that a motion to quash the indictment on the grounds that it is invalid be made at the Plea and Case Management Hearing. It would be open to the prosecution to apply either for Counts 3 and 4 to be deleted or for leave to be granted to prefer two fresh indictments out of time, one containing Counts 1 and 2 and the other containing Counts 3 and 4. The original indictment could then be stayed. In my view, the prosecution are most likely to pursue the latter course to which the judge will almost certainly agree.

Assault and violent disorder

7. As far as the counts of violent disorder and causing grievous bodily harm are concerned, Mr Hanson's primary defence is that of alibi. There is some doubt about this, in that his recollection of the events of the afternoon is unclear, and there is no statement as yet from Vicky Bryant or any of the others who may have been present in the various public houses in question that afternoon. It follows that those instructing me should as a matter of urgency take statements from these potential alibi witnesses. In doing so, of course, such times as the witnesses can recollect will be crucial, together with any reasons they might have for remembering dates and times. Those instructing me will no doubt be aware of the provisions of s 6A of the Criminal Procedure and Investigations Act 1996. The date of birth of any alibi witnesses must be given. Where the name or address of the alibi witness in question is not known, information should be given to assist in identifying and finding the witness. At present the only alibi witness I have included in the defence statement is Vicky Bryant. I have been unable to include her date of birth as it is not in the papers I have before me. Once the process of taking statements from the potential alibi witnesses has been completed, it will be necessary to update the defence statement.

8. Mr Hanson's possible defence of alibi throws into question the strength of the prosecution's identification evidence. The evidence as to Mr Hanson's presence depends largely on what PC Kemp says about 'Man 2', whom the prosecution allege to be Mr Hanson, and the consistency between the description of that man and Mr Hanson

on arrest. When PC Kemp's description of the man who assaulted him is compared with PC Keith's description of Mr Hanson on arrest and Mr Hanson's description of himself in interview, it is apparent that there are a number of similar features. However, by itself the description is rather bland and could fit a large number of people.

9. The prosecution's case is strengthened by three other pieces of evidence. First, in her statement Nuala Carroll says, 'I also think I recognised John Hanson in the crowd that had gathered round'. PACE 1984 Code D 3.12 requires that whenever a witness has purported to identify a suspect and the suspect disputes being the person the witness claims to have seen then an identification procedure must be held unless it is not practicable or would serve no useful purpose. If Mr Hanson is particularly well known to Ms Carroll then the police decision not to hold an identification procedure may be justifiable. However, there is nothing to suggest that this is the case on the face of the papers and it would appear that the police were under a duty to hold an identification procedure. If so, there is a strong argument for excluding her purported identification under s 78 PACE 1984 at trial. The courts will take a breach of Code D3.12 very seriously and, if there has been a breach in this case, there is a likelihood that Ms Carroll's identification will be excluded at trial.

10. Second, the man in the brown jacket (who is apparently, on the prosecution's case, Mr Hanson) drove off in a blue Vauxhall Cavalier—the same colour and make of car as Mr Hanson was driving when he was arrested (see PC Keith's statement). PC Robinson noted that the first three letters of the registration were 'CLP'. The registration of the car Mr Hanson was driving began with the letters 'CLY'. However, I note that Mr Hanson has given an explanation as to how Tony Mead came to be driving the car and it may be that he was the man seen getting into the car.

11. Third, PC Kemp recalls that Mr Spring shouted at the group and in particular started at 'Man 2' to 'Get him off me...or you're out of my house and back on the fucking street'. It is clear from the custody record that Mr Hanson gave Mr Spring's house as his address. However, Mr Hanson states in his proof of evidence that Anthony Mead was also staying at Spring's house and so Spring could equally have been directing his words to him. Copies of the transcripts of the interviews with the other defendants, and in particular Anthony Mead, should be obtained to see whether they contain any statements supporting Mr Hanson's case.

12. In my view, the identification of Mr Hanson as a participant in the assault is relatively weak. In the light of this, it is very surprising that no prosecution witnesses appear to have been invited to attend an identification procedure in accordance with PACE Code D, and the police failure in this regard can clearly be raised at trial in order to underline the weakness of the evidence of Mr Hanson's presence. Incidentally, it appears from Mr Spring's interview that PC Kemp knew Mr Hanson, and was responsible for his conviction on an earlier offence. The facts surrounding this allegation need to be ascertained from Mr Hanson. If it is true, it means that PC Kemp's failure to mention that he recognised 'Man 2' means that it is very unlikely that it was Mr Hanson.

13. In the interview Mr Spring stated that Mr Hanson was a participant in the violent disorder and assaulted PC Kemp by kicking him in the face, an action which PC Kemp attributed to 'Man 2'. The interview is not evidence against Mr Hanson and an application should be made to exclude the prejudicial parts of it at trial under s 78 PACE 1984. In my view, the trial judge is likely to accede to this application.

14. If Mr Spring gives evidence at trial to the same effect as his interview the jury will have to decide which, if either, defendant they believe. Mr Spring may attempt

to support his case by seeking to adduce evidence of Mr Hanson's bad character, although no application is disclosed in the papers. Under s 101(1)(e) of the Criminal Justice Act 2003, a defendant's bad character may be admitted where it has substantial probative value in relation to an important matter in issue between the defendant and a co-defendant. Mr Spring may argue that Mr Hanson has a propensity to commit offences of violence and that this propensity is of substantial probative value as it makes Mr Spring's account of Mr Hanson's role in the incident more credible. Mr Hanson has previous convictions for offences under s 4 of the Public Order Act 1986, Affray and Actual Bodily Harm which may be capable of establishing such a propensity. If I am provided with the details of his previous convictions, I will be able to give Mr Hanson further advice about the likely outcome of any application made by Mr Spring. From Mr Hanson's proof of evidence it appears that he does not propose to give evidence against Mr Spring and, as a result, evidence of Mr Hanson's bad character will not be admissible in relation to the issue of his credibility.

15. I note that Mr Spring also has previous convictions. If Mr Spring gives evidence which is consistent with what he says in interview, he will be deemed to have given evidence against Mr Hanson and evidence of Mr Spring's previous convictions will be admissible. While not every previous conviction is capable of having substantial probative value on that question there is a reasonable prospect that the judge would admit Mr Spring's previous convictions for theft, taking a vehicle without consent and affray for that purpose. Mr Spring also has a previous conviction for affray. It would be open to Mr Hanson to apply to adduce this conviction at trial on the grounds that it shows a propensity to commit offences of the kind with which he is presently charged but I have two reservations. First, as there is only one previous conviction of this nature the judge is unlikely to take the view that it is evidence of propensity. Secondly, it could trigger an application by Mr Spring to adduce Mr Hanson's bad character if one has not been made by that stage of the trial. Mr Hanson was convicted of the same offence on the same occasion and if both previous convictions are ultimately placed before the jury, Mr Spring's conviction is unlikely to advance Mr Hanson's case. However, without knowing the facts of the previous conviction I cannot reach a conclusive view.

16. The effect of Mr Hanson's interview also needs to be considered. The fact that he refused to answer questions relating to the assault could potentially lead to adverse inferences being drawn under s 34 of the Criminal Justice and Public Order Act 1994 which could strengthen the case against him. In order to confirm this, it is necessary to know whether he was cautioned prior to or during the interview about the effect of the refusal to mention matters which he might later wish to make use of in his defence. For this reason, and also to check the accuracy of the transcript generally, I will need to listen to a tape of the interview and would be grateful if those instructing could request a copy from the CPS.

17. As those instructing are aware, under s 101(1)(d) of the Criminal Justice Act 2003, a defendant's character may be admitted as part of the prosecution case where it is relevant to an important matter in issue between the prosecution and the defence. As noted in paragraph 14 above, the court may find that Mr Hanson's previous convictions are evidence of a propensity to commit offences of violence. Such a propensity would most obviously be relevant to the issue of whether Mr Hanson committed the offences of Violent Disorder and Causing Grievous Bodily Harm with Intent. However, the Prosecution may also seek to adduce the evidence in relation to the offence of Attempted Robbery being an offence which involves the use or threat of force. Once I have details of Mr Hanson's previous convictions I will be able to advise

more fully. Should evidence of a propensity to commit offences of violence be admitted in relation to any offences, it will also be relevant to the credibility of Mr Hanson's defence in relation to those charges (*R v Campbell* [2007] 2 Cr App R. 28). With regard to the driving charge, Mr Hanson has no previous convictions for such offences and, as a result, no issues as to his bad character arise.

Attempted robbery

18. As far as the attempted robbery is concerned, there are substantial gaps in the evidence which need to be filled before Mr Hanson can be properly advised. In particular, according to Mr Hanson's proof of evidence, there appears to be an in-store video on which he is alleged to have appeared. A copy of the CCTV footage and Mr Hanson's further instructions on it need to be obtained, so that I can assess its likely evidential weight. Again, there is the failure to hold an identification procedure, which means that, in the absence of an admissible video, the prosecution will find it difficult to prove that it was Mr Hanson who attempted the robbery.

19. In addition, there is the question of the words which Mr Hanson is alleged to have uttered on arrest at the police station: 'I only tried to rob the place'. Its admissibility ought to be challenged, under s 78 of PACE 1984. It is remarkable that the custody record entry for 21:10 hours states that these words were uttered on arrest and yet Mr Hanson had been arrested shortly after 19:30 hours by PC Keith; and was booked in by PS Waller at 19:45 hours. This anomaly needs explanation at the least, and is likely to undermine the admission it contains, even if the judge rules that it is admissible.

20. Leaving aside the question of whether Mr Hanson was involved in the incident at the off-licence, there is the question of whether he had the capacity to form the necessary intent. In his proof of evidence, he raises points relating to his state of mind. In my view it is necessary to obtain expert evidence on the likely effect of the combination of Prozac and alcohol upon his mental state. I would be grateful if instructing solicitors would obtain an expert's report dealing with this issue.

The driving charge

21. The driving charge is stated to have been added to the indictment under s 40 of the Criminal Justice Act 1988. In fact, it cannot have been added under that provision, since 'driving while unfit through drink or drugs' is not one of the charges which appears in s 40. That means that the charge can only have been dealt with at the Crown Court if it was sent under s 51(3) of the Crime and Disorder Act 1998. Sight of the notice listing the offences for which Mr Hanson was sent for trial will settle this question definitively. If the charge was committed by the magistrates under that provision, then it can only be dealt with if Mr Hanson is convicted of one of the indictable offences presently on the indictment and the court is satisfied that the summary offence is related to that offence. If it was not sent to the Crown Court under s 51 by the magistrates, then it cannot in any event be dealt with.

22. On the evidence before me, Mr Hanson does not have a defence to this charge and appears to concede that he was unfit to drive.

Action to be taken

23. It will be apparent from the points made above that there are a number of actions which I advise my instructing solicitors to take. In particular, I would ask that:

(a) statements be taken from Vicky Bryant and anyone else who may be able to establish Mr Hanson's presence in the various public houses in question on the afternoon in question;

(b) a copy of the CCTV footage be obtained from the CPS as a matter of urgency. If there are any difficulties in making a copy available, arrangements should be made for it to be viewed at the police station;

(c) an early conference be arranged in order to obtain Mr Hanson's instructions on various of the matters canvassed above, and advise him more fully;

(d) the CPS be asked for the schedule of unused material, a copy of Mr Hanson's tape of interview, summaries of the interviews of the co-accused, copies of the criminal records of the co-accused and any witnesses, the crime report sheets and any relevant radio/telephone messages;

(e) once the schedule of unused material has been served, the defence statement be updated to include with any unused material sought;

(f) the defence statement be updated to deal with the additional matters set out in paragraph 5, once these have been clarified;

(g) a map of the estate be agreed;

(h) expert evidence be sought as to the effect of combining Prozac and alcohol in the way in which Mr Hanson did.

24. The case is not yet in a state where the Plea and Case Management Hearing Questionnaire can be completed, but that position should be reached once a conference with Mr Hanson has been held. I would be grateful if those instructing me could arrange a conference as soon as possible.

25. If I can be of any further assistance, please do not hesitate to contact me in Chambers.

Mahendra Dhoni

2 Atkin Building
London WC1

<u>IN THE CROWN COURT SITTING AT OXTON</u>   T0155/09

REGINA

v

JOHN HANSON

and

Others

_____

DEFENCE STATEMENT

_____

1. Nature of the defence

Mr Hanson was not present at the time of the alleged offences of violent disorder and assault.

On the 11th July 2009 Mr Hanson was living with his co-defendants Mr Nicholas Spring and Mr Anthony Mead at 27 Fountains House, Upton. At 10 am that morning Mr Hanson left the address to attend an appointment with a solicitor to collect some money he had just received by way of inheritance. He left behind the keys to a blue Vauxhall Cavalier, registration mark CLY 853X, which he had borrowed from Vicky Bryant, of 13 Onyx Close, Upton, on 10th July. Vicky Bryant is the owner of the vehicle and Mr Hanson's girlfriend.

At about 12.30 pm Mr Hanson went to the Three Bells public house, Bow Avenue, Upton where he stayed until about 2.30–3.00 pm at which time he left and went directly to the Coach and Horses public house, Bow Avenue, Upton, where he met up with Vicky Bryant and some of her friends.

Shortly before 4 pm he left and went to the Ratcatcher public house, Upton High Street, Upton. Whilst at the Ratcatcher public house a group of people including Anthony Mead, Simon Bratt, Kieran Bratt and Louis Bucknell entered. Anthony Mead had the keys to the Cavalier and an argument ensued about him driving it. Mr Hanson then took the keys back.

With regard to the offence of attempted robbery on Michael Kelly at Kelly's Off-licence, Mr Hanson has no recollection of the events constituting this alleged offence. During the course of the afternoon of 11th July Mr Hanson consumed a considerable amount of alcohol. He had also taken prescription Prozac tablets and believes that he may have accidentally taken more than the daily dosage. In the circumstances he was unable to form the intent necessary to commit the offence.

2. Matters of fact on which the accused takes issue with the prosecution

With regard to the offences of violent disorder and causing grievous bodily harm with intent, the accused takes issue with the prosecution case that he was present on the Abbey Estate on the afternoon of 11th July, that he assaulted PC Kemp and that he participated in the violent disorder. The reason why the accused takes issue with the prosecution case is because he was not present on the Abbey Estate but was at either the Three Bells public house or the Coach and Horses public house.

With regard to the offence of attempted robbery, the accused takes issue with the prosecution case to the extent that he cannot recall any of the events that took place.

However, even if he committed the *actus reus* he did not have the requisite intent. The accused challenges the evidence that he made the admission on arrest that has been attributed to him. This admission was not entered into the custody record for a substantial time after it was alleged to have been made even though PS Waller claims that a record was made contemporaneously.

3. Points of law

The accused was unable to form the specific intent required for the offence of attempted robbery.

Applications will be made under s 78 of PACE 1984 to exclude:

(i)the identification of Mr Hanson by Nuala Carroll as no identification procedure was held in accordance with PACE 1984, Code D 3.12;

(ii)the admission allegedly made by Mr Hanson on arrest at the police station;

(iii)those parts of the police interview of Nicholas Spring which are prejudicial to Mr Hanson and in particular the allegation that he was present at the time of the Abbey Estate incident and assaulted PC Kemp.

4. Alibi

The accused was present at the Three Bells public house, Bow Avenue, Upton between approximately 12.30 pm and 2.30–3.00 pm and the Coach and Horses public house, Bow Avenue, Upton between approximately 2.30–3.00pm and 4 pm. At the Coach and Horses public house he was in the company of Vicky Bryant of 13 Onyx Close, Upton.

5. Disclosure

Please disclose the following items on the unused material schedule which are capable of assisting the defence case or undermining the prosecution case:

[INSERT UNUSED MATERIAL SOUGHT ONCE CPS HAS SERVED UNUSED SCHEDULE]

6. Declaration

I, John Hanson, have read and understood this defence statement. I agree with its contents and confirm that it is consistent with my instructions. I understand that if I give evidence which conflicts with it, the prosecution may apply it in evidence and use it to cross-examine me.

Signed:

Dated:

Index